CONTENTS

A newcomer to the game would be excused for thinking shinty had something to do with skittles

100 YEARS OF SHINTY
CEUD BLIADHNA IOMAIN

(left): centenary logo

(below): the perfect dribbling action. Ken MacIntosh (Newtonmore, right) in action in the 1981 Camanachd Cup Final at Glasgow

SHINTY!

Shinty is one of the fastest and most exciting of games — also one of the oldest and most influential in the world of sport. Shinty (*Camanachd*) — known as Hurling in Ireland, and Shinny in Canada — is the fore-runner of Ice-Hockey. First introduced into the Scottish Highlands from Ireland some 1500 years ago, it has been taken by Scots all over the world.

This book celebrates the formation and development of the Camanachd Association — shinty's ruling body — one hundred years ago. It is both a definitive account and an entertaining one, telling of the wild heroes of the sport, the legendary characters and their club; it highlights the achievements, the journeys to Ireland and to Cape Breton to compete and share this unique game of courage and speed; and it shows the often hilarious and uneasy moments in a feast of photographs drawn from numerous and previously unpublished collections.

PALAEOLITHIC SHINTY PLAYER
(HOMO CAMANACHDIENSIS)
FOUND IN PEAT BOG IN SKYE

The Author

Hugh Dan MacLennan's early enthusiasm for shinty began at Lochaber High School in Fort William, for whom he played in the seventies. From winning a Blue as a player for Glasgow University, he continued to play first for Fort William and then Inverness, where his professional career as journalist and broadcaster developed a link when he received the first ever *Shinty Reporter of the Year Award* in 1990 from Marine Harvest, a sponsor of this sport.

Kind Regards

Hugh Dan.

22. 05. 93.

Donald Mackay of Broughty Ferry's award-winning picture of Newtonmore's John MacKenzie in full cry at a Camanachd Cup Final in Fort William

SHINTY!

Hugh Dan MacLennan

BALNAIN BOOKS

in association with

The Camanachd Association

Printed in Hong Kong by Wing King Tong Co. Ltd.
Colour origination by Wing King Tong
Type & filmset in Garamond by Hiscan, Inverness
Design & typography by Balnain

Published in association with
the Camanachd Association
by
Balnain Books
Druim House, Lochloy Road,
Nairn IV12 5LF

British Library in Publication Data:
A catalogue record for this book is obtainable from the
British Library

ISBN 1 872557 18 X

ACKNOWLEDGMENTS

Lean gu dlùth ri cliù bhur sinnsire

This book represents one of the Camanachd Association's most significant investments in its future, not just in finanical terms, but as an acknowledgement of the debt those involved in the greatest game on earth owe to the many outstanding individuals who have contributed to its past.

Its production would not have been possible but for the magnificent support of all the member clubs of the Camanachd Association who have contributed material relating to their own clubs (some with a greater sense of urgency than others!) and also a number of individuals who have made crucial contributions.

It is unfair perhaps to single out individuals, but I owe a great debt to the following for their advice and material which was most gratefully received: Rob Ritchie, Newtonmore; Brendan Harvey, Belfast; Duncan MacLennan (Lovat), Inverness; Alister Chisholm, Boleskine; Malcolm Fraser, Inverness; Neil Campbell, B.E.M., Strachur; David MacMaster, Strathpeffer; Angus MacKenzie, Ferintosh; Alastair MacKellar, Inverlochy; Gordon Gilchrist, Ayr; Lachie Galbraith, Glasgow; Martin MacDonald, Inverness; Donnie MacKinnon, Uig.

I am indebted also to the editors and staff of various newspapers who have assisted in this project with unfailing courtesy and understanding, and also given permission for material to be used: *The Inverness Courier; The Oban Times; Badenoch and Strathspey Herald; People's Journal/Sunday Post;* and Runrig *(Cutter and the Clan).*

A number of photographers also have to be thanked, principally Ewen Weatherspoon of Inverness whose own work features in the book and who patiently undertook a number of commissions copying large numbers of old prints for inclusion; Donald MacKay, Broughty Ferry, for his outstanding contribution to shinty photography in recent years; Ken MacPherson, Inverness; Stuart Cunningham, Glasgow; John Paul, Trevor Martin, Gordon Gillespie, all of Inverness; David Cruickshank, Cumbernauld; and Willie Urquhart of Skye.

The centenary volume was a hugely ambitious project for the Camanachd Association to undertake. Its production is due in no small measure to the enthusiasm and commitment of the Chairman of the Centenary Committee, Donnie Grant. As Editor of this volume, I would like to thank him and also Association President Ken Thomson for their support, advice and consideration over the last eighteen months.

Finally, I owe a great debt of gratitude to my fellow scribes who have sustained an effort beyond the call of any duty to ensure that this book saw the light of day. Special thanks to Jack Richmond, Newtonmore, for permission to use material from his unique archive of the game and also for his advice; Hugh Barron, Inverness, for his outstanding scholarship, attention to detail and patience in proofing the whole book virtually single-handedly; John Willie Campbell, Gorthleck, for access to his own unique collection of records of the game and his contribution to the chapters dealing with the early years of the twentieth century; and to Coll MacDougall for his assistance throughout.

It is never easy to produce a book by committee, and certainly not a production of this size. There was never a point when we didn't speak to each other. Harsh words were spoken at some points, but on the whole there was a collective will and appreciation of the task in hand which sustained us throughout and now affords us the opportunity to present the Camanachd Asscociation with what we feel is a suitable tribute to the past hundred years.

The whole undertaking would never have reached this stage had it not been for the enthusiasm, commitment, understanding, and above all patience of Simon and Sarah Fraser of Balnain Books. Relationships between publishers and authors are often fraught and rarely easy. The past few months have been at times trying, given the enormity of our task. Their quite remarkable application to the project has, however, ensured its eventual appearance.

I should also thank my friends, family and colleagues, particulary at BBC *Highland* and *Radio nan Gàidheal* for their infinite patience in difficult circumstances. There were times when the BBC studios must have appeared to be no more than a *poste restante* office for contributions being sent from far and wide. My periods of prolonged disappearance and insistence on talking about nothing else apart from 'The Book'

are now, I trust, fully explained. My especial thanks to Kathleen Scott who will be glad to know that life can now return to some semblance of normality.

My apologies to anyone I may have missed out, but every contribution to this book, no matter how small, was greatly appreciated.

All those named above are, of course, absolved from any of the blame for sins of omission and commission perpetrated between these covers. Responsibility for these and any errors of fact which may have crept in, despite our best efforts, rest with me alone as editor.

Hugh D. MacLennan
April, 1993

The Camanachd Association wishes to acknowledge the major financial contribution made by the following organisations towards the publication of this centenary volume:

An Comunn Gàidhealach

Bank of Scotland

Commun na Gàidhlig

Glenmorangie

Highlands and Islands Enterprise

Marine Harvest

West Highland Free Press

The Camanachd Association would also like to acknowledge the financial assistance received from the following towards the production of the book. Without their help, the project would not have been possible.

A.J. Ferguson Transport, Spean Bridge
Aberdeen University Shinty Club/Athletic Association
Alex Fraser (Contractors), Inverness Ltd
Allan MacPherson-Fletcher of Balavil
Anderson Shaw and Gilbert, Inverness
Argyll and Bute District Council
British Alcan Primary & Recycling Ltd.,
Lord Burton of Dochfour
Lochaber Smelter
Cànan Earranta, Sleat
Cumming's Hotel, Inverness
Alan Gammie, Edinburgh
Gleaner Oils & Gas
Lord Gray of Contin, P.C. DL.
Highland Fuels Ltd., Inverness
Holland House Electrical Co., Ltd., Inverness
Hugh MacRae & Co. (Builders) Ltd., Inverness
Innes & MacKay, Inverness
Inverness Courier
Inverness Insurance Centre, Inverness
James Dingwall, (Culbokie) Ltd.
Sir Andrew Forbes-Leith, BT
John Fraser, Silvercraft, Inverness
Sir Russell Johnston, M.P.
Charles Kennedy, M.P.

Keyline Builders' Merchants
Kingussie Golf Club
Kyles Camans, Tighnabruaich
Loch Insh Watersport & Skiing Centre
McCormack's Garage, Kingussie
MacKenzie Butchers, Newtonmore
George Maclean, Inverness
MacRae & Dick Ltd., Inverness
MacVicar & MacInnes (Argyll) Ltd.
Ray Michie, M.P.
Moray Firth Finance, Inverness
Sir Hector Munro, M.P.
Oban Times Ltd.
Priory Hotel, Beauly
Ross and Cromarty District Council
Royal Hotel, Portree
Scottish Hydro Electric plc.
Scott Oswald & Co., Inverness
Silverfjord Hotel, Kingussie
Tanera Camans, Fort William
The Press and Journal
Treecraft Woodwork, Dornoch
Tulloch Construction Group Ltd., Inverness
West Highland Woodlands
William T. Fraser & Son, Inverness

The first hundred years: Ewen Weatherspoon's summary of organised shinty
under the game's ruling body — the Camanachd Association

The exiles' spectacle : The Club of True Highlanders playing shinty on Blackheath Common in London, in the early 19th century

Illustration by R.R. MacIan, of Grant of Glenmoriston, (*The Clans of the Scottish Highlands*, 1845)

Portrait by Henry Raeburn of the Hon. John Hay MacKenzie of Cromartie, with caman and ball, in the 1790's

Action from the historic
1992 Camanachd Cup Final,
Glasgow; Fort William's first win

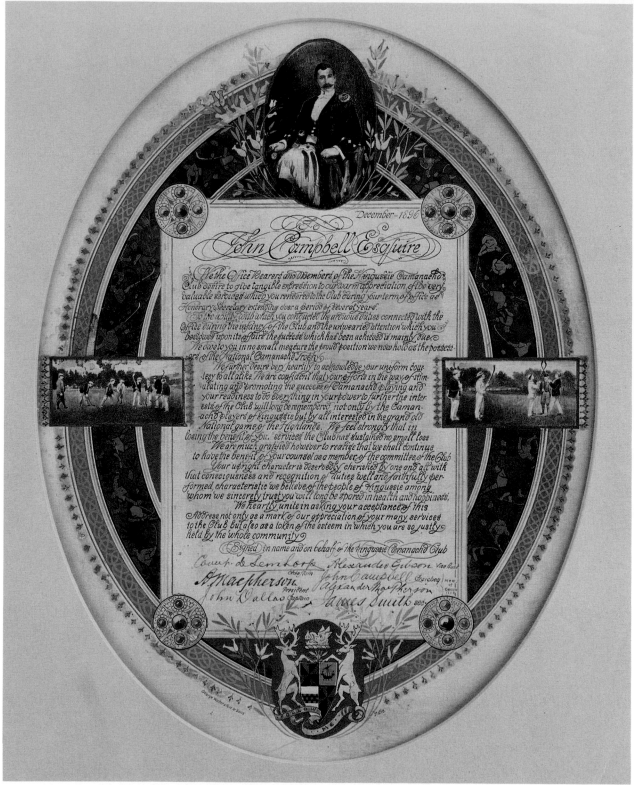

Presentation scroll from the Kingussie Club in 1896, to John Campbell, first Secretary of the Camanachd Association

Kingussie's 1984 Grand Slam winners;
(in Victoria Hall, Kingussie, where the Camanachd Association was formed in 1893)

Early days

The Spoils of Victory

(*above*): the Camanachd Cup Final 1992

(*below*): Glenurquhart, 1990-91 season

The title page of the Littlejohn Album, held in Aberdeen University Library.
The album details the background to the donation of the Littlejohn Trophy for play
between university clubs

THE UPROARIOUS MELEE

O! Muster, my lads, for the shinnie,
Come, rush like the waves of the sea;
Come, sweep as the winds from the
*   heavens,*
Nor these than the Gael more free.

Shinty, in Gaelic *iomain* or *camanachd* is Scotland's national game. Of this there is little doubt. The modern game is, however, only the development of a stick and ball game whose origins go beyond history into legend. A game fit for princes and kings in whose courts, indeed, it is said to have begun.

The game's antiquity is not in any doubt and has been most ably delineated in two important volumes which precede this one— Rev J. Ninian MacDonald's classic work *Shinty* and Roger Hutchinson's more recent, and commendable, *Camanachd*.

The purpose of this volume is not to trace the historical roots of what its exponents have frequently referred to as "the ancient and noble game" or, quite simply, the best game in the world. That has been done elsewhere, but what has not been adequately celebrated to date is the spirit and organisation of the game which has taken place specifically over the last hundred years since the formation of the

Camanachd Association, shinty's ruling body.

The expression "camanachd" itself has as its root "Cam", meaning a turn or twist. The word "shinty" itself, a much more modern term, is of more uncertain origin. It is possibly a derivation or corruption of the Gaelic word "sinteag" meaning a leap or stride.

Although the ancient and noble game (referred to, incidentally, by one modern Doctor Johnson as "hockey, without the rules") is played mainly in areas which are now primarily English-speaking, the original terminology of the game was Gaelic. The game's Gaelic roots and the

from Bede's Life of St. Cuthbert. The saint was 'too fond of games' as a boy

Camanachd Association's appreciation of that will be evident from the pages which follow.

Shinty's trail may be followed here, there, and everywhere, blazed across the story of social life in these islands for hundreds of years. Perhaps no stronger testimony to its one-time popularity could be adduced than is found in the variety of names by which it has been known in different districts.

From the root "cam" in Caman (the curved stick) arose the variants — Cammock, cammack, camac, camok, camoke, camake, camocke, camog, camag, camawg, cambock, cambok, cambuc, cambuck, etc.

From the "hooked" stick we have — Hockey, hockie, hawky, hawkey, etc.

Perhaps the earliest use of this variant is found in the Galway Statutes, 1527, where amongst prohibited games is included —

"the horlinge of the litill balle with hockie stickes or staves." (Hist. MSS., Com. 10th, Rep. app. V., 402).

Bandy (the bent stick) was also a term in common use, likewise "bandy-ball," and in Norfolk and Suffolk, "bandy-hoshoe."

Hurling or hurley became the English equivalent used in Ireland (which must be carefully distinguished from Hurling as practised in Cornwall). In Cheshire we find "baddin," in Lincolnshire "crabsow," in Fifeshire "carrick," in Dorsetshire "scrush," and in Gloucestershire "not" (from the knotty piece of wood used as a ball). In other districts we find "chinnup, camp, crabsowl, clubby,

humney, shinnup, shinney-law, shinney,"
etc.

In recent years the term "Shinty" has come into general use amongst English speakers; whereas in the last generation it was more usual to speak of "camack." Thus in *Edinburgh Evening Courant*, January 22nd, 1821 — "On Christmas and New-Year's Day matches were played at the camack and football." Gaelic speakers continue to use the term "camanachd," which has been applied to the pastime from time immemorial; although, as has been observed, in the oldest writings, "ag iomain" (the driving or urging) is of most frequent occurrence.

(Rev. J. Ninian MacDonald: *Shinty — A Short History* ,1932)

"As a means of physical development I claim for shinty the highest place. Cricket, shinty and golf would do more preventative work against consumption than many dream of. Without a doubt we would have no need of sanatoria. If an earnest worker doubts this assertion, let him start a shinty club in a country district or village and watch the results. Clumsy, top-heavy, slouching lads speedily grow alert and active, quick of eye and nimble of foot, new blood in their pulses, and fresh thought in their brains. I have watched these desirable results with the greatest delight. Why, there was hardly a shinty player in Scotland but volunteered for service in the South African War. All Gaels should support a game of which they have every reason to be proud."

(Dr Campbell, Oban, quoted in *Transactions of the Gaelic Society of Inverness*, Vol XXX, p.53)

"Two boys at play" (from a MS. Book of Prayers of 14th Century)

The Second Statistical Account of the Parish Alvie says that the principal amusements of the people were "camack matches, raffles and dancing", but Sir Aenas MacKintosh describes the Camack or Shinty matches as follows:

"Playing at Shiney is thus performed — an equal number of men dran up on opposite sides, having clubs in their hands, each party has a goal, and which party drives a wooden ball to their adversary's goal, wins the game, which is rewarded by a share of a cask of whiskey, on which both partys get drunk. The game is often played upon the ice, by one parish against another, when they come to blows if intoxicated, the players legs being frequently broke, may give it the name of Shiney.

"Many people remember their father's stories of this rather ferocious game. In Strathdearn, at the time of the New Year, the ball was hit off the High Road, at the old boundary between Moy and Dalarossie, it was then played over walls and fields and ditches until it got too dark to see, or till it ended in a free fight, almost the entire male population joining in the fray. The celebrations that took place after the game were far from pussyfoot".

"A Highland landscape with a game of shinty" (att. to D. Cunliffe c.1840)

Extract taken from *Notes Descriptive and Historical, Principally relating to the Parish of Moy in Strathdearn*.

The claim that shinty is Scotland's national game is not, however, an idle one. The game is now, thanks to modern coaching techniques and substantial sponsorship, widening its horizons, but it should be remembered as this account of the organised form of the game begins, that hundred years ago, the boundaries of active shinty clubs were, at various times before then, much more widespread.

Club names such as Cottonpolis, Manchester (the first established in England), Bolton Caledonian and London, may have ceased to exist many years ago, but they are part of the remarkable history of an Association which was formed in 1893, ironically, in the same year as the whisky distilling company MacDonald and Muir was formed in Leith, the ancient port of Edinburgh.

The link may not be all that obvious, but the history of the Association which follows is one of special friendship and related development.

Register of High Kirk Session of Glasgow

16 October, 1589.

That there be no playing at golf, carri or shinny, in the High Kirk or Kirk-yeard, or Blackfrier Kirk-yeard either Sunday or work-day"

(Liber Collegii Notre Domine, p.lxviii)

"They use for their diversion short clubs and balls of wood; the sand is a fair field for this sport and exercise in which they take great pleasure and are very nimble at it; they play for some eggs, fowls, hooks and tobacco; and so eager are they for victory that they strip themselves to their shirts to obtain it."

Martin Martin, *Description of the Western Isles* c.1695

BANDO

Although rugby football dominates sport in south Wales, and soccer the north, both are comparatively recent in their popularity as organised games. Alongside them in the nineteenth century there were other more traditional games which were also widely distributed, but which did not survive industrialisation and urbanisation. Among these was 'bando' which has a certain similarity to shinty in Scotland and hurley in Ireland. Unlike these, however, it was never established on an organised basis with clearly defined rules and a framework of arranged matches. It remained very much an informal game vaguely remembered by the rapidly dwindling older generation whose memory extends back to the turn of the century.

Playing bando (or bandy) is documented in many parts of Wales in the nineteenth century and often mentioned in the descriptions of the childhood of eminent Welshmen of the period such as Lloyd George and the less well-known John Elias, a Calvinistic divine who dominated Methodism in north Wales at the beginning of the last century,

The Camanachd Centenary Medal

and who would certainly have taken a very different view of the game later in life. Most of these references, unfortunately, testify to the popularity of bando but give very few details of how it was played. The bando stick was a rough bent stick not unlike that used in hockey. It was preferably of ash and the ball was made of yew, box or crab apple. Glamorgan coalminers often used a pick handle or a shovel handle as a convenient substitute and hit a ball of rags or a tin. The game could be played on the street (like football), as its rules were apparently very flexible. Along the Glamorgan coast it was generally played on the sea shore, and the sandy beach near Margam and Kenfig, close to the site of huge modern steelworks, was the scene of many exciting matches played by the Margam bando boys, one of the most famous of the teams in the first half of the nineteenth century.

The players also took their bando seriously enough to practise by long-distance running before the game. Two examples of a bando stick are preserved in the Welsh Folk Museum; both are approximately 2'3" long with a curved end of about 6". One stick is 1" thick and oval in section and also has a leather strap handle; the other is circular in section and has no handle.

Trefor M. Owen. *Shinty Yearbook*, 1975-6

Is binne glóir mo chamain fhéin
na guth nan eun no ceòl nam bàrd;
's ni binne fuaim air bith fo 'n ghrèin

"HOW THE PUNTERS SAW IT..." Glasgow reacted curiously after the Camanachd Cup Final at Old Anniesland — A tough game left many punters thinking football was more like a Sunday school picnic — the Glasgow newspapers were equally bewildered as the morning reports showed; one described the exhibition as "a disgrace' while another said: "...a man's game in which there are no big stars——only survivors." Yet another said: "Shinty can come back any time."....
Reproduced from The Glasgow Herald *by kind permission of Jimmy Turnbull*

na pòc air ghleus o liathroid àird.

(More sweet the tone of my own stick than voice of birds or music of bards; and nothing, under sun, so sweetly sounds as a smack with skill on a lofty ball.)

On the shinty-field no social distinctions have ever obtained; from the chief to the lowest clansman each and all have vied in generous contention. "On the turf, as under the turf, all men are equal."

Camanachd calls for gifts, physical and mental, of no mean order. Naturally it is no pastime for weaklings or degenerates; nor is it an exercise wherein the slow-witted or dullards will be found to shine. It makes demands on stamina, on soundness of wind and limb, on brain as well as muscle, on prowess, on manliness and courage, for which in few other games will a parallel be found...

A finished caman-wielder must, therefore, be a first-class athlete. Ability to deal lightning strokes on the ball at so many angles on the ground, in the air, whilst speeding over the turf, as well as whilst stationary; the free play of each and every muscle; the easy poise of the body on fleet yet steady feet — these are some of the qualities that one looks for in a first-class player, and these are the qualities which make such a one a picture of force and strength, but also of perfect grace and carriage."

Rev J. Ninian MacDonald O.S.B

a mid air dual between Strathglass and Glenurquhart

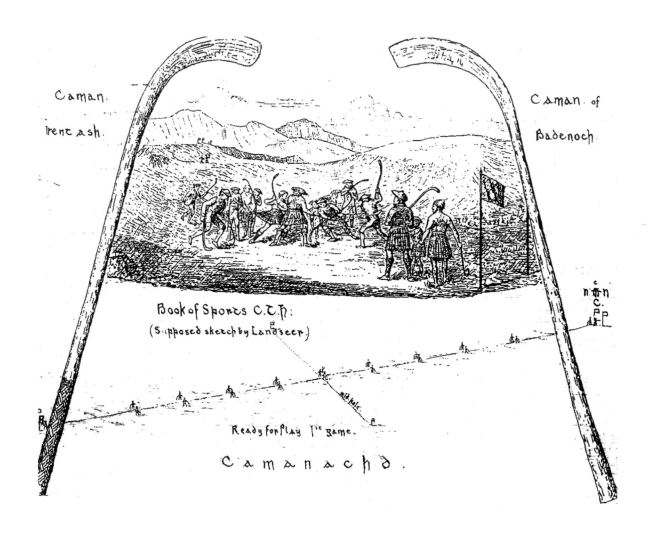

Caman.
Irene ash.

Caman. of
Badenoch.

Book of Sports C.T.H:
(Supposed sketch by Landseer.)

Ready for play 1st game.

Camanachd.

Early rules of shinty — *A guide to team formation from the book of the Society of the True Gael, 1881. The diagram apparently indicates that the Society's members preferred to play eleven-a-side, and to adopt a strangely linear formation at the throw-up, the start of play. There is also a distinction drawn between a Badenoch and an ash-caman*

AN INTRIGUING WEB OF WAYWARD STRANDS

shinty *shin'ti*, **shinny** *shin'i*, *ns.* a game like hockey, of Scottish origin, played by teams of 12: the slim curved club (the caman, also **shin'ty stick**) or leather-covered cork ball (or substitute) used therein. [Perh. from Gael. *sinteag*, a bound, pace.]

caman, -ain, *pl.* -ain [& camanan,] Club for playing shinty, hurley, or golf. Not a cricket-bat, as given in some dictionaries, as *caman* must have a curve in it. 2(DU) see camag, 4.

——achd, s.f. Shinty, hurley, golf.

iomain, *pr.pt.* ag iomain, *v.a.* Urge, drive slowly as cattle. 2 Toss, whirl, roll. 3 Conduct. 4**Drive anything forward on the ground, kick forward, as a football. 5 Play as at shinty, football, or any driving game. Iomainidh iad, they shall drive; 'gan i. 'sa chath, *driving them backward in battle*; am bheil thu dol a dh'iomain? *are you going to play?* ciod e an iomain? *what game?*; a dh' i. chaman, am ball iomain, *or* am ball iomanach, *shinty*.

Shinty — or camanachd, as it is traditionally known in the Gaelic-speaking West Highlands, is an ancient game. Introduced to North-West Scotland along with Christianity and the Gaelic language nearly two thousand years ago by Irish missionaries, the game can safely lay claim to being Scotland's national sport.

There is no doubt that the game was popular at various stages virtually nationwide. It is to be found from the windswept rocks of St Kilda to the more hospitable and gentler plains of the borders. Indeed, it is claimed that golf was born out of shinty players practising, alone or in pairs, the art of driving the ball with the caman, or stick.

The game is also to be found on a much wider plain — the world-wide stage with exiles taking the game to the furthest flung corners of the globe — from South America to the war-ravaged wastes of Europe through two world wars, to the two dozen camain issued to the squadrons of the Lovat Scouts during the Boer War, to the Maritime region of Canada, where the game was re-introduced in 1991 by a party of players from the Kingussie and Skye Clubs.

Kingussie in 1880

INVERNESS COURIER

July 13, 1842

The fourth of April being a holiday, the sons of the mountains, resident in this province, had determined to try a game at shinty for the auld lang syne. Though the weather was very threatening in the morning, the players were not to be daunted, but crossed the bay in boats, and marched to the ground (a plain situated at the foot of the mount, from which Montevideo derives its name), under the inspiring strains of the bagpipes, to the tune of 'The Campbells are coming', where they were greeted by a large concourse of people, assembled to witness the game.

After sides were called, and a few other preliminaries arranged, playing commenced, and was carried on with great spirit until four pm, when the players sat down on the grass and partook of an asado de carvo con cuero (beef roasted with the hide on), and plenty of the real Ferrintosh (Aldourie and Brackla being scarce). Dancing then commenced and the Highland fling by Messrs MacLennan and Macrae; Gille Calum, by Captain Maclellan; Sean Truise, by Mr MacDougall, and several other dances and Scotch reels were greatly admired.

At half past seven o'clock, the backpipes (sic) struck up the 'Gathering', and the whole, forming two deep, marched from the field to the place of embarkation, to the tune 'Gillean na Feileadh', amidst loud cheering, and still louder vivas from the natives.

Shinty, as with many other aspects of Highland heritage and the Gaelic language in particular, has been frequently threatened, both by Statute and under the influence of other movements in

COPY OF THE GENERAL ORDERS ISSUED BY A.J. LIST, SUPERINTENDENT OF COUNTY POLICE, EDINBURGH, FROM 1840 TO 1843: REVISED AND APPROVED BY THE SHERRIFF APRIL 1842
Many complaints having been made of boys playing at "shinty or football" upon the public roads, the Constable is directed to put an immediate stop to it: and if the players do not discontinue after being cautioned, they must be summoned to the Road Court, agreeably to article 21 of the bills headed "Public Roads".

Police Notice 1843

The two earliest-known photographs of play

society. That the game has survived the combined assaults of Royal edicts against popular and 'uncontrollable' games, as well as the Sabbatarianism which followed the Reformation and outlawed the playing of sports on the day of rest, (not to mention the rapid erosion of the Highland way of life as described by historians such as Jim Hunter and Roger Hutchinson in his excellent history of the game, *Camanachd*), is a tribute to the people involved in the setting up of the organisation which drew this intriguing web of wayward strands together one hundred years ago — the Camanachd Association, shinty's ruling body.

A series of hugely interesting and memorable exhibition matches 100 years ago were the immediate catalyst leading to the formation of the Association which has seen the game develop from a series of loosely organised (and sometimes

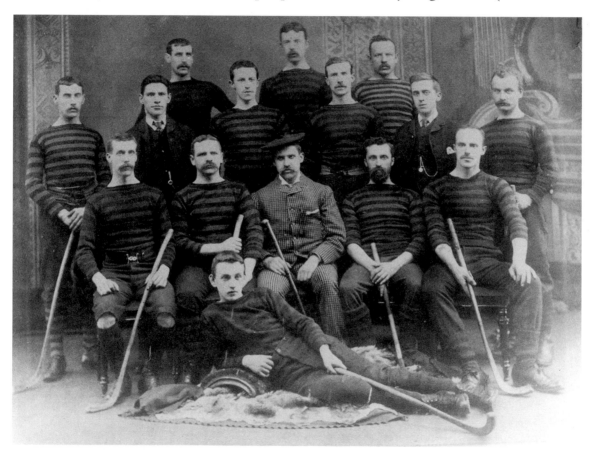

Inveraray, 1882 — one of the earliest teams to be photographed

barely organised) clubs and structures, into an efficiently run and progressive organisation with some forty clubs competing on a regular basis, commanding national media attention and significant sums of sponsorship, both from commercial organisations such as The Glenmorangie Distillery company (the sponsors of the game's premier competition the Camanachd Cup), multi-national fish-farmers Marine Harvest who sponsor the national leagues, and local authorities such as Highland Regional Council who have made significant investments in funds to enable clubs to improve their facilities.

Shinty in its organised form has come a long way since it fought to survive in the glens of the Highlands and much further afield, in public parks as far from its main heartland as Wimbledon, Manchester, Cottonpolis; and even in Grampian

Region where the Aberdeen North of Spey Club appears to have been one of the earliest formed, in the 1840's.

The Highlands of Scotland were, and still are, the heartland of shinty, though as Roger Hutchinson quite dramatically illustrates, there was feverish activity in shinty terms on both sides of the border, in what he refers to as 'a fantasy world of Celtic twilight'.

It was usual in the Highlands, however, to have the principal games of shinty at New Year or Old New Year. In these contests, often between two districts or parishes, there was no limit as to the numbers taking part with players arriving and departing at will, and often play continued from the forenoon until darkness fell.

Play was, quite simply, lacking in any system with every man chasing after and hitting the ball which could be stopped by hand, foot or home-made caman. In Badenoch it was the aim of each player "a bhith far an robh 'm ball" — to be where the ball was. There were, of course players who exercised considerable skill in company of all ages, even in those chaotic times.

In many districts, the games died out however towards the middle of last century, but tended to continue in places such as Badenoch, Lochaber and Strathglass where interest never waned and the annual 'cluidh-bhall' was kept up, even into the present century.

The modern, organised form of shinty therefore is only to be found from the mid to later 19th century. By this time there had been a considerable drift of Highlanders into the towns and cities of the south and clubs began to be formed as a means of retaining territorial identity, as well as for social reasons.

By the end of the century, greater mobility, mainly due to improved means of transport, helped to make the game more popular and gradually games began to be organised between clubs located at considerable distances apart. Gradually the local rivalries began to be replaced with a more competitive, ambitious atmosphere.

The earliest mention of an organised club (an exception, as it was in existence in the first half of the 19th century), seems to be that in the *Inverness Courier* of January 11, 1849, where it is reported that the members of the North of Spey Shinty Club, Aberdeen, met on the links on January 1st 'for conducting the long established Celtic game'. The players were divided into two sides and hail keepers (goal keepers) appointed.

Their coats were then taken off and the ball thrown up, the play continuing for nearly two hours. Those wearing 'red signals' were the winners. In the afternoon, led by a piper, the whole company proceeded to the North of Scotland Hotel for a repast, after which Mr Sutherland, who was chairman, complimented the club on the orderly manner in which the contest was played. After an appeal was made, the club agreed to contribute to the Culloden monument.

Meanwhile Vale of Leven appear to have been formed around 1856 and it is understood that the players were members of a famous football club who engaged in shinty from time to time. An early notice of their activity appears in the *Lennox Herald* of January 11, 1849:

Sir,

Owing to the success that the Glenfruin players met with in the late contest with the Gareloch men we are glad to understand that they are anxious to have a match with the Vale of Leven players. If so, we would be happy to meet them at an early date and arrange a match with them and, should they wish, we will play with 20 men against their 25. An early answer, through the Herald, will much oblige.

Robert McGowan,
Alexandria

A further challenge appeared among the advertisements of the *Inverness Courier* on January 1, 1870:

Shinty players of the Vale of Leven, Dunbartonshire would be glad to have a match with the Inveraray, Badenoch, Lochaber, Inverness or Sutherland, men for £50 or £100 a side. Twenty players to play on each side; and they agree to take £15 and go any distance within 100 miles of Dumbarton or give that sum to any party who accepts the Challenge, and who agree to come to Vale of Leven to have it played out. Communications to John Sinclair, Seaforth House, Bridge of Allan, will be attended to.

The same issue of the *Courier* contained the comment:

'The fine old game of shinty is wearing somewhat out of date but we think there are

Kingussie

players enough in the north to accept the challenge. The stakes however are too heavy; why not have a game for honour, or for a cup, medal or some other trophy.'

The challenge appears to have died the death, however, and no other mention of it is to be found until much later. Mr Donald Campbell, J.P., Kingussie, when speaking of shinty in former times after a

'cluidh-bhall' in January 1905, said the challenge by Vale of Leven was accepted by Badenoch but nothing further was heard.

At a supper held after Glasgow were beaten at Burnbank in February 1876, reference is made in the *Highlander* newspaper that Vale of Leven had never been beaten at shinty and that before this game

36

Glasgow Cowal 1895

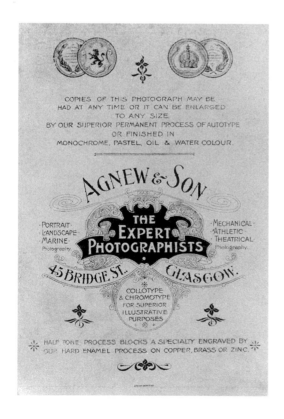

had always won by more than three hails (goals). In April of the same year, in another game, John Morrison of Glasgow scored a hail, believed to be the first hail against Vale of Leven. In February 1877, a match 'to decide the championship of Scotland' was played at Summerton Park, Govan in which Vale of Leven defeated Inveraray by 4 hails to 1. The club was one of those represented at the meeting eventually held to form the association on October 13, 1877.

The defeat which Inveraray suffered in February 1877 was avenged at New Year, 1878 in a game with Vale of Leven. This game, again described as being for the championship of Scotland, took place at Winterton Park, Inveraray. Play lasted for one and a half hours with fifteen players on each side and Inveraray won by 12 hails to 1. The ground was roped off and

Glasgow Cowal 1901-04

at half time the hard wooden ball used regularly by Inveraray was changed in favour of one of a softer material.

Several goals had been disputed in a game in which Cowal provided the opposition and it was suggested in the report that in future two trustworthy men should be stationed at the posts to decide. The writer of the report gave it as his view that Vale of Leven must adopt a humbler title than 'Champions of the World' and congratulated Cowal on keeping their temper under great provocation from Vale of Leven.

The various shinty reports in the *Highlander* between 1874 and 1881 indicate that the earliest clubs were outwith the Highlands in Edinburgh, Glasgow, London and even in Manchester and Bolton. An account is also given of a game in Birmingham in connection with the Celtic Society in that city in December, 1878.

The oldest club then in existence was the one in Edinburgh, 'Cuideachd Chamanachd Dhun-Eideann'. On January 1st 1874, the annual game was held in the Queen's Park, the day being as boisterous as on the occasion of the clubs' first match with the 93rd Regiment (The Sutherland Highlanders) two years before.

It was a club rule to play on New Year's day, however bad the weather. The players began to assemble at noon and the time was called at 3pm. The Chief, MacDonell of Morar, was present along with honorary members including Sheriff Nicolson and D. MacKenzie, Advocate. 'A great and enthusiastic crowd thronged the park'.

A year later, play was again held on the Queen's Park which was covered by six inches of snow. Two sides, reds and blues under the new chieftain, Hector Campbell of Achnacloich, and Alex R. Forbes, secretary, played for some time, all wearing Highland dress. At the Annual Business meeting held on December 4 of that year, attempts were made to have a match with the newly formed Glasgow club. The sixth anniversary of the founding of the club was held in February, 1876. Attempts to discard playing in Highland dress were overthrown on that occasion and the numerical and financial state of the club was described as 'prosperous'.

At the close of the season in April, 1877, during which there was play every Saturday from October, and a match with Glasgow, it was remarked that the game should be played 'according to use and wont in the Highlands'.

THE PENNY MAGAZINE
for the Diffusion of Useful Knowledge
January 31, 1835.

THE GAME OF SHINTY

In the Highlands of Scotland it is customary for persons to amuse themselves, in the winter season, with a game which they call "shinty". This sport has a considerable resemblance to that which is denominated "hurling" in England, and which Strutt describes under that name. The shinty is played with a small hard ball, which is generally made of wood, and each player is furnished with a curved stick somewhat resembling that which is used by golf players. The object of each party of players is to send the ball beyond a given boundary on either side; and the skill of the game consists in striking the ball to the greatest distance towards the the adversaries' boundary, or in the manoeuvering to keep it in advance of the opposing side. Large parties assemble during the Christmas holidays, one parish sometimes making a match against another.

In the struggles between the contending players many hard blows are given, and frequently a shin is broken, or by a rarer chance some more serious accident may occur. The writer witnessed a match, in which one of the players, having gained possession of the ball, contrived to run a mile with it in his hand, pursued by both his own and the adverse party until he reached the appointed limit, when his victory was admitted. Many of the Highland farmers join with eagerness in the sport, and the laird frequently encourages by his presence this amusement of his labourers and tenants.

In 1877 play was held at Stockbridge instead of Queen's Park, where play had been held for many years, and in a game there it appears that handling of the ball was permitted as 'by a united rush the ball was literally carried through the hail'.

The club's season in 1881 closed on April 2nd with a game between sixteen from Badenoch and sixteen other members. Duration of play was one and a half hours which seemed to be usual about this time. The club, which was described as 'strictly confined to Highlanders' continued to play at Stockbridge. The New Year game held there in 1888 lasted from one pm to three pm with a pause at two pm. The Chieftain at the time was A. Mac-

from the Penny Magazine

Donald, merchant, Dublin Street who was from Strathglass. By 1891, play was being held at Inverleith. In that year the Edinburgh University club was formed and it was followed by Edinburgh, Sutherland in 1894 and Edinburgh Northern Counties in 1896. By the end of 1896 the Edinburgh Shinty League was in being.

The popular bardess of Skye — Mairi Ni 'n Iain Bhain — composed a stirring song on a match played on New Year's Day, 1876, at Strathbungo, Glasgow, between teams with thirty players a side, one lot in the kilt, the other in knickerbockers! With a large contingent of followers, they marched to the field of play, pipers in the van and in the rear, a horse, with cart laden with provisions — bannocks in plenty, abundance of cheese, 'agus deur beag de'n Tòiseachd, a chur spreigidh

"Sans Peur."

SUTHERLAND

➤*SHINTY CLUB*◄

SEASON 1893-94

Secretary and Treasurer.

WALTER M. FORSYTH,
18 RAEBURN PLACE, EDINBURGH.

GROUND.

INVERLEITH PARK.

PRACTICE.

SATURDAY AFTERNOONS AT 3.30.

Rules of the "Camanachd Association."

1. EACH Team shall number 16 Players, who shall be *bona-fide* Members of the Club for which they play, and no individual shall play for more than one Club during one season.

2. The field of play shall not be less than 200 yards long by 150 yards broad, nor more than 300 yards long by 200 yards broad. In Cup Matches the maximum obtainables must be played.

3. The Hails shall be 12 feet wide and 10 feet high, attached by a fixed cross bar above.

4. The time allowed for playing a game shall be one hour and a half, with an interval of five minutes at half-time. Teams to change sides after each Hail is scored, but if no Hail is scored by half-time, ends shall be changed, and no further change to take place.

5. Nothing but Hails shall count.

6. When both Teams are ready, the Referee, standing in mid-field, shall throw the ball straight in the air, between two opposing players.

7. No player shall use his hands or club to hold or push his opponent, neither shall he trip, hack, jump at, or throw him by the use of his leg or club. A set blow will be given as a penalty for every foul granted by the Referee, but a Hail from such blow will not count.

8. Rough or unruly play will not be tolerated, and any player observed wilfully infringing any of the Rules shall be expelled the field of play, and shall not be replaced by a fresh man.

9. A player disabling an opponent must retire from the game, unless the Referee declare the man so disabled to be in fault.

10. When the ball is sent from the field of play through the Hail-posts and under the cross-bar connecting them, the Hail is won, even should it graze the posts or bar, or be sent through by one of the defending side.

11. The ball may be stopped by the hand, but if caught must be immediately dropped. No player shall be allowed to run with or throw the ball.

12. The ball to be played with shall consist of cork and worsted with a covering of leather, and shall measure 7½ to 8 inches in circumference.

13. When the ball passes the side lines, the player first reaching it must bring it within the line, and if no opponent challenges him, can take a set blow, but if challenged he must take 16 yards within the line, and drop it between himself and his opponent.

14. When the ball passes the Hails without scoring, the Hail-keeper has the option of sending the ball afield with either hand or club.

15. Players are prohibited from playing with spikes in their shoes, and no iron plates or metal of any kind shall be allowed on the clubs.

16. If the ball be sent from the field of play past the Hails on either side by a player of the defending side, it shall be taken back 15 yards in front of the point at which it was sent out of play, and thrown up by the Referee between two opposing players.

17. When the ball is thrown in the air, as provided for in Rules 6 and 7, the two players shall stand with crossed clubs, and no other player allowed within 5 yards till the ball is hit.

18. Each competing Club to choose two Umpires and between them one Referee for each Match.

19. At the commencement of the game, and after each Hail is scored, the players shall take the places allotted to them by their respective Captains.

20. Except in a scrimmage, no opponent shall be allowed to stand within 5 yards of the Hails unless the ball be in play in front.

21. No person admitted to the field of play during the course of a Match except the Referee, Umpires, and a club-bearer for each Team.

"SANS PEUR."

The Club Membership is open to all Highlanders, Natives of the County, and their friends.

ANNUAL SUBSCRIPTION.

Honorary Members,	-	5s.
Playing Members,	-	1s.

Member's Name.

....

Peter J. Duffy, Printer, 385 High Street, Edinburgh.

First rules!

anns na gillean,' (and a small drop of Ferintosh, to put smeddum into the lads). It is evident she was elated by the occasion:

Gach fleasgach gun mheang,
Le chaman 'n a laimh,
's a chnapag le srann 'g a fògradh leo.

(Each lad without flaw,
with his stick in his hand
as he sent the ball humming forward.)

In passing it is interesting to observe that the term ''cnapag'' is the equivalent of the Old Scots ''Knottie,'' a by-name for a shinty-ball; while another, ''humie,'' is suggested by the word ''srann'' (hum) in the same verse.

On Old New Year's Day, 1877, the Gaels of Greenock challenged their compatriots of Glasgow to a match in which no less than sixty a side took part. This formidable contest is also celebrated in song by the same poetess.

Camanachd Ghlaschu le Mairi Nic a'Phearsain (Mairi Mhor nan Oran) 1876

Chan fhacas a riamh,
A leithid de thriall,
Air sràidean Ghrianaig cò-lamh ann.
(There never was seen such a procession
on the streets of Greenock, at one
time.)

'S i seo a'Bhliadhn' Ur thug sòlas dhùinn,
'S iad gillean mo rùin a thogadh mo
shùnnd.
'S i seo a'Bhliadhn' Ur thug sòlas dhùinn.

'S iad gillean mo ghraidh,
Tha 'n Glaschu nan sraid,

Is fhada bho ait' an eòlais iad.

'S ann goirid roimh'n Challainn
A chruinnich an comunn,
'S a chuireadh an iomain an òrdugh leo.

Nuair thainaig an t-am,
Gun chruinnich na suinn,
'S bha caman an laimh gach òigeir
dhiubh.

Aig aon uair deug
A rinn iad an triall,
Le piob 's bu bhriagh' an còmhlan iad.

Nuair rainig na sair
Gu ionad a'bhlair,
Gun chuireadh gun dail an òrdugh iad.

Bha glaineachan lan
Dhe'n Tois'eachd a b' fhearr,
Is aran is caise còmhla ris.

Bha bonnaich gun taing
Is pailteas dhiubh ann,
'S clann-nighean nan gleann 'gan
còcaireachd.

Nuair roinneadh na laoich
'S a ghabh iad an taoibh,
Bha mis' air an raon toirt cò-dhail
dhaibh.

'S e 'n sealladh as breagh'
A chunnaic mi riamh,
Gach oigear gun ghiamh 's a chòta dheth.

Gach fleasgach gun mheang,
'S a chaman 'na laimh,
'S a' chnapag le srann 'ga fògar leò.

Bha cuid dhiubh cho luath
Ri feidh air an ruaig,
'S cha chluinnt' ach 'A suas i,
Dhòmhnaill,' leo.

42

*'S ann ann a bha'n eadhlain
Le glagadaich chaman,
'S gach curaidh cur fallais is ceòthain
    deth.*

*Bha duine gun chearb,
Le siosa-cot dearg,
'S cha bhiodh am boc-earba còmhla ris.*

*Fear eile gun ghiamh
'S a chiabhagan liath
Chuir 'tigh' i bharr fiacail mòran diubh.*

*'S e duine gùn tùr
Nach fhaiceadh le shùil,
Gu robh iad bho thùs an òige ris.*

*Nuair chuireadh am blàr,
Gun choisich na sàir
Le pìob gu Sràid an Dòchais leò.*

*Suidhibh, a chlann,
Is gabhaidh sinn rann,
Gu'n cuirear an dram an òrdugh dhuibh.*

*Gun dhealaich na suinn,
Mar thainig iad cruinn,
Le'n cridheachan coibhneil, 's b'òrdail
    iad.*

This song first appeared in the *Highlander* on January 29, 1876. The game it refers to was played on New Year's Day 1876 in Queen's Park Glasgow. It was the first game played by the Shinty Club which had been formed by the Highland Society. Mary MacPherson, the famous Gaelic poetess, was one of the ladies who helped prepare the players' meals.

It would appear that Manchester was the first club to be founded in England. It isn't clear when, but it certainly appears to have been in existence in April, 1876. In the previous year, on the 1st of January, Manchester Highlanders and their friends had engaged in a game with sides under Robertson, Strathspey, the President and MacPherson, Ardnamurchan. On Christmas, 1876, there was a match with the Caledonian Club with thirty on each side. Of the Manchester team, all but two spoke Gaelic and of the Caledonian, only the captain was a non-Gaelic speaker.

In April of the same year the Manchester club claimed to be the only one in England, but in fact another was being formed in the city at that time.

Until 1896, there was no limit to the extent of the field of play — a plain, a mile, or even two, in length being a common area. Thus, Principal Shairp of St. Andrews, in a poem descriptive of a match he witnessed in Glen Dessary in 1876, states:

*It was a level piece of ground,
two miles or more from west to east.*

A beach of firm sand, where available, was a favourite venue:

*Mar bhall de arca air tràigh 'ga sir-ruith,
le buille-bharach o laimh gach aoinfhir.
(Like a ball of cork, keenly pursued on a
    strand,
with a master-stroke from every hand.)*

So we have it in a lament, declaring the sorry plight of his clan, on the death of that redoubtable Royalist, Sir John MacLean, chief of Duart, in 1716. Apropos, there is record of a thrilling tussle that took place in 1821, between the Campbells of Argyll and the MacLeans of

Mull on the shore of Calgary, where the local team 'won a decisive victory.'

Also, there was no limit to the duration of the period of playing, a stretch of four to five hours being common, or until dusk terminated the contest. The poem by Principal Shairp, already quoted, in description of a game, has so many interesting observations on the mode of playing which then held, that one is tempted to quote fairly freely from the ballad:

... Loch Arkaig stirred, from shore to shore the call was heard;
to Clunes it passed, from toun to toun,
that all the people make them boun,
against the coming New Year's Day,
to gather for a shinty-fray within the long Glen Dessary.

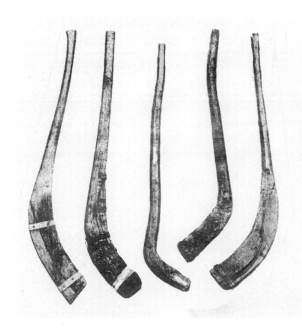

some early camans

Blue, frosty, bright the morning rose that New Year's Day...
Crisp was the sward beneath their tread, as they westward marched:
and at their head the piper of Achnacarry blew the thrilling pibroch, "Donald Dubh."
This challenge the piper of the glen as proudly sounded back again,
... till far-off rang the tingling crags to the wild war-clang of the pibroch that,
loud to battle blown, the Cameron clan had for ages known.
To-day, as other, was the same, it summons to the peaceful game.
From the braeside homes, down trooping come the champions of Glen Dessary,
some in tartan filibegs arrayed, the garb that tyrant laws forbade,
but still they clung to, unafraid;
some in Rome-woven tartan trews, rough spun, and dyed with various hues,
by mother's hands or maiden's wrought:
... but all with hazel camans slung their shoulders o'er,
men old and young with mountaineer's long, slinging pace move cheerily down to the trysting place.
It was a level space of ground two miles and more from west to east,
... on that long flat of green they take their stations:
on the west the men of Dessary, Kingie, Pean Glen,
ranged 'gainst the stalwart lads who bide down long Loch Arkaig, either side.
The ground was ta'en, the clock struck ten as Ewan, patriarch of the glen,
struck off, and sent the foremost ball Down the strath flying
... Now fast and furious, on they drive:
here youngsters scud with feet of wind, there, in a melee, dunch and strive;
the veterans outlook keep behind.
Now up now down the ball they toss,

now this, now that side of the strath.
.. Any many a stroke of stinging pain in
    the close press was gi'en and ta'en,
without or guile or ire. So all day long
    the clansmen played,
and to and fro their tuilzie swayed
    untired,
along the hollow vale; and neither side
    could win the hail. ...

A club known as Bolton Caledonian Shinty Club had been formed by December 10, 1877 when over fifty members had been enrolled and it was agreed that the rules of the Manchester club were to be observed *pro tem*.

On December 26, play, 'in the true Highland fashion, although the majority were good, stiff Lowland Scotsmen', began at nine am. By noon each side had scored five times, and after refreshments the captains 'tossed for the final run of the goal and conquering game and in 15 minutes the hail was scored'. At a dinner held in July 1878 the membership was reported as being almost a hundred and the hope was expressed that matches would be held at Rugby, Stafford or Crewe.

Manchester and Bolton played in February, 1879 on the ground at the former, Old Trafford. They had previously agreed to play in any weather. In the second game, at Folds Road, Bolton in March which was drawn 1-1, there were seventeen on each side and sides were changed after the first hail. The intervention of the umpires and referee was required several times as the clubs had been playing to differing rules before this encounter.

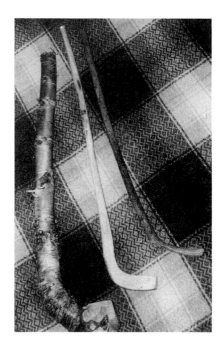

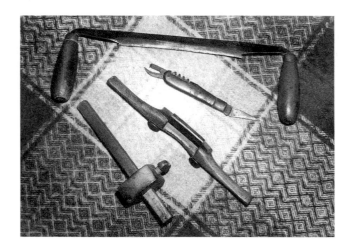

Stages in the making of a caman from native birch

There were no Highland surnames in the Bolton team, but several in that of Manchester. A further game was played between the clubs in November 1880 for the benefit of the Bolton Infirmary. The difficulty of getting practice in a busy manufacturing town was briefly noted at a dinner of the Bolton Club in October 1879 and also that at play on the previous Christmas the members had shown their enthusiasm by playing for about one hour in knee-deep snow. The Manchester and Bolton Clubs met in April, 1881 and this appears to be the last notice of these clubs.

Shinty was also played around the same time in London, with the 1989 Shinty Yearbook detailing the first recorded match in 1823. Details of matches played by Highlanders there in the 1830's are given in Alexander MacDonald's important paper on the history of the game published in the Transactions of the Gaelic Society of Inverness (Volume XXX). *'Shinty : Historical and Traditional'*. He quoted a song about a game played at Blackheath in 1836, written by David MacDonald, an Inverness bard. The song was published in his book *The Mountain Heath*. Alexander MacDonald also refers to a game played in Copenhagen Fields in London, organised by 'The Society of True Highlanders' in June, 1841 and recorded in James Barron's *Northern Highlands in the Nineteenth Century*, Vol II. The *Inverness Courier* gives an account of play held at Blackheath Common at Christmas, 1846 in which sixty young Highlanders 'under the judicious guidance of our friend MacPhee' took part. It was a 'keen, spirited contest' lasting several hours. At the end 'many came forward and subscribed sums for a new set of shinties'. A further report of play organised by 'The Society of True Highlanders' appears in the *Inverness Courier* of June 26, 1865. This play took place on Wimbledon Heath which was found to be a better ground than Blackheath which had been the venue for games in previous years. The teams, each of 15 players, under the captaincy of Messrs Scott and MacGregor, played three games. The first was won by Scott's team, the second by McGregor's and the deciding one by Scott's.

A report of a meeting held in the Caledonian Hotel, Adelphi, London at the end of December 1877 for the purpose of forming a shinty club appears and it was followed by another meeting on January 4, 1878. It was reported on this occasion that it was 'the intention of the executive while giving due attention to the athletic part of the programme not to lose sight of social questions affecting the Highlands and welfare of Highlanders generally'.

Rules were to be formed and membership was to be confined to Highlanders (not necessarily Gaelic speaking) and sons of Highland parents. The object of this was 'to prevent the discontent at present in the London Scottish Rifles owing to the Scottish Cockneys on its ranks'.

John MacDonald Cameron and Archibald MacTavish were described as Chieftain and Captain respectively at a further meeting held on January 18, 1878. By March of the same year, The London Highland Camanachd Club was fully constituted and working with rules adoped and the following office bearers: Patron, Rt. Hon. Lord Lovat; Chief, J.W. Malcolm of Poltalloch; Chieftain, Donald Grant; Captain, J. MacDonald Cameron, F.C.S. There were thirty playing members and 50 camans had been ordered. The first appearance of the club soon followed on Wimbledon Common with play lasting an hour and a half, using the Northern Association's rules.

It was hoped that better camans could be acquired and that Northern Clubs could assist in providing them. At the next game on the same field on Easter Monday, there were many spectators, some of them impeding play in their excitement and keen-ness to witness the 'novel and exciting event.'

When agreement had been reached as to the length of the field of play, boundaries were traced at both ends. Each was called a "tadhal" (goal or hail), and sometimes a "bair," *(genitive barach)*. The stroke that sent the ball over this line was called "buille-bharachd", or "buille-chollaid"; cf. a poem by Eoghan MacGhilliosa:

Nuair thig bliadhn' ur oirnn,
bi' buidheann luthor a' cluich na dulain
*   air aodann lom;*
le darach laidir an laimh gach armainn,

's e cur na barach gu laidir teom.
(When comes the New Year,
an agile band will engage in the
*   challenge on a close-cropped plain,*
with stout "oaks" in the hands of
*   stalwarts*
scoring goals with strength and skill.)

When, as often happened, a game was played between men in the same district, protagonists were named and one, gently tapping his fellow, would say: *Buailim ort* (I hit you). The other would answer: *Leigim leat* (I let you choose). Then the selection would proceed, each picking a player until all who wished to participate were placed in the teams.

Any advantage presented by the field, as slope, direction of wind, etc. was decided by one of the leaders who, tossing his caman in the air, would ask his opponent to guess whether bas or cas (head or haft) would first touch the ground. If he guessed aright, he would tell his opponent to state his choice. On scoring a hail, the sides were changed.

The Annual General Meeting of the Highland Camanachd Club, London in October was well attended, most of the company wearing the club uniform — Norfolk jacket and knickerbockers of Lovat Mixture, grey knitted Kilmarnock bonnet and hose to match. The patron was Lord Lovat and the President was Rt. Hon. Lord Colin Campbell, M.P. A report in the *Highlander*, taken from The Field of December 26, 1878 states that a friendly game was played between the club and the Club of True Highlanders. The name of the latter, which organised games in 1836 and 1865, does not appear to occur again.

The London Club's first important match was a game with Glasgow at Summerton Park, Glasgow on April 12, 1879. This was a twelve-a-side match lasting from 4.20 to 5.45pm and Glasgow won by six hails to one. At the social following the game, reference was made to Robert Fraser, late captain of Glasgow and 'father of the London club'.

The last report of the Highland Camanachd Club of London appears in the *Highlander* newspaper (which ceased

Furnace Excelsiors approx. 1890. The captain Donald Campbell 'The Drover' is seated in the centre of the group. He was reputed to be the foremost player in the Furnace area at the time. Furnace Excelsiors were the forerunners of the Furnace team which went on to lift the Camanachd Cup in 1923.

in 1881) in January 1880. *The Northern Chronicle*, which commenced in 1882, has a report on a game at Wimbledon between the London Inverness-shire Camanachd Club and the Ross-shire Association which had recently started a shinty club. The more experienced Inverness-shire club won, having had the advantage of having played together for two years.

At Wimbledon on December 26, 1891, play was held by twenty-four members of 'L.S.S.C.' which would appear to be the London Scottish Shinty Club. On the same field at the same time the London Northern Counties Camanachd Club, described as a 'rival club', also held a game. Some weeks afterwards a letter by 'Seann Chamanachd' stated that the report of the

Caberfeidh Shinty Club — 1888 (back row, left to right): Bob Lunn, John Munro (Strathpeffer Hotel), John Macrae (Tarvie), David Bryden, Johnnie MacKay (Mason), David Ross (Joiner), Murdo MacGregor, Murdo MacLeay, Roddie Munro, Kenny Sinclair
(middle row, left to right): David Gordon, Alex Christie, John MacMaster (Vice-Captain), Willie Gunn (Captain), Donald MacKay, Danny Graham, Sandy MacDonald, Mr Anderson Forester.
(front row (middle), left to right): William MacKenzie, James Cameron
(front row, left to right): George Munro, William Campbell, Colin Munro, Dan Sinclair. (boys at rear, left to right): Alick MacKenzie, David MacKenzie.

play by the London Scottish Shinty Club was 'bogus', only mustering a few players, some of whom had been expelled from the old club, the London Northern Counties, which was formerly known as the London Inverness-shire Association Camanachd Club.

By the autumn of 1892 a host of clubs had come into existence. Besides those of - Strathglass, Brae-Lochaber, Kingussie, Newtonmore and Glen-Urquhart already mentioned, there were those of Glencoe, Ballachulish, Insch, Vale of Laroch, Vale of Leven, Dunally, Ardkinglas, Lochgoilhead, Dalmally, Oban, Bunawe, Strachur, Furnace, Inveraray, Kiltarlity, Inverness, Grantown, Strathpeffer, Alvie, Glasgow Cowal, Aberdeen University, Edinburgh University, Edinburgh Camanachd, London Scottish, London and Northern Counties, to which Beauly, Glenmoriston, Fort-Augustus, Invergarry, Spean-Bridge and others were soon added.

Shinty, Rev. J. Ninian MacDonald, OSB

The London and Northern Counties Club was one of those represented (by James Campbell) at the inaugural meeting of the Camanachd Association and took part in the opening season of the Camanachd Cup, which was offered as the game's premier competition. A gathering of the London Highland Athletic Club was held at Stamford Bridge on Monday, June 7, 1897 one of the events being a shinty contest between London and Northern Counties and Beauly, the winners of the Camanchd Cup that year and described as 'Champions of the World'.

The Champions!

Beauly eventually ran out winners by 6 hails to one, their opponents' counter apparently allowed out of respect for exiled friends. The appellation 'Champions of the World' followed, although their title was hotly disputed in Scotland! A second game with the Ireland United Hurling Club was drawn, each team scoring four hails.

Meanwhile back in Scotland, the first of several clubs was formed in Glasgow between the founding of Edinburgh Camanachd Club in 1870 and the one in Manchester in 1876. This was Comunn Camanachd Glaschu which was established in November, 1875 under the auspices of the Glasgow Highland Association, membership being open only to members of that association. The letter reproduced here details the background to the formation of organised shinty in Glasgow.

The Old "Comunn Gaidhealach Glaschu".

To the editor of the "Oban Times".

Portree

Sir —

In further reminiscence of this Society, which is now almost forgotten, one portion of its work seems to have become very firmly established, and that is the fostering of the game of shinty.

In November, 1875 at a meeting in the rooms in 30 Hope Street, the writer made a suggestion to the effect that the Society should start a Shinty Club. The proposal was received with acclamation, and at once a committee was formed to get it set agoing, and everyone set to get a shinty team from home. At that time, as far as I know, there was no organized club in existence, with the exception of the Edinburgh and London clubs.

At the Vale of Leven, some of the members of the once-famous Vale Football Club played shinty occasionally, and at Inverary the young men of the town kept up the game among themselves. It was arranged in Glasgow that play should begin in the Queen's Park on New Year's Day, 1876, when sixty young men mustered with their camans. Under the management of Mrs Macpherson, the Skye Poetess, the creature comforts of the gathering were provided in the shape of home-made oat-cakes, scones, cheese, etc.

Mrs Macpherson composed a song for the occasion, which is printed in page 183 of her book. So many joined the Club that it became over-crowded, and a dispute arose as to the dress to be worn at play. Some wanted to keep up the nationality of the club like the Edinburgh and London clubs who always played in the kilt. The greater part, however, preferred knickers, with the result that there was a division, the majority adopting the knickers. Ultimately, however, so many joined that it was found necessary to break up into district and other clubs. These included the Glasgow Cowal, Inverary and other district clubs as well as the "Fardach Fhinn" or the Fingal Lodge of Good Templars.

The advocates of the kilt formed themselves into the "Ossian", but latterly it was found that the big majority of members belonged or had a connection with Skye, so that the name was changed to the "Skye", of which I had the honour of being the first secretary. Immediately after, other clubs

early (Irish) players

were formed all over the country. I remember the late Captain Chisholm of Glassburn wrote for a copy of the rules of the Glasgow club, which, I am afraid, would not satisfy the players of today. The rules were printed in Gaelic and were as follows:-

RIAGHAILTEAN COMUNN CAMANACHD GHLASCHU.

1 — Bithidh an Comunn so air ainmeachadh "Comunn Camanachd Ghlaschu".

2 — Bithidh gach camanaiche 'n a' bhall de Chomunn Gaidhealach Ghlaschu.

3 — Bithidh deich slatan a dh' astar eadar an da phost a bhios aig gach ceann d' an achadh.

4 — An uair a theid am ball seachad air taobh cearr nam post, buailidh an ceann-stuic air ais e.

5 — Chan fhaod fear sam bith am ball a thogail bhar an làir no thiligeadh le laimh an deigh a ghlacadh 's an athar.

6 — Chan fhaod fear beantainn ri fear eile le laimh no caman air son a chumail air ais.

7 — Chan fhaod fear sam bith a bhi steòcaireachd air chul nan ceann-stuic.

8 — Chan fhaod droch fhocal a bhi air a labhairt air raon na h-iomain.

9 — Theid connspaid sa bith a dh'éireas a shochrachadh leis an dà Cheannard agus buill sam bith a thaghas iadsan.

Tha e air iarraidh le luchd-dhreuchd a' Chomuinn so gun dlú-lean gach camanaiche ris na riaghailtean, agus gun gluais e e fein anns gach dòigh mar dhuin'-uasal agus mar Ghàidheal air son cliù a' Chomuinn agus ònair a dhùthcha.

(translation:)

RULES OF GLASGOW SHINTY CLUB

1 — This Club shall be named "Glasgow Shinty Club".

2 — Each shinty player shall be a member of the Glasgow Highland Society.

3 — There shall be a distance of ten yards between the two posts at each end of the field.

4 — When the ball goes past the outside of the posts the hail keeper shall strike it back.

5 — No one may lift the ball up from the ground or throw it with his hand after catching it in the air.

6 — No player may touch another with his hand or club in order to keep him back.

7 — Nobody may hang about behind the hail posts.

8 — No bad language may be used on the shinty field.

9 — Any dispute which arises will be settled by both captains and any members they choose. The office bearers of this Club request that each player closely follows the rules and that he conducts himself in every way as a gentleman and as a Highlander for the reputation of the Club and the honour of his native district.

I understand Captain Chisholm, who was a most enthusiastic Highlander, was the means of starting several clubs in the North.

The shinty of those days was very different from that of today. Then it was a case of every man running after the ball at the same time; no order, no system. But one game with the Vale of Leven opened our eyes, and we were not long in taking a lesson. We had the advantage of being trained by Harry MacNeil one of the crack players of the famous Queen's Park Football Club. Now, after a lapse of 48 years, the game is as popular as ever it was in the old days, and long may it continue.

— I am, etc.

J.G. MacKay.

John G. Mackay, O.B.E., a merchant in Portree, was born in Sutherland and spent his youth in Lochalsh where his father was a schoolmaster. He took a leading part in the land reform movement last century. Articles by him were published in the *Transactions of the Gaelic Society of Inverness* and his book, *The Romantic Story of the Highland Garb and Tartan*, appeared about the time of his death in 1924.

Rapid progress was made and camans were supplied through James Sinclair from 'Land of Lorne'. Rules were drawn up and printed in Gaelic and various

matches followed between Glasgow and Vale of Leven, a club of such standing that Glasgow was considered rash to challenge it, and also between Glasgow and Springburn.

These early matches all attracted a good number of spectators. Differences regarding rules and operation of the club led, however, to a split within Glasgow Camanachd. The issue which brought matters to a head was the clothing to be worn at play. One faction preferred knickerbockers of 42nd tartan with dark blue jerseys and stockings of red and black

Alexander MacKellar, the Tighnabruaich man who became captain of the all-conquering Glasgow Cowal team, and modern shinty's first great tactician

and this was adopted at the Annual General Meeting. The other faction decided to continue wearing kilts and formed the Ossian Shinty Club, with Mr John MacQueen of Skye as Secretary.

It was described in December, 1876 as 'fast advancing towards a high point in proficiency of play and numbers'. In addition to shinty, Highland dancing and gymnastics were indulged in by members during the winter.

During March 1879, Ossian, which appears to have had a short and chequered career, broke up. But from it arose 'The Skye Shinty Club' which was formed at a meeting at Dewar's Hotel on March 25. Having elected office-bearers, it was decided to remain as a kilted club and in the following month Macleod of Macleod accepted an invitation to become Chief.

A number of letters on the vexed question of whether to wear knickerbockers or kilts appeared in the *Highlander* in May and June, 1878. William Lockhart Bogle was one of those who wrote in an attempt to reconcile the disagreeing parties. A letter from J.G. Mackay, at that time Secretary of Ossian, was described as 'breathing Mars throughout', while that of Henry Whyte (Fionn), had 'an impartial tone'. Whyte, a member of the Glasgow Club was one of the best known Gaels of his day. A native of Easdale, he was a prolific writer and a Gaelic bard. He died in 1913. John G. Mackay whose career is given in Martin MacDonald's *Skye Camanachd* (1992) died in 1924.

The matter of dress also took up a considerable amount of the time of members of the Fingal Club, *Comunn Camanachd Fhinn*, which was formed in April, 1877 from members of the Fingal Lodge of Good Templars (Fardach Fhinn) a Highland Lodge which had been established three years earlier. The players are reported to have used Gaelic as their means of communication whilst at play.

The Club's name was changed at the AGM of April, 1880 to Glenforsa and it was agreed that henceforth the dress at play should be knickerbockers of MacKenzie tartan. Play was to be held at Glasgow Green on Saturdays.

Early in March 1877, arrangements were being made by natives of Cowal and Inveraray resident in Glasgow to form shinty clubs to represent their districts. This led to the formation of Glasgow Cowal by the middle of March and they began to play at Southside Park, fielding teams on at least seven occasions that year.

At about the same time the Glasgow Inveraray Club had been formed, taking the number of clubs in the city to five. Glasgow Inveraray and Cowal met on a number of occasions up to 1881 and met notably in the first final of the Glasgow Celtic Society Challenge Cup in April, 1879. This was a contest between two sides each of fifteen players with two umpires and one referee and was won by Glasgow Cowal, captained by shinty's first superstar, A. MacKellar, by six hails to nil. It was observed, as was to happen often, that the losing team lacked the system and combined play of their opponents.

The Celtic Society Trophy is, in fact, shinty's oldest competition and the Society celebrated its Centenary on June 23, 1979 with its cup final at Allan Glen's Sports Ground at Bishopbriggs, now home of Glasgow Mid Argyll. The Society itself had been formed on October 31, 1856 for the purpose of 'preserving and promoting the language, literature,

The Celtic Society Trophy

music, poetry, antiquities and athletic games of the Highlanders'. No fewer than four Presidents of the Camanchd Association have come from the Society's Directorate: Archibald MacPherson, Angus Cameron, Dr John D. Murchison and Donald M. Skinner, the Association's Chief in its Centenary Year. A succession of prominent Highlanders have represented the Society with distinction.

'In the early years of the century, even Ibrox Park, Glasgow, was used as a venue.'

SHINTY MATCH AT IBROX PARK, GLASGOW. GLASGOW COWAL V. KYLES ATHLETIC

The exhibition match played by the above well-known clubs at the Glasgow Rangers' Highland Gathering on Saturday last turned out, as was expected, the most attractive event on the programme. Notwithstanding the inclement weather that prevailed, there was a crowd of 10,000 present. When the shinty teams stepped on the field they were enthusiastically received by the vast assemblage.

The referee, Mr Wm. M. Smith, Campsie, lost no time in starting the game. Cowal were the first to move with freedom, and some nice passages took place amongst the blue and white players. James Campbell at centre was driving the ball well on towards the Kyles goal, but MacLachlan and Munro, assisted by Tom Nicolson and MacPhail, kept the Cowal forwards from getting too near MacKellar. After eight minutes' play MacCorquodale and Montgomery, by nice combination, carried the ball well in towards goal, where MacInnes sent in to MacKellar, and MacVicar following up smartly beat the Kyles custodian amidst great cheering. From the centre Cowal again returned, and in a tackle with MacPhail, Munroe of Cowal was accidentally injured and had to retire. Despite this handicap, Cowal maintained their advantage till half-time, when they led by 1 goal to 0.

The game was resumed in brisk fashion, and some grand bouts took place between James Campbell and Hugh Nicolson, the centres of their respective clubs. Duncan MacLachlan, the clever left centre of Kyles was playing a pretty game. Kyles had a bigger share of the game this half, with the result that Peter Campbell and Fowler had to look lively on several occasions to prevent them from scoring. Five minutes from time Kyles, after a beautiful bit of combination in front of Sinclair, succeeded in equalising the score, MacKellar beating the custodian in clever fashion. The equaliser was well received by the spectators. The closing minutes of the game were brimful of excitement, each side striving to gain the ascendancy, but time was called with the result a draw — 1 goal each.

The introduction of shinty at Ibrox games will go a long way to popularise the game in the south, as was evident from the keen interest manifested in the match by the spectators.

A page from the Littlejohn album, presented to Aberdeen University in 1905

GRECIAN ATHLETES AND EVENING POTATIONS

In the accounts in the *Highlander* of these games played in the period 1874 to 1881 there are many references to rules and the desirability of having these fixed and to be observed by all clubs. Disputes during matches became frequent and the need for having a governing body became an urgent matter. One of those who felt keenly about this was William Lockhart Bogle who was for some time captain of Ossian. A well known artist, he was the son of a Glasgow merchant, Hugh Bogle, and Alexa, daughter of Rev John MacRae, minister of Glenshiel and Glenelg. Some of his boyhood was spent in

Wester Ross, a district with which he maintained close connections and in 1883 he was behind the formation of the Lochcarron Club.

In April, 1877 he had a letter in the *Highlander* stating that the time had come to have rules for universal use, as the bitter disputes which arose often engendered ill feeling and he felt that the rules of some clubs which stated that the Captain should settle all disputes were not satisfactory. In a report, in the same month, in which the activities of the Edinburgh Camanachd were reviewed, the writer gave it as his view that the game should be played according to use and wont in the Highlands and not by adopting 'innovations and dodges' from other games such as football. He went on to say that if unanimity is to exist between clubs, rules must speedily be assimilated and suggested that two office bearers from each club, the captain and secretary, together with a well-known player and member should meet and arrange rules. Again, in the same month, 'Camanaich Og' wrote in a similar strain. Reference was made to off-side play. He told how, in the old way of playing, several teams were allowed to strike on any side and it was generally recognized that when hitting the ball the club was held left hand above right and that this was the best way as it showed more play and less danger. In a game which he had recently seen, when the ball was thrown up, one man always struck his opponent's club aside and turned his back, caused by not having a right and wrong side. As some clubs did not have such a rule the other had to do the same or be at a disadvantage.

A further letter from "W.L.B.", William Lockhart Bogle, appeared in May. Stating the urgency of achieving early standardization of rules, he suggested a meeting of representatives to arrange bye-laws which could be published in the *Highlander*. The eleven clubs to be represented were named by him, Vale of Leven, Edinburgh, Ossian, Glasgow, Glasgow Inverary, Glasgow Cowal, Fingal, Inverary, Greenock, Tobermory and Manchester. Finding that no move to have such a

meeting had been made by July, he again wrote expressing his surprise that the secretary of the Edinburgh club "having the precedence of action being the first established club" had made no arrangements for the delegates to meet and adjust satisfactory association rules.

The delegates eventually met on 13th October 1877 in Whyte's Temperance Hotel, Candleriggs, Glasgow and it was agreed to form a Shinty Association. The clubs represented were Vale of Leven, Glasgow, Inverary, Ossian, Cowal and Fingal. Captain James Menzies, 105th Glasgow Highlanders, was elected President; Mr M. Leitch, 74 Parson Street, Secretary; and Mr M. MacKellar, 31 Raeberry Street, New City Road, Glasgow, Treasurer.

The Constitutional Rules which were drawn up were:

CONSTITUTIONAL RULES

I The Association shall be called the Shinty Association.

II That the committee consist entirely of two representatives including Office Bearers from each club, and that each club be entitled to send three representatives to the Annual General Meeting which shall be held in September each year. That each club subscribe to the funds of the Association ten shillings annually.

III When the ball passes the touch line it shall be taken ten yards inside and thrown up between the player in possession and his opponent opposite where it crossed the line.

IV No one shall be allowed to lift, throw or kick the ball during play.

V The ball to be used shall be of cork, covered with worsted and then with or without a covering of leather.

VI When the ball passes the goal posts by whomsoever it is struck the ball shall be taken ten yards inside and thrown up by the umpire opposite where it passed through.

VII That in the event of a player getting disabled his opponent at commencement of play retires.

VIII No one shall be allowed to push, trip, catch or charge.

IX Should no goal be taken before half time, sides shall be changed and the ball thrown up in mid-field by the umpire.

X Profane language strictly prohibited.

Origins for the design of the Littlejohn Trophy —a page from the Littlejohn Album

The hope was expressed that the Association would be the means of stimulating the formation of new clubs. It had been seen of late that the game could be played as scientifically as any other field game and it was hoped that it would in future be played according to scientific rules.

Similar rules were drawn up at a conference of Argyll clubs at Inverary on 13 October 1880. There was an additional one stating that the goal posts should be 5 yards apart and from 10 to 12 feet in height with a cross bar. These rules were accepted by the Inverary club and are printed in an extract of the minutes of the club by Alasdair MacIntyre in the Shinty Year Book, 1973-74.

It is surprising, as Alister Chisholm remarks in *Shinty in Glasgow — the first five year*s (Shinty Year Book, 1989), that no rules were laid down by the association concerning the dimensions of the playing pitch, the duration of the game and the number of players on each side. The usual number in games held about this time was fifteen.

There were some objections concerning the rules which had been formulated. 'Fideag'*, whose letter appeared on 29th October 1877 commented on the heavy subscription levied by the Association. (Each club had been asked to subscribe to the funds of the Association the sum of ten shillings annually.) He, as one who had played in Inverness-shire and elsewhere for twenty-five years, felt that having an umpire was unecessary except to decide in important games and that the fourth rule was a decided innovation which should never have been passed, especially as to lifting and kicking, the first of these being indispensable for the 'fideag' when available and the second unavoidable when there is little room to work the caman. The tenth rule he found to be totally uncalled for and claimed that a draft of proposed rules should have been published earlier and circulated to clubs for information.

Instances of lifting the ball by players have been noted in some of the newspaper reports. In a game held by the

First and last pages of a letter from Strathglass Shinty club — pre 1893 — when several clubs were endeavouring to rationalise the rules of the game. Strathglass and Capt. Chisholm of Glassburn in particular played a crucial role in the formation of the Association.

---

*Dwelly's Gaelic dictionary defines 'fideag' as "the act of drawing up the ball, hitting it while still in mid air and sending it, at a somewhat high trajectory, to the other end of the field". As he says the word was given to him by A. Henderson, Ardnamurchan, it may not have been in use in the northern Highlands.

Manchester club on Good Friday, 1876 "one of the reds caught the ball as it reached the ground and ran with it until he threw it in" and in the annual game between married and single members of Edinburgh Camanachd in March, 1878 it was reported that "by a united rush the ball was literally carried through the hail".

A Gael in Bradford, A.A. Cameron, had a letter in the *Highlander* in May 1878 in which he objected to the word 'camanachd' being used and suggested the more euphonious 'cluich iomain' or 'cluich bhall'.

Captain James Menzies presided at the Annual General Meeting on 6th Septem-

from the Littlejohn album

ber 1878 in Dewar's Hotel of the 'Glasgow Association' as it was named in the report. Vale of Leven, Furnace, Glasgow, Inverary, Glasgow Inverary, Ossian, Cowal and Fingal were the clubs represented on this occasion when minor alterations were made to the rules. A letter was read from the Glasgow Celtic Society stating that they intended to present to the Association a silver cup for competition by the various clubs connected with it. Games in connection with this trophy were arranged and took place during the months which followed. Glasgow Cowal lodged a protest to the Association against Vale of Leven after the game played in February and this resulted in a replay being ordered. This was to take place on the same ground on 22nd March with umpires and referee appointed by the Association. Because of an error this game did not take place and the ruling was that Glasgow Cowal should claim the tie. In the final in April 1879 Glasgow Cowal beat Glasgow Inverary by 6 hails to one, each side having 15 players. The teams at this, the first final, were —

Cowal: P. Kerr, James Campbell, Alex MacKellar, captain, D. Smith, W. Bell, John MacKellar, P. Weir, D. Clark, D. Urquhart, John Barr, P. Cairns, D. MacLaren, D. Campbell, A.M. MacKellar, W. Orr.

Inverary: M. Leitch, P. Ferguson, J. Purdie, H. MacKellar, D. Maclachlan, J. MacArthur, A.M. MacKellar, H. MacAlpin, A. MacNicol, J. Campbell, C. Richardson,

D. Fletcher, D. Munro, J. Leitch, A. Mac-Callum. The umpires were H. Whyte and Mr Byron and the referee was John Elder of the Celtic Society.

The chief business at a special meeting held in the Athole Arms Hotel on Wednesday 9th July was the presentation of the Celtic Society Cup to Glasgow Cowal. Mr Duncan Smith, Vice President of the Glasgow Celtic Society, was in the chair and also present were Captain James Menzies and Mr J.G. Mackay, President and Vice President of the Association and Mr A. MacTavish of London Camanachd. The chairman presented the cup.

The report described the cup as being of 'chased design' and bearing the inscription 'Clanna nan Gaidheal ri guaillaibh a cheile. Challenge Cup presented by the Glasgow Celtic Society, 1879. Winners — Cowal Club; A. MacKellar; captain.'

At the Annual General Meeting held in Dewar's Hotel on 6th September 1879 two new clubs were admitted to the Association, these being Glencoe and Vale of Laroch. Office Bearers were appointed. President, Captain James Menzies; Vice President, D. Macpherson; Secretary, Mr Munro, Glasgow Inverary; Treasurer, Mr Orr. It was reported also that there were several amendments to the rules but none of much importance. It appears that one of these concerned the number of players on each side as a report of a friendly game between Glasgow and Glasgow Inverary later in September states that it was played 'according to the new rules of the Association' with twelve on each side.

There was a strange occurrence at a friendly game in October between Cowal and Glasgow Inverary. Inverary opened the scoring and Cowal soon equalized but this goal was disputed. Shortly after this 'the game ended in a most complete and unfortunate stampede, the true cause of which seems difficult to determine'. Play had lasted for only 30 minutes.

The final on 10th April 1880 was between the recently formed Glencoe Club and Vale of Leven and was played at Summertown Park. Vale of Leven, whose captain was J. Smith, won by 4 hails to 2 over this club which was new to competitive shinty. The following year, however, Glencoe won the cup, their captain being J. Kennedy.

A note in the *Badenoch Record* of 4th May 1957 tells that the last final 'of the original competition of the old Association' about 1888 took place between Furnace and Inverary and that there had been a dispute. It then stated that Inverary placed an interdict on the cup and the competition was not completed. Dunollie had been winners in 1886 and Inverary in 1887. Oban were winners in 1889 and 1890. A list of the clubs which won the Celtic Society Cup along with the names of the captains appears in the *Shinty Year Book* of 1975-76.

As the *Highlander* newspaper continued only to 1881 no further reports of the Association have been noticed. It ap-

The Strathglass team, flanked by their pipers and with Archibald Chisholm at their heart, before the great game of 1887.

pears that it ceased to exist or was in abeyance as in a letter to the *Inverness Courier* of 26th February 1892 'Buaileam ort' asked 'where is it now and these clubs?' He went on to say that Edinburgh Camanachd had not joined the Association and never disputed any of the rules and that an association was simply 'a mean copy of that detestable game, football!' Another writer to the same number of the Inverness Courier, 'Shinty Player, High Street, Kingussie' said that his club would welcome rules for all games and that those of Kingussie might serve as a model. The Badenoch Record of 2nd January 1948 contains notes by John

Cameron who stated that about 1887 the Newtonmore Club of which he had been secretary had its rules printed and copies had been sent to others for approval.

In the Northern Highlands there was a gradual awakening of interest and the first club there was formed at Strathglass, for long known as a stronghold of the game, in 1880 with Captain Archibald MacRae Chisholm of Glassburn as Chief. A 'Constitution, Rules and Regulations of Comunn Camanachd Straghlais' and 'Rules and Regulations for the Game of Shinty' were drawn up that year and were printed in the history of the club which appeared in 1980. 'It is a particular rule of Strathglass Shinty Club' ran a report of play at Struy in January 1887, 'that ardent spirits shall not form any part of the refreshment given by the club to its members' and 'this commendable rule is strictly enforced'. The founding of Lochcarron followed in 1883 and in 1884 Glenurquhart came into being. The first contest in 1887 between Strathglass and Glenurquhart at the Bught in Inverness aroused great interest and a revival of game in Inverness and district which resulted in a club being formed there later that year. The Rules and Bye-Laws of Play of the Inverness Club are to be found in its history published in 1987. The enthusiasm engendered by the first contest between Strathglass and Glenurquhart in

The men of Glenurquhart preparing to face the undefeated Strathglass

March 1887 caused the formation of a club known as the Wanderers in Inverness. It was composed of natives of Glenurquhart living in Inverness and its life was short, being mentioned on only one occasion.

About this time in Badenoch, a district in which interest had never really waned during the early part of the century, keen contests were being held between Kingussie and Newtonmore and clubs were formed in these places. Although accurate information is not available it appears that these great rivals came into existence about 1887 or 1888.

Reminiscences of Auchnagoul

Mary MacVicar, nee MacNaughton, aged 90. (Shinty Yearbook. 1992-93.)

Shinty was the only game the boys played when my father was a boy at Auchnagoul, (3 miles South West of Inveraray). All the best players there, when they reached their teens, were generally picked to play for Inveraray. The Inveraray team had won all their matches played at the surrounding district and felt they could tackle the Vale of Leven, the reputed Champions of Scotland.

So, in December 1878, they set off feeling they could beat the Champions. They played their shinty in a pack. All running with the ball, feeling they would be sure to win.

They were amazed that the Vale did not run with the ball, but passed it to a member of their team stationed at strategic points, such as backs, centres and forwards. They all passed the ball so quickly, that when an Inveraray man went to try to get the ball, it would be away at the other side of the pitch.

I never heard how many goals the Vale had scored. They would be too numerous to count. The Inveraray team went off the pitch one by one. When their numbers were so depleted, they stopped the game.

Profiting by that practical lesson, the Inveraray team practised passing the ball either forward or back, never letting it rest, so that, at the return match the following year, they beat the Vale by 12 goals to 2!

My brother was talking to Willie Stewart about shinty and he told him about a shinty match he and Charlie Guthrie played against my father and Peter Munro, to decide whether the town players or the Auchnagoul players were the best — the winners to get a bottle of whisky.

They tossed a coin for the choice of ends. The referee got them going and they changed over at half time. My father and Peter won the bottle of whisky. I am sure they would be in need of a drink, after an hour and a half running all over a full sized shinty pitch.

The ball at that time was made of birch wood and it travelled very fast. It could also be hit a very great distance. The only time my mother went to a shinty match, Archie Munro the goalkeeper got his eye knocked out by the birch ball. When my mother saw that, she fainted. That was in 1889.

I think it was after that they started to play with the leather ball. After the First World War ended a few shinty enthusiasts got the southern shinty teams going again. Kyles still had the Nicolsons and their name combined with previous victories made it more difficult to beat them.

Furnace, Inveraray and Kyles Athletic were equally good. Furnace were the first to break the Kyles monopoly. At that time the south teams were sure to beat the north.

A club at Aberdeen University was in existence by 1889*. In December of that

---

*R. Hutchinson in *Camanachd* gives 1861 as the year of its foundation.

year a match, described in the *Inverness Courier* as the first one the university club ever played, took place at Seafield, Inverness between the students and a club formed by employees of the Locomotive Department of the Highland Railway in Inverness. This Inverness club, which also was founded in 1887 and continued only for a few years, won this game and a return one at the Duthie Park in Aberdeen. The Edinburgh University Club was formed in 1891 and it was not until 1901 that Glasgow University Club was formed with Angus J. MacVicar, who later became the well known minister at Southend, Kintyre as its first captain. He and two Ross-shire students, Murdo MacRae and Murdoch MacKenzie, were behind the founding of the club about which there is an account in the Shinty Yearbook of 1971.

The first occasion on which a club from the south played in the Northern Highlands was on 29th March 1891 when Edinburgh Camanachd played Kingussie at Ruthven on a terrace near the old barracks. A great number of spectators saw the home team win by 3 hails to 2. All the Edinburgh players were from the northern districts and almost all were Gaelic speakers. This game was generally considered to have been a good exhibition of skill and was free from any dispute.

It was not so at a game held a week later at Castle Leod, Strathpeffer, where Caberfeidh and Lovat each scored one hail. There was a long and annoying delay in starting the game because of a disagreement over one of the rules and the account of the game again stressed the need to have an association and standard rules.

A meeting between Kingussie and Edinburgh was arranged to take place at Inverleith in February 1892 but because of a dispute concerning the size of the field Kingussie refused to play and departed, thus causing ill feeling between the two clubs.

The increasing popularity of the game at this period in the north was shown by Kingussie receiving an invitation from a body of influential people in Elgin to play an exhibition game there. The consequence was that Kingussie met Caberfeidh in early April 1892 at Linkwood Park, about one mile from Elgin, before a crowd of several hundred. Kingussie won by three hails to nil and both captains expressed the hope that there would soon be an association. The ball used was the Kingussie one which was described as smaller than a tennis ball and very hard whereas the Caberfeidh ball was soft and larger than an ordinary cricket ball. The camans used by Kingussie were lighter than those used by Caberfeidh.

At play held by the Strathglass Club at Cannich in January 1887 a hockey regulation ball from London was tried out but was found to be too heavy and hard and in its place one made by a member, Alex. MacKenzie, a farmer from Beauly, was used and was found to be preferable.

The Kingussie Camanachd Team 1891-92

John Cameron, to whose notes in the *Badenoch Record* of 21st February 1948 reference has been made, there stated that the first time a leather ball was used was in a famous contest at Dalchully in Laggan between Badenoch and Lochaber 61 years before. In the first half the old hair ball (ball gaosaid) was used and in the second, the leather one. The old ball was made of cork and horse hair made into twine around it. In diameter it was twice the size of the leather one and three times as heavy. There were no goal posts or nets on that occasion and the players had no recognized positions. When a player retired injured a substitute was allowed. John Cameron, a shoemaker, was aged 82 when he wrote and he had made many balls for the Newtonmore club in its early years.

It is evident that by about 1890 combined play was becoming more usual. A report of a game between Caberfeidh and Kinlochewe a year later than the Elgin

68

The distinctive person of Donald Campbell, honorary captain of Kingussie Camanachd at the time of the club's Highlands versus Lowlands clash with Glasgow Cowal in the 1880's.

one stated that Caberfeidh had learned 'from the crack Kingussie team in combining.' The remarkable skill in passing and combining by Kingussie was a feature of a match they played with Lochaber in February 1893. Newtonmore too were showing similar skill at this time and one report told that all their players could handle the club with the left hand.

Challenge after challenge appeared in the press as clubs sought to establish their right to the title of 'Champion'.

INVERNESS COURIER

KINGUSSIE AND NEWTONMORE SHINTY.
to the Editor.   Kingussie, 1st March, 1893.

Sir,

In the Northern Chronicle of to-day we observe the following astounding advertisement, viz.:- "As Kingussie failed in playing Newtonmore Shinty Club, we are now ready to go halfway to meet any team in Scotland as may be arranged. — Shinty Secretary, Newtonmore." We have only to refer the boastful advertisers to their geographies to learn that Lochaber is in Scotland, where in the latitude of 4 to 1 it can be seen sitting on Newtonmore's neck with Kingussie 5 degrees higher still ruling the roost. Since the formation of the Kingussie Club three years ago we have played no fewer than thirteen matches and never yet suffered defeat. In the list of clubs beaten by us are Newtonmore, Edinburgh, and Grantown.

A team is now formed consisting of the best players in these three Clubs, and this combination seeks to play Kingussie under the name of the Newtonmore Club.

Kingussie agreed to play them on Saturday first, reserving the right to publish the match as Kingussie versus a combination of Newtonmore, Edinburgh, and Grantown Camanachd Clubs. On hearing this, the would-be Newtonmore Club refused to play, and now cover their cowardice by inserting the above advertisement, with a view to bring discredit on our Club, who not only offered to play them as already stated on Saturday first, but are still open to play on any other suitable day that will meet the convenience of the already defeated "Lochaber no more" combination, who would like to palm themselves off as the Newtonmore Shinty Club.

Signed in name and on behalf of the Kingussie Club. JAMES D. PULLAR, Captain.

JAMES GRANT, Vice-Captain.

JNO. CAMPBELL, Secretary.

In his book *Shinty. A Short History of the Ancient Highland Game*, Rev. Fr. J. Ninian Macdonald, O.S.B., tells of the great hold which the game had taken in the various parts of the Highlands by 1893 and says "A match played between the Kingussie and Glasgow Cowal Clubs on April 3rd of the same year was described as one of the finest exhibitions of the game ever seen. It formed a culminating point in the renaissance. It aroused such intense and widespread interest that a general meeting of all supporters of the game was convoked at Kingussie in the following October."

This game between the leading north and south clubs was described as a memorable one and was attended by many from all over Badenoch and further afield. Business in Kingussie was suspended on that Monday afternoon which, being a Glasgow holiday, enabled many of the Glasgow Cowal supporters to attend. Play began at 1.15pm. The ball used was smaller than the one to which Kingussie was accustomed and Cowal had lighter camans. Each club had different rules and the teams were of fourteen players each with an umpire. The only hail scored was by Glasgow Cowal five minutes before the end. Kingussie wore scarlet jerseys and white knickerbockers while Glasgow Cowal, whose photograph appears in the *Celtic Monthly* of 1893, wore grey striped jerseys and black knee breeches. Later in the same year the *Celtic Monthly* tells of a six a side tournament arranged within Glasgow Cowal and that in 1897 a match was arranged with Dublin Hurling Club.

The various statements expressing the desirability of having a governing body came to fruition in the autumn of 1893.

The *Inverness Courier* of Friday 29th September 1893 has the following notice on the subject —

SHINTY

Proposed Central Shinty Association.

Some time ago Mr L.A. Macpherson of Corrimony, Mr John Macdonald of Keppoch (Captain of the Lochaber Club), and other influential gentlemen interested in the game, entered into communication with the officials of the Kingussie Shinty Club regarding the desirability of forming a central organisation to draw up rules for the guidance of the various clubs in Scotland, and asking the Kingussie Club to call a conference at Kingussie, as a central place, of delegates from these clubs, so far as they were known. In compliance with the request a meeting of members of the Kingussie Club was held on Tuesday evening — the Chieftain (Provost Macpherson) presiding — to consider the suggestion. After a full discussion it was resolved to call such a conference at Kingussie on Tuesday, 10th October next, at one o'clock, and Mr John Campbell, the Secretary, was instructed to prepare a circular to be sent to the several clubs inviting them each to send two delegates to Kingussie on the day fixed.

The meeting took place as arranged and the minute reads as follows:-

At Kingussie and within the Victoria Hall there on Tuesday, 10th October 1893 at a Meeting of Representatives of various shinty clubs throughout the country, held for the purpose of forming a Camanachd Association.

On the motion of Mr John MacDonald, Keppoch, captain of the Brae Lochaber Club, C.J.B. Macpherson, Esq., of Balavil was called to the chair and Mr John Campbell, Hon. Secretary of the Kingussie Club, Clerk of the Meeting.

There were also present from Aberdeen University — Kenneth MacLennan and Malcolm MacBean: Alvie Club — Macpherson of Balavil and Peter Stewart: Brae Lochaber — John Macdonald and A.H. MacDonald: Glenurquhart — L.A. Macpherson and Mr Macdonald: Grantown — A. Grant and J. Grant: Insh — Malcolm Smith and Murdoch MacGregor; Invergarry — John Macdonald and John Campbell; Inverness —; Kingussie — James D. Pullar and John Campbell; Laggan — Dr Campbell and D. MacKillop; London Northern Counties — James Campbell; Newtonmore — John Cameron and Maj. Cattanach; Strathglass — J.B. Grant; Strathpeffer — H.F. Gunn; Kinlochewe — H.F. Gunn.

A letter from Captain Chisholm, Strathglass was read regretting his inability to attend the conference and wishing it every success.

The Clerk stated that as secretary to the Kingussie Club he had been requested by the members to call this conference in terms of letters which they had received from several influential gentlemen throughout the country desirous of having a Central Association formed to regulate the Game of Shinty. The circular calling the meeting was then read, together with a list of thirty-five Clubs to which it was sent. Letters favourable to the formation of an Association were also submitted from the following clubs, viz:- Glasgow Cowal; Inverary; Ballachulish; Edinburgh University; Edinburgh Northern Counties; Edinburgh Camanachd Club; Fort William;

Captain Archibald Macra Chisholm of Glassburn — First Chief of Camanachd Association, 1893-1897

Spean Bridge; Furnace; Inverness; Oban; Strachur.

On the motion of Mr Macdonald, Keppoch, seconded by Mr Macdonald, Glen Urquhart, it was unanimously resolved to form a Shinty Association.

Print of Rules drafted for the guidance of the meeting were then submitted, and these having been taken up seriatim were, with several alterations and amendments, adopted as the playing rules of the Association.

It was resolved that each club joining the Association pay an Annual Subscription of 10/-.

It was further resolved that the Office Bearers consist of a Chief, a President and three Vice Presidents with a Secretary and Treasurer: and the following were appointed to these offices, viz:—

Chief — Captain Chisholm of Glassburn. President — Lord Lovat. Vice Presidents — Cluny Macpherson. C.J.B. Macpherson of Balavil. L.A. Macpherson of Corrimony. Secretary and Treasurer — Mr John Campbell, Kingussie.

It was resolved the first Annual Meeting of the Association be held in Inverness on one of the Northern Meeting days and one member from each of the Badenoch Clubs was appointed along with the Secretary to carry on the business of the Association until then.

On the motion of Mr H.F. Gunn, Strathpeffer, Mr C.J.B. Macpherson of Balavil was thanked for presiding and a similar compliment having been paid to the Clerk the meeting after a sitting of five hours ended.

(signed) C.J.B. Macpherson Chairman of meeting.

The *Inverness Courier* report of the above stated that among others present were Mr James Macdonald, builder, Kingussie; Mr John Cattanach, slater, Newtonmore; Mr D. MacBean, Inspector of Poor, Alvie; Mr Mackintosh, bootmaker, Kingussie; Mr James Crerar, printer, do; Mr Thomas Warren, do; Mr John Campbell, High Street, do.

The same account also stated:—

"With considerable forethought the Kingussie Club had previously drawn up draft rules for the consideration of the conference. These draft rules were printed and submitted to the delegates so that the course of business was very much facilitated, as each rule was taken up and discussed, and if found not satisfactory, adjusted and adopted.

A rule that was the subject of considerable discussion had reference to the size of the field for play. The dimensions suggested were as follow: — "Not less than 250 yards long by 150 yards broad; not more than 300 yards long by 200 yards broad." Mr Gunn and several others referred to the great difficulty that many clubs experienced in obtaining a field so large for practice, and held that it would be unfair to such clubs if such a minimum as that suggested was adopted by the Association. It was ultimately agreed to reduce the minimum to 200 yards long by 150 yards broad. The conference, which lasted for about five hours, finally agreed upon the following rules:-

1. Each team shall number 16 players, who shall be bona fide members of the Club for which they play, and no individual shall play for more than one Club during one season.

2. The field of play shall not be less than 200 yards long by 150 yards broad, nor more than 300 yards long by 200 yards broad. In cup matches the maximum obtainable must be played.

3. The hails shall be 12 feet wide and 10 feet high, attached by a fixed cross-bar above.

4. The time allowed for playing a game shall be one hour and a half, with an interval of five minutes at half-time. Teams to change sides after each hail scored; but if no hail is scored by half-time, ends shall be changed, and no further change to take place.

5. Nothing but hails shall count.

6. When both teams are ready the referee, standing in mid-field, shall throw the ball straight in the air, between two opposing players.

7. No player shall use his hands or club to hold or push his opponent, neither shall he trip, hack, jump at, or throw him by the use of his leg or club. A set blow will be given as a penalty for every foul granted by the referee, but a hail from such blow will not count.

8. Rough or unruly play will not be tolerated, and any player observed wilfully infringing any of the rules shall be expelled the field of play, and shall not be replaced by a fresh man.

9. A player disabling an opponent must retire from the game unless the referee declare the man so disabled to be in fault.

10. When the ball is sent from the field of play through the hail-posts and under the cross-bar connecting them, the hail is won, even should it graze the posts or bar, or be sent through by one of the defending side.

11. The ball may be stopped by the hand, but if caught must be immediately dropped.

No player shall be allowed to run with or throw the ball.

12. The ball to be played with shall consist of cork and worsted with a covering of leather, and shall measure 7 to 8 inches in circumference.

13. When the ball passes the side lines the player first reaching it must bring it within the line, and, if no opponent challenges him, can take a set blow, but if challenged he must take it 10 yards within the line, and drop it between himself and his opponent.

14. When the ball passes the hails without scoring, the hail keeper has the option of sending the ball afield with either hand or club.

15. Players are prohibited from playing with spikes in their shoes, and no iron plates or metal of any kind shall be allowed on the clubs.

16. If the ball be sent from the field of play past the hails on either side by a player of the defending side, it shall be taken back 15 yards in front of the point at which it was sent out of play, and thrown up by the referee between two opposing players.

17. When the ball is thrown in the air, as provided for in rules 6 and 17, the two players shall stand with crossed clubs, and no other player allowed within 5 yards till the ball is hit.

18. Each competing club to choose 2 umpires and between them 1 referee for each match.

19. At the commencement of the game, and after each hail is scored, the players shall take the places allotted to them by their respective captains.

20. Except in a scrimmage, no opponent shall be allowed to stand within five yards of the hails unless the ball be in play in front.

21. No person admitted to the field of play during the course of a match except the referee, umpires, and a club-bearer for each team.''

The Annual Meeting of the Association was held within the Burgh Court House, Inverness on Friday, 21 September 1894. Mr C.J.B. Macpherson of Balavil was in the chair and the following clubs were represented. Alvie — C.J.B. Macpherson of Balavil and Mr Peter Stewart, Feshie Bridge; Aberdeen — Mr B. Davidson and Mr G.A. Reid, Aberdeen; Laggan — Mr Donald MacKillop, Blargie; Grantown — Mr J. Grant, Grantown; Camerons — Captain Malcolm and Sergeant MacLean, The Barracks; London N.C. — Mr D. MacGillivray and Mr A. Davidson; Kingussie — Mr Ewan Campbell, Kingussie and Mr R. Stewart, Perth; Invergarry — Mr John MacGillivray and Mr Harry MacRaild, Glengarry; Strathglass — Mr J. Grant, Erchless; Inverness — Mr Alex Macpherson and Mr D. MacGillivray, Inverness; Glenurquhart — Mr Macdonald, Drumnadrochit; Caberfeidh — Mr Gunn, Strathpeffer; Kinlochewe — Mr Gunn, Strathpeffer.

The Office Bearers appointed for the ensuing year were President, Lord Lovat; Vice Presidents, Cluny, Balavil and Corrimony; Chieftain, Captain Chisholm, Strathglass; Secretary and Treasurer, Mr John Campbell, Kingussie.

The meeting revised the Rules of the Game and the following alterations were made:

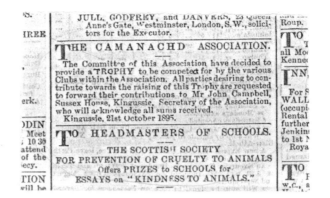

(above): The beginnings of a trophy

(below): An early drawing of the Camanachd Challenge Cup, designed by Hamilton and Inches, Edinburgh.

*The Camanachd
Association Challenge
Trophy*

Rule 1. That each team number 12 or 16 players instead of 16 at present.

Rule 2. That the field of play for a team of 12 shall be not more than 250 yds by 100 yds nor less than 150 yds by 70 yds. The field for a team of 16 to be not more than 300 yds by 200 yds and not less than 200 yds by 150 yds.

Rule 3. That the hails be 12ft wide by 10ft high attached by a cross bar above and provided with nets fixed at a distance of not less than 4ft 6in behind the goal line and attached to the cross bar and uprights.

Rule 4. That teams play half time each way instead of changing ends after each hail is scored.

Rule 7. That the word "charge" be added before the word "trip".

Rule 13. That a clause be inserted to the effect that when the ball passes the side line it shall be taken in 16 yds and thrown up between two opposing players.

Rule 16. That the word "intentionally" be inserted between "be" and "sent" in the first line of this rule.

Rule 18. That two linesmen be added in addition to the two umpires and referee.

It was at this meeting that the question of having a trophy for competition among the clubs of the Association was considered and it was decided to leave the matter over to the next meeting in order to give the various clubs time to fully consider the proposal.

At the Annual General Meeting of 1895, on the motion of Lord Lovat, it was unanimously resolved that there should be competition among the various clubs for such a trophy and, in order to keep down the expenses of the competing clubs, four divisions be formed, the clubs in each division to compete among themselves according to ballot, then the leading clubs in each division against each other. A committee was formed to raise funds for the trophy and to frame rules for its competition. At this meeting amendments to the rules of play were submitted by the Glengarry Club these being:—

1. That the ball to be played with should have a fixed weight, not lighter than 3 oz. and not heavier than 4 oz., at the same time keeping to regulation size.

2. That rule 17 be altered, so that "no player be allowed within ten yards," instead of five yards as at present.

3. That in order to facilitate linesmen's duties there should be two on each side of the field — four in all.

The Association unanimously adopted the first amendment, and gave effect to it in a clause added to rule 12 of play; but the second did not appear to commend itself to the meeting, and was withdrawn, while the third was lost on a division.

The draft of rules prepared by the secretary in connection with the proposed trophy were revised by the committee and adopted at a meeting in Inverness on Thursday, 17th October 1895. The secretary was instructed to send a copy of the proposed rules for the trophy to all known shinty clubs throughout the country, whether associated or not, along with a circular calling a meeting of the Association for 16th November and an intimation that entries for the competition would be received up to 12th November. The secretary was also asked to apply by public advertisement for subscriptions in the *Inverness Courier, Northern Chronicle, Elgin Courant, Oban Times* and *People's Journal* and was authorized to receive and acknowledge all sums for that object on behalf of the committee.

OBAN TELEGRAPH
December 20, 1895

INVERARAY v RANGERS (Ardkinglas)

These clubs met in a friendly game upon Ardkinglas Park, Cairndow, on Saturday last. Heavy rain had fallen during the early morning and forenoon, but in the afternoon the weather improved slightly, only one shower falling during the progress of the game. The Inveraray were not out at full strength, some of the juniors thus being given an opportunity of showing their paces. The following are the teams:

Rangers — Goal, Gregor Macgregor; backs, Hugh Clark, Duncan Mackellar; half-backs, Nicol Luke, Thomas Jones; centres, John Macnicol, Duncan Macvicar, Hugh Brodie; forwards, Duncan Macnicol, Hector Urquhart (captain), Peter Macnicol, Donald Macintyre. Umpire, Mr P. Brodie.

Inveraray — Goal, Joseph Buchanan; backs, John Sinclair, Robert Campbell, half-backs, Ernest Smith (captain), Alastair Macarthur; centres, Peter Macgregor, James Lawson and Dugald Macdonald; forwards, William Stewart, Andrew Paterson, Charles Macarthur and James Stewart. Umpire, Mr E. Maccallum. Rev J.S. Barrowman, Strachur, acted as referee.

The game started shortly after 2 p.m. Inveraray having won the toss, played with the wind at their backs. On the ball being thrown up, the Rangers made some progress towards their opponents' goal but the Inveraray backs cleared well up field, and their forwards getting possession scored the first goal within 5 minutes of the start. On resuming Inveraray kept up the pressure, but the home defence was good. At last the Rangers came away, and the

Two details of the Camanachd Association Challenge Trophy

Inveraray goal had one or two narrow escapes. Inveraray again began to press, and the Rangers goal once more fell, this time to a high shot from the left. Play now settled down somewhat, but was mainly confined to the Rangers' territory. Half-time found Inveraray leading by 2 goals to 0. On changing ends play was begun with much more dash, each goal being visited in quick succession, and the backs on both sides were taxed to their utmost. Inveraray again began to press round the Rangers' citadel, and scored a third and fourth goals. The Rangers now played up with great dash, and kept up a hot siege on the Inveraray goal, but could not get an opening. Inveraray again transferred operations to their opponents' goal, and for the last fifteen minutes of the game kept hovering round the Rangers' posts. The final result was — Inveraray, 4 goals; Rangers, 0.

The rules for the competition, after revision and slight amendment, were duly approved at a general meeting on Saturday, 16th November in Inverness. It was also resolved that, because of the difficulty involved in visiting Portree, the Skye club would play competition games on the mainland on ground to be arranged by the trophy committee which would be composed of one representative from each competing club, five to form a quorum. Meetings of this committee were to be held at Kingussie unless otherwise arranged.

Mr Duncan Macpherson, Gun and Fishing Tackle Maker, Drummond Street, Inverness, had sent a letter asking the Association to accept a hickory caman to be presented to the captain of the trophy winning team. The caman was gratefully accepted and Mr Macpherson thanked. This presentation of a silver mounted caman by Mr Macpherson became an annual feature at these meetings and his nephew Mr John Macpherson, who had a long connection with the Inverness Club

and with the Association, continued the custom.

For the purpose of dividing the country into playing districts and balloting for the first round of the competition, the committee met at Kingussie on Friday, 29th November, 1895. The result of the balloting was as follows.

Northern District, Rogart v Inverness, Caberfeidh v Beauly, Lovat v Nairn. Portree, a bye. Central District, Newtonmore v Grantown, Alvie v Laggan, Kingussie v Insh. Western District, Glengarry v Spean Bridge, Brae Lochaber v Ballachulish. Southern District, London Camanachd v Glasgow Cowal.

The first mentioned club in each case had choice of ground and ties were to be played on or before 10th January.

The various rounds having been played, the final tie of the Camanachd Cup took place at Inverness on 25th April, 1896. The report of the *Inverness Courier* follows.

KINGUSSIE V. GLASGOW COWAL

Great interest was centred in the match which was played in Inverness on Saturday. The occasion was the final match of the Camanachd Cup competition — a competition which has been the means of raising the flagging interest in the fine old Highland pastime of shinty. The contending teams were the Kingussie and Glasgow Cowal, two brilliant exponents of the game, and the contest might be fitly termed a fight between the North and South. The Cowal Club came

North with a terrorising name, but it was quite on the card that the Badenoch warriors would grimly fight for the honour that was at stake. Thanks to the energy of Mr Campbell, Secretary of the Association, who carried out all the arrangements, the park at Needlefield, where the match was played, was put into good condition for the game. The day was practically observed as a holiday in Kingussie, and the special train which conveyed the team to Inverness brought over 400 persons desiring to see the contest. From strath and glen ardent enthusiasts flocked into Inverness, the streets of which contained an unwonted number of wearers of kilt and knickerbocker. The Glasgow team arrived on Friday night to be in trim for the contest. The weather seemed in a smiling mood, but just before the match began, it grew murky, and a drizzling rain fell which rendered the playing pitch a bit slippery. Notwithstanding the charge of a shilling, crowds flocked to the match, and there must have been about 1000 persons present. The money drawn at the gate reached the sum of £41. As the teams lined up on the field, the crowd anxiously weighed up their physical abilities. The Cowal team looked a smart, wiry, well-built lot. Their opponents are heavier, and look as if possessed of more stamina and grit. On the whole, from outward physical appearance, there is little to choose between the teams.

The following were the teams:- Kingussie — Goal, John Campbell; backs, J. Campbell and A. Macpherson; half-backs, A. Gibson, Dallas, and Pullar; forwards, Grant, Cumming, Robertson, Campbell, and Ross (captain). Cowal — W. Robinson; backs, P. Campbell and D. Martin; half-backs, Dun. Morrison and John Macinnes; centres, D. Robinson, A. Campbell, and A.B. Ferguson; forwards, Peter Macinnes, Thomas Scott (captain), J. McCorquodale, and A. Crawford.

The ball has been thrown up by Referee Macgillivray, and the commotion around the ropes is hushed. The Cowal start well, but Gibson of Kingussie strikes the ball towards Cowal territory. Back it comes with unerring accuracy, and Cowal has the first bye. The Kingussie team looked unsettled and, taking advantage of this, the Glaswegians are playing well; their striking is sharp and sure, and Tom Scott plants a fine shot, but Campbell saves with a timely stroke. Still the Cowal players keep the ball in Kingussie territory. Again and again Dallas of Kingussie, by most determined and really brilliant play, averts danger, and frustrates his opponents, who are essaying for hails. Matters look as if Cowal will score, but their forwards are a bit lax, and are often outplayed by Kingussie defence. The game opens out to some extent. The Badenoch men are beginning to play to some purpose and with more method. The forwards are getting more of the ball, and, encouraged by the slogans of their enthusiastic supporters, who are as demonstrative as Highlanders ought to be, they play up and make the acquaintance of the Cowal custodier. The Cowal still look the more likely to score, but the Kingussie defence seems impregnable, and the Kingussie forwards, no doubt inspired by the brilliant play of their own defence, re-awaken to a sense of their responsibility, and, by powerful striking, rush into their opponents' territory. Pullar, Gibson and Dallas stand out prominently. The characteristics of the play of the teams were most diverse. The men of the hills — Kingussie — fought in the most impetuous manner. Their striking was vigorous and de-

Kingussie — 1896 First winners of the Camanachd Association Challenge Trophy
(back row):John Campbell, A. MacPherson, John Campbell, A. MacPherson
(middle row): Col-Sergt. MacDonald, J.D. Pullar, James Grant, James Smith, Alex
Cumming, John Campbell
(front row): Alex Gibson, John Dallas, Provost MacPherson, D. Campbell, Wm. Ross, Alex
Campbell

termined. The city men — the Cowal — hit sharp and sure, and their players up till now, at any rate, with more finish than their opponents. The play was carried with unabated vigour from side to side, and from goal to goal. Ultimately, with a dash and impetuosity that was well nigh irresistible, the men from Badenoch press their opponents, and Ross has the satisfaction of scoring the first goal for Kingussie, after seventeen minutes' play. On resuming, the Cowal came away beautifully, and in a twinkling a rare shot flies directly over the Kingussie uprights. The Glasgow men assault most severely, and it does surprise many that they do not score. A. Macpherson and Johnnie Campbell are ever to the fore, and defy the best efforts of the Cowal players to score. The Badenoch men are now asserting themselves more strongly, and on pressing they are again dangerously near scoring. The back division are plying their camans to some purpose, and are sending the ball well in. A. Campbell snaps the ball, and by a scorching shot scores the second hail for Kingussie, amid the loud and prolonged demonstrations of the spectators. Nothing succeeds like success, and it would seem as if Kingussie were really to be masters of the situation, as they hurried away for more hails. The Cowal again assert themselves. The tall, lanky centre is undoubtedly as finished and competent a player as any on the field, and by his work the team makes progress. Again the weakness of the forwards is seen, and the two Kingussie backs find no difficulty in keeping their goal clear until half-time is called.

Resuming, the Cowal made a fine effort to reduce their opponents' score. By clear, sharp, timely striking, their forwards, who are clustering about the vicinity of the Kingussie uprights, receive likely chances but are thwarted, or send the ball bye. The players are not only using their clubs, some are adepts at accurate stopping with hand and feet, and this lends some variety to the play. The Kingussie fly away. A. Ross catching the ball in the air, deftly sends a shot for the Cowal uprights, but it passes over the bar. The pace did not slacken. It was wonderful how the players maintained the high rate of speed and energy required. The ball was carried from one hailpost to another. A. Macpherson was working with much power for the Kingussie team, his powerful striking being of immense service. Fouls were awarded both sides, but it gave neither any advantage. Cowal look like scoring, and are worthy of a point on play, but their forwards cannot cope with the Kingussie defence. We thought that this was owing to the fact that some of the centre players lay too far back when pressing. Kingussie had also opportunities of scoring, but they also failed to register another point. Towards the close of the game, Cowal made a plucky effort to score, but the wary Kingussie defenders were not caught napping, and amidst intense excitement, Kingussie carried away victory, and won the championship. The scores were — KINGUSSIE, 2 hails; GLASGOW COWAL, 0. The news of the victory of the home team was received with much satisfaction in Kingussie and district, and the players were accorded an ovation on their return, pipers playing lively airs, and others carrying lighted torches, assembling at the station, and marching through the town, while bonfires were lighted above the burgh and two on the farm of Dunachton.

Needlefield, where the match was played, was a piece of ground situated between Longman Road and Cromwell's Fort.

Perhaps the earliest minor trophy was a silver mounted caman presented in or before March, 1892 by Mr C.G. Kennedy, Victoria Villa, Newtonmore and at one time in Edinburgh. It is also referred to in 1895 and 1898, the competing teams being Aberdeen, Edinburgh, Inverness and Newtonmore.

Another minor competition was set afoot during the period in which the Association was arranging its own competition.

In November, 1895 Donald Campbell, a merchant in Kingussie and a son of the Badenoch bard Dòmhnal Phàil nan Oran, presented a silver cup to the Badenoch clubs to be held for a year by the winning team. He was a great shinty enthusiast who had by that time attended the annual "cluidh-bhall" at Cluny for over forty years. In later years the second teams of Kingussie and Newtonmore competed with the smaller clubs in Badenoch and Strathspey.

Glasgow Cowal

In December, 1896 it was reported that there was a newly formed Edinburgh Shinty League. By this time, in addition to Edinburgh Camanachd and Edinburgh University, Edinburgh Northern Counties and Edinburgh Sutherland were active.

Mr John Campbell who had been Secretary and Treasurer of the Association since its inauguration intimated his resignation at the Annual General Meeting at Inverness on Friday 18th September, 1896. The Chairman of the meeting, Mr Macpherson-Grant, Yr., of Ballindalloch and Invereshie, moved that there be recorded in the minutes "the cordial thanks of the Association to Mr John Campbell for the important and valuable services rendered gratuitously by him in its interests ever since its inauguration; and likewise the Association's warm appreciation of the zeal, ability and efficiency with which Mr Campbell discharged the duties of Secretary and Treasurer since the date of his appointment to these offices in 1893".

Mr Campbell had been involved over many years in the public life of Badenoch as Inspector of Poor, Collector of Rates and Town Clerk of Kingussie. As an officer in the Volunteer Force he served in the South African War and as a Territorial in France early in 1915 when he was wounded. He attained the rank of Lieutenant-Colonel and was awarded the Territorial Decoration. He died in 1934.

His successor as Secretary and Treasurer was Mr D.P. MacGillivray of the Bank of Scotland, Inverness.

It was decided at this meeting that the Trophy Competition should start on 1st November instead of 1st December as in the previous season and that the Trophy Competition Committee should consist of the Council of the Association instead of one member of each club entered.

The question of presenting badges to the cup-winners and runners-up was dis-

The gold medal presented to John Campbell, first secretary and treasurer of the Association, in appreciation of his work by the Kingussie club.

cussed at the Annual General Meeting in Inverness on Friday, 17th September 1897 and it was resolved that these be procured and presented after the final.

A great loss was sustained by the Association on learning of the death, on 19th October, of Captain A.M. Chisholm of Glassburn who had been its Chief since its inauguration in 1893 and whose founding of the Strathglass Club in 1880 had been the means of reviving interest in the game throughout the Highlands.

The Tain, or Macdonald and Muir Cup seems to have been presented by that firm in Leith about 1897. An association was formed early in January 1898 for the running of the competition, the officials being Dr Gillies, Mr Charles Rattray and

MacDonald & Muir Trophy. Drawing by Jack Richmond

Mr Duncan Mackenzie, Tain. Mr Norman E. Mackenzie was a delegate on behalf of the Tain Club. Other clubs which usually entered were Lairg, Rogart, Kincardine, Contin, Fodderty and Caberfeidh. It is of interest to know that after many years in abeyance this cup has been found and has been the trophy used in the Glenmorangie indoor six-a-side championships at Aviemore now played for at the Aviemore Centre Contest.

The *Inverness Courier* report said:

"The victory of the Kingussie team was a very popular one. The team left Inverness by train at 7pm and was accompanied by a large contingent of supporters. The engine was gaily decorated with Macpherson tartan ribbons, and the engine driver and fire-man had donned the Kingussie jerseys. The train steamed out of the station amidst the loud cheers of a large number of persons who were on the platform. On their return, the players were accorded an ovation, pipers playing lively airs and youths carrying lighted torches, assembling at the station, and marching through the town, with bonfires lit above the burgh".

Northern Chronicle
April 14 1897

Camanachd Cup Final 1897
FINAL MATCH FOR THE HIGHLAND CUP

The Final match in the competition for the shinty trophy took place at Inverness on Saturday afternoon, the teams being Brae-Lochaber and Beauly. Beautiful weather favoured the event, which was looked forward to with much interest, particularly in the country districts; the result being that the largest crowd ever seen at a shinty match assembled in the Haugh Park. The attendance was estimated at about 3000, about two-thirds of them were not townspeople. A special steamer brought the Lochaber men and a large contingent of friends to Inverness; Beauly sent hundreds by train, and every strath and glen in the eastern portion of the county contributed their quota of interested spectators. By the way, the Haugh Park proved an excellent theatre for play, and regret was expressed on all hands that a piece of ground, so beautifully situated and laid out, and so convenient to the town, should have been allowed to pass into private hands for building purposes.

Physically the Lochaber men made the best impression when they took the field, but those who had on previous occasions watched the Beauly play, freely predicted their defeat, and events, as it turned out, warranted their confidence in the team. The ball had not been knocked about many minutes when it became evident that the Beauly men were quicker and more alert in their movements, and had practised a clever system of play to which their opponents were not accustomed, and to which they could not respond. Slim and agile, the Beauly players outraced their bigger brethren, manipulated the ball more cleverly, indulged in passing of remarkable accuracy, and altogether maintained the mastery of the game from beginning to end. On the other hand, Brae-Lochaber played strong and determinedly according to their system, long hitting being their forte, with a weak attack, and a slowness on the ball of which their more nimble opponents took full advantage. Play was, in these circum-

stances, mostly confined to Lochaber territory, where the spectators, by a sort of instinct of the impending result, gravitated in largest numbers.

The teams lined up as follows shortly after three o'clock.

BRAES OF LOCHABER:- Goal, Donald Macarthur; backs, Donald Mackintosh and Archy Kennedy; half backs, John Macdonald, Dugald Macdonald, Allan Macdonald and Archy Macarthur; forwards, A.W. Macdonald, Huntly Macdonald, James Macdonald, Alexander Macdonald and John Mackintosh.

BEAULY:- Goal, K. Forsyth; backs, Tom Forbes and Archie Chisholm; half-backs, T. Fraser, Don Macpherson, Ewen Macdonald and Donald Cameron; forwards, William Cameron, J. Forbes, T. Fraser (captain), W.J. Macrae and A. Macaskill.

Lochaber pressed at first, but soon realised the strength of their opponents, and after the first hail, which was scored by a long shot from Macaskill, their game was more on the defensive side, with an occasional rush, which, but for its impetuosity, might have secured good results. When the second half began with two goals to the credit of Beauly, Lochaber played doggedly in the defensive, but all their determination and hard hitting was in vain; Beauly kept up an incessant bombardment, and three other goals were added. This scoring, by no means, however, represents what the score might have been with better luck, not a few goals being missed by an inch or two or a yard or more, while on one occasion the ball actually lay within the precincts of the net, in line with the posts. There is no necessity for particularising the players; on each side every man played all he knew. Beauly all through, and in all situations, gave a pretty exhibition of the game as now practised, and their victory by 5 goals to nil was popular and deserved. Lochaber took their defeat with philosophic calm, and left the field with the evident intention of profiting by their experience of the afternoon.

We are requested by the Beauly Shinty Club to record their huge appreciation of the very courteous and gentlemanly treatment they received from their opponents in this important match. They have played, says our correspondent, many keenly contested matches during the season, but rarely have they been privileged to meet so honourable a company of sportsmen, as their friends from Brae-Lochaber.

Mr Duncan MacTavish, a grain merchant in Inverness and of an old Stratherrick family, in January 1898 presented a cup

Beauly — Camanachd Cup Winners 1897, 1898

at a meeting of the Inverness Club. The idea was to stimulate interest in the district and competition for the cup was held open to clubs in the Northern District which had been eliminated from the Camanachd Cup and others desiring to enter. Portree were the first winners of this cup in Inverness. In November 1904 the MacTavish Association drew up new rules to place it on a basis that would ensure the successful resuscitation of the competition which did not take place in the 1903-04 season. The participating clubs were grouped in two divisions, those north of Beauly and those south of

Simon, Lord Lovat, the first President of the Camanachd Association, and its chieftain between 1898 and 1933.

it. All ties were to be completed before the later stages of the Camanachd Cup.

Soon after receiving a protest from Glasgow Cowal on 9th February 1898 concerning the early stoppage of play in a tie with Inveraray, a rule was added to those already in force "that a referee shall have full and sole power to decide before or during any stage of a match whether it should be continued or not in view of weather, state of ground or any other circumstance".

The Beauly Club won the Camanachd Cup in 1897 and in 1898, both finals being in Inverness. In 1898 they beat Inverary by 2 hails to 1 at Seafield (which seems to be at or near Needlefield, the scene of the 1896 final). The Inveraray team which had not previously played in the north travelled overnight and in the early morning went to inspect the pitch. A prominent player of the Beauly team, Ali MacAskill who worked in Inverness, went to join them and was not recognized. He pretended to be completely ignorant of the game and asked the Inverary men about it. One of them showed him how to use a caman — not as a walking stick! Listening to their conversation, Ali heard some of the Inverary men say that the only man in the Beauly team who had a reputation and who would require to be carefully watched was MacAskill. The Beauly team was famous at this time, as was Kingussie, for its accurate short passing and combined play. It was said Beauly learned this from football. When shinty declined in popularity about 1880 and football clubs were formed in Inverness the game was played for some years in Beauly.

Lord Lovat was unanimously elected to succeed Captain Chisholm of Glassburn as Chief at the Annual General Meeting on Thursday, 22nd September 1898. He was succeeded as president by Mr John Macdonald, Keppoch. A sub committee was named to arrange the appointment of a new secretary, Mr D.P. MacGillivray having resigned. Mr MacGillivray, who had been engaged in banking in Scotland and in Egypt died in 1919. He was referee at the first final in 1896 and later represented the Perth Club at meetings of the Association and continued to act as a referee. The family to which he belonged was an old one in Strathdearn and several members of it became prominent as breeders of cattle. During the year up to the 1898 Annual General Meeting eight clubs had become members of the Association, these being Oban, Inverary, Furnace, Foyers, Kyles, Lairg, Strathdearn and Perth. The Glasgow Cowal Club intimated withdrawal of membership, claiming that they had been treated unfairly. Some amendments to the rules, proposed by different clubs, were considered and passed. It was also agreed that the Skye Club be placed on the same footing as other clubs. Another rule agreed upon was that in allocating the money drawn at the final, some extra allowance be made to the club coming from a distance. Immediately after this meeting the committee asked Mr James P. MacGillivray, Bank

of Scotland, Inverness, to become Secretary and Treasurer and this appointment was made. Mr MacGillivray, a brother of the previous secretary, was of a family which had a long connection with shinty.

Later in the year, Lord Lovat, as President, had written to the Glasgow Cowal Club regretting the circumstances which had caused them to withdraw from the Association and hoping that they would withdraw their resignation. Their reply stated that they were willing to rejoin on condition that the Argyllshire clubs be formed into a district of their own and that the Southern District be comprised of Edinburgh, Glasgow and Perth and the winners of these districts meet and decide which should enter the semi finals. The reason for the request was to curtail travelling expense. It was unanimously agreed to re-admit the Cowal Club.

For the first time the final of 1899 was played at a venue other than Inverness. Perth was chosen and Mr D.P. MacGillivray was referee. Ballachulish defeated Kingussie by two hails to one in this game which was played on the North Inch. The attendance was disappointing being less than 800. Inverness was chosen as the venue for the final in March, 1900 which resulted in a draw. The replay was won by Kingussie who defeated Furnace by the only hail of the game at Perth on 21st April.

In May 1900 there is a brief report of a game between Caberfeidh and Muir of Ord in the Strathpeffer Junior Cup and in the same month Rogart and Lairg played in connection with the Wallace Trophy. No information about these trophies has been obtained.

The Balliemore or MacRae Cup was presented about the beginning of the century by Lt. Col. John MacRae-Gilstrap. Clubs such as Lochgilphead, Millhouse and Bute competed with the junior teams of Inverary and Cowal, the finals being played at Balliemore.

Some alterations to the rules were passed by the council in September, 1900. One of these was "The ball may be stopped by the hand but not caught. No player shall be allowed to run with, kick or throw the ball". Another was "No person admitted to the field of play during the course of the match except the referee, players, linesmen and goal judges."

At the time of this meeting Lord Lovat was in South Africa in command of the Lovat Scouts which he had raised for active service there. It was proposed by Mr Donald Skinner, Oban, that the Association should record its appreciation of Lord Lovat's splendid services to the country and that a copy be sent to him in South Africa. It was drawn up as follows.

"The Camanachd Association respectfully offer their heartiest congratulations to the Right Honourable Lord Lovat, Chief of the Association, on his patriotic action in raising a Corps of Scouts and Sharpshooters at a critical time in the history of the Empire. The members of the Association are proud to have him as their Chief and they feel that in what he has done he has nobly maintained the traditions of his House. They are delighted to hear that the Corps has won honour and fame for itself in the great South African Campaign now happily drawing to a close and they express the hope that his Lordship and the gallant men of the Corps may return in safety to their country. They are glad to hear that many shinty players, members of the Association, have followed the noble example of their Chief."

Mr Ewen Campbell, Kingussie, proposed at a later meeting of the Council that a presentation be made to Lord Lovat on account of his action in raising the Corps for service in the South African War and for his invaluable services to the cause of shinty. The secretary was accordingly asked to circularize all clubs with a view to obtaining subscriptions towards the proposed presentation.

It had been proposed that an exhibition game between teams representing north and south should take place at the Glasgow Exhibition on 5th October 1901 but after consideration the proposal was dropped as the size of the ground available was only 110 x 65 yards which was deemed to be inadequate for a display of the game.

The season 1900-01 saw fewer games played as 'the war had told severely on the game, probably more so than on any other sport'. Nearly every club had felt the loss of players who had served in the war. At this Annual General Meeting in Inverness on Friday, 20 September 1901 it was also stated that the gate money at the final between Ballachulish and Kingussie in Inverness was a record one and

(above): Kyles Athletic, pre 1900

(right): Skye 1898, first winners of the MacTavish Cup

the bank balance (£35.12s.6d) was the largest to date. A motion that the headquarters of the Association should be in Perth was turned down on the casting vote of the Chairman, Mr John Macdonald, Keppoch. Later in the year two new clubs, Clachnacuddin (Inverness) and Govan were admitted as members of the Association and took part in the competition of 1901-02. By April 1902 the Captain Robertson Reid Cup for junior teams in Badenoch had been in existence.

The resignation of Mr James P. MacGillivray, Secretary and Treasurer, was intimated at the Annual Business Meeting in 1902. He had been appointed to a post in banking in London and became secretary of London Camanachd the following year. After some service in banking in Hong Kong he returned in 1924 and along with Mr John Macpherson provided finance and a cup to inaugurate the MacGillivray League Cup Competition.

He was succeeded as Secretary and Treasurer by Mr John C. Mackay, Inverness, who was on the staff of the *Inverness Courier*.

It was at this meeting, at the conclusion of business, that Lord Lovat, C.B., D.S.O.,

Col. Jock MacDonald.
1889—1980.
"I'm still the king!"
Capped for Scotland at
rugby, the incomparable
Colonel Jock was a son of
Harry MacDonald,
Viewfield, Portree, a
founder member of Skye
Camanachd.
Colonel Jock's first love
was, however, shinty and
from 1969 until his death
in 1980 he was the highly
respected Chieftain of the
Skye club. In a remarkable
link with the past, Colonel
Jock was in the crowd at
Skye's famous MacTavish
Cup Final victory in 1898,
the first time the cup was
played for

was presented with an illuminated address along with a silver cigar box from the Association and shinty players generally. Mr John Macdonald, Keppoch, as chairman handed over the gift and Lord Lovat in his reply made reference to shinty being played by the Lovat Scouts while on war service in South Africa.

Major A.W. Macdonald, D.S.O., Brae Lochaber, younger brother of Mr John Macdonald, Keppoch, was chairman at the Annual Business Meeting held at Inverness on Friday, 18th September, 1903. These brothers and their father, Donald, of Keppoch and Ben Nevis Distillery, had done much in earlier years to foster the pastime. They were grandsons of John Macdonald, well known as "Long John". A proposal by Mr D. MacCorquodale, Glasgow Cowal, that the field of play be not more than 180 yards by 80 yards nor

Kingussie — 1900

(left): Kyles Athletic 1901
(below): Newtonmore 1902

less than 140 yards by 70 yards was turned down. Other decisions made were 'that none but the hail keeper be allowed to stop the ball with the hand' and 'that when the ball passes the hail keeper without scoring, the hail keeper must send the ball afield with his caman from the 7 yards semi-circle'. There was also discussion about the venue of the final and it was decided that it should be played at different centres including Glasgow.

The entrants for the 1903-04 Trophy Competition included two new clubs, Edinburgh University and the Cameron Highlanders, the first military team to compete.

The Lovat Cup was presented by Lord Lovat in 1904 to be played for annually at New Year between Lovat and Beauly

on each other's ground in alternate years.

Mr John C. Mackay, Inverness, who had been Secretary and Treasurer since 1902 intimated his resignation at the Annual General Meeting in Inverness on Friday, 23rd September, 1904. His successor was William Macdonald Fraser who had for some time acted as assistant secretary. He was a playing member of the Inverness Club and one who took a lively interest in the affairs of the Association and in several sports. A native of Strathspey, he was proprietor of Mackintosh and Co., wine merchants in Inverness, and died in 1946. The auditor, Mr Andrew Macdonald, Sheriff Clerk, also tendered his resignation at this meeting and was succeeded by Mr Norman T. Russell, Oban, at a fee of one guinea.

SEMI FINAL FOUGHT AND WON

by Malcolm MacDonald, Newtonmore

Hurrah for the team who has triumphed
again,
The gallant Clan Fraser fought hard on
the plain.
Though beaten by Laggan on the banks of
the Spey,
The team of Lord Lovat pure shinty can
play.

Proud Laggan in hundreds have come
from the west,
The horses and drivers were all of the
best.
Craigdhu blessed the players in their gay
four-in-hand,
Captain Tolmie, the hero, he was in
command.

The heroes of Lovat arrive at mid-day,
To play with brave Laggan on the banks
of the Spey,
In hundreds the people went down to the
Dell
Yet who could be victors, no one could
tell.

The day it was cold and the pitch it was
keen,
The stalwart young players lined up on
the green
The referee his duty knew how to perform,
Better ruler of shinty never was born.

The game now is started and fast flies
the ball,
The teams on their mettle respond to the
call
The heroes of Laggan press hard on the
foe,
Two byes and a beauty for nothing they
go.

The fight now is raging all over the field
The Frasers, pressed backwards, their
camans did wield,
They dashed swiftly forward though not
at the Boer,
From a desperate scrimmage they open
the score.

The veterans of Laggan press forward
again,
Redouble their efforts and hard was the
game
The forwards work smartly and Grant
nets the ball
The deeds of their fathers the lads did
recall.

Brave Cattanach in goal proved one of
the best,
By the blunder of others proud Laggan
was blest
MacDougall from Crathie was the best on
the field
The doctor, by magic, the veteran healed.

The back line and centre played in grand
style,
Though pressed by Clan Fraser close upon
time
The veterans of Laggan had the best of
the play;
Let your motto be 'Conquer' on the great
final day.

The score now is equal and they play
extra time,
The ball swiftly travels along the whole
line;
Brave Laggan plays grandly and once
more they score,
Last quarter, though pressing, they did
not add more.

Both teams are a joy to their own
Highland home
Their names greatly honoured wherever
they roam,

John MacDonald of Keppoch, officiating at the 1899 Camanachd Cup Semi-Final, held at Keppoch. Kingussie v. Caberfeidh (Alick Falconer, Kingussie, left) note the flag used for field-marking

*The veterans of Laggan swift, healthy and
  strong,
Their prowess in shinty is the theme of
  my song.*

*Great was the struggle and many did fall.
Though bleeding and wounded, they
  stuck to the ball,
The pace never slackened, and tested the
  men
But sound in the wind are the teams
  from the glen.*

A contest which seems to have been the first of its kind, between teams representing North and South, took place on 29th April 1905 at the Dell, Kingussie with about 1000 spectators. The North won by 3 hails to 1. The teams consisted of the following players:-

North: A. Mackintosh, Kingussie; John Campbell, Laggan; D. Middlemas, Newtonmore; William Dallas, Kingussie; George Campbell, Kingussie; A. Mackintosh, Alvie; Donald Tolmie, Laggan; A. Macdonald, Alvie; Angus Mackenzie, Kingussie (captain); Archd. Mackenzie, Kingussie; D. Cattanach, Laggan; Hugh Campbell, Lovat.

South: Turner, D. Maclachlan, A. Benn, Glasgow Caledonian; H.J. Mackenzie, M. Montgomery, D. MacGregor, J. Campbell (captain), Cowal; D. MacPhail, F. Smith, Govan Argyle; J. MacCorquodale, M. Fowler, H. MacInnes, Cowal.

The referee was Mr J. Smith, Campsie.

An Honorary Vice President of the Association, Mr Alex. Littlejohn of Strathcarron, Ross-shire, had kindly given a prize of £20 for the best essay on the game of shinty. Dr Campbell, Oban, who was present at the Annual General Meeting at Inverness on Friday, 22nd September 1905 moved the thanks of the Association to Mr Littlejohn for his liberality which would give a much needed stimulus to the game as he did not think that the number of teams was increasing as rapidly as it was hoped. Dr Campbell also advocated that steps should be taken to popularize the sport in the army and in schools.

Further gifts by Mr Littlejohn, who had been a stockbroker in London, were intimated at a meeting of the Council at Perth on 28th October of the same year. These were a framed photograph of the vase which he had presented to the universities of Scotland and a copy of an illuminated album, painted in water colours, illustrative of the game of shinty. The photograph and a copy of the album

Four trophies: The Camanachd Association Challenge Trophy, Skeabost Horn (front), Celtic Society Cup, Littlejohn Vase

were later gratefully received and were handed over to the Inverness Free Library for safe keeping.

The Littlejohn Vase which was presented to Aberdeen University in 1905 and offered for contest among the Universities of Edinburgh and Glasgow was to be played for on a Home and Away league basis. In December 1910, Glasgow defeated Aberdeen by 4 hails to 3 at King's College. The report stated that this was the revival of the competition which had been dormant for five or six years.

A suggestion was made by Lord Lovat at the Annual General meeting on Friday, 21st September, 1906 that, in order to make the game more popular in the north, an exhibition game be played on the last day of the Northern Meeting. It was agreed to approach the Northern Meeting Sports Committee regarding this proposal. The committee did not at first favour the idea, believing that the ground was too small and that there might be danger to the spectators.

The opening round of the Skye Camanachd Association Cup which had recently been donated for competition "by a local gentleman" (Mr Peter D. Robertson of Scorrybreck) was played on 23rd February 1907. A field at Edinbane had been provided by Mr R.C. Robertson Macleod of Greshornish. The first entrants for this trophy, The Robertson Cup, were Portree, Portree Juniors, Braes, Bernisdale and Edinbane.

Short reports of games for the Gleann Mhor Cup are found in the years 1906, 1907 and 1910. Participating clubs in these years were Foyers, Fort Augustus, Glengarry, Glenmoriston, Spean Bridge and Achnacarry. No information is available about the donor of this cup which Spean Bridge was allowed to retain after winning it in 1912, 1913 and 1914.

Fifteen clubs entered for the Trophy Competition of 1907-08, the same number as in the previous season. Lovat, Perth and Glasgow Caledonian had dropped out and their places taken by Portree (Skye), Grantown and Gleann Mor (Fort Augustus). The Skye team was drawn to play against Beauly in the first round, the game to be played at Strathcarron. Having beaten Beauly, Skye was drawn to meet Newtonmore and this game was scheduled to take place at Dingwall.

The matter of having an exhibition game at the Northern Meeting in September, 1908 resulted in the Sports Committee agreeing to this provided the Council of the Association undertook all risks. As this was agreed, invitations were sent out to all clubs connected with the Association and the following agreed to send teams to compete — Inverness, Newtonmore, Lovat, Grantown, Kingussie, Lochaber, Beauly and Laggan. It was suggested that two games be played, one on Thursday the other on Friday with six players in each team and the duration of the game twenty minutes. The following clubs were selected to play — Inverness v Lovat on Thursday, Newtonmore v Brae Lochaber on Friday. The Northern Meeting Sports Committee set aside £10 towards expenses and offered to provide badges for the winners. The secretary of the Association was appointed to referee both matches.

In the 1908-09 season Wester Ross made their first appearance in the Trophy Competition and were drawn to play Beauly in the first round. The cup in 1909 was won by Newtonmore for the third season in succession and for the first time the final was played in Glasgow. The gate money did not come up to the Association's expectation but the financial position was, on the whole, fairly satisfactory.

Eighteen clubs had notified the Council at a meeting in Perth of their intention of taking part in the Trophy Competition of the season 1909-10, Paisley and Strachur for the first time and Perth and Skye after

Newtonmore, winners of the Camanachd Cup for the first time in 1907, on the steps of the Duke of Gordon Hotel, Kingussie.. Lord Lovat, Chief of the Association, standing beside the cup.

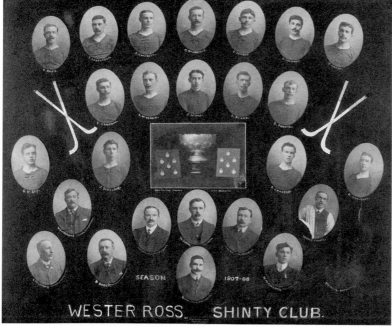

Four clubs

(top): Glasgow Skye
(left) Wester Ross

an absence. Portree were to play on the mainland and on the same conditions as formerly.

Following a suggestion by Dr Campbell, Oban, at a previous meeting of the Council, that the Association should consider the matter of supplying camans at a cheap rate to schoolboys, a letter from Mr John Macpherson, Inverness, was read at a meeting of the Council at Inverness on Saturday 27th January, 1910. Mr Macpherson stated that he was prepared to supply camans for boys at a reduced price of 2/9d each if a quantity was purchased at a time, this sum being 1/- less than the usual price charged.

As the day of Lord Lovat's marriage was approaching it was the unanimous wish of those present at the Annual General Meeting in 1910 to present him with a silver-mounted caman as a marriage gift. The representatives had agreed that their clubs would contribute 5/- each towards the presentation. The Secretary in his report referred to the final played at Kingussie in which Newtonmore, by defeating Furnace, established a record in winning the trophy for the fourth year in succession. When discussion turned to the state of the game, some of the members felt that it was becoming less popular and that an effort be made to stimulate greater interest.

On behalf of the Inverness Club Mr John MacAskill moved "That the Council shall consist of one representative appointed by each club affiliated to the Association instead of members appointed at the Annual Meeting." This motion was adopted.

Early in 1910 the *Inverness Courier* reported that Mr Arthur V. Hussey, a chemist at Foyers, had presented a cup to be played for annually by Stratherrick and Foyers and any other team.

(left): Furnace, 1912
(above): Strachur, 1910

1910 for Glasgow Cowal —

(above): c.1910., with Captain James Galbraith, centre row, second left.

(right): 1909-10 League Championship medal, won by James Galbraith

The inauguration of the Strathdearn Association was suggested by Mr John MacAskill, a native of Strathdearn who had a farm near Inverness and was secretary of the club there. He was a tireless worker on behalf of the game. At a meeting in Tomatin in January 1911 conditions on which Colonel Mackintosh of Balnespick donated the Strathdearn Cup were laid down and in March the newly formed Strathdearn Club was defeated in the first final by Inverness. In the following season a team from Duthil, (Carrbridge) took part. As well as Strathdearn, Foyers, Duthil, Stratherrick, Grantown, Beauly, Lovat, Strathglass, Caberfeidh, Strathconon and Lochcarron were all winners of this cup in the years up to 1939.

To John McQueenDedicated to my dear friend Mr. John McQueen, Glasgow Skye Shinty Club, on the occasion of his leaving for New Zealand. November 21, 1911

*When Skye were making history upon the
   shinty field,
A gallant played among them who could
   the caman wield,
And long shall Skye remember how on
   Strathbungo's green,
They were led on to victory by Captain
   John McQueen.*

Chorus:

*Kingussie Snowdrops —
Winners of the Campbell
Cup, April, 1912*

*Then give a cheer to the dear young lad,
    our comrade staunch and true,
'Tis sad indeed we all now feel to bid
    him fond adieu,
He's sailing o'er the ocean to New
    Zealand far away,
So give the lad three hearty cheers,
Hooray! Hooray! Hooray!*

*A son of the Scottish Highlands armed
    with a Highland heart,
Who with his Isle of Islands is somewhat
    loath to part,
His thoughts return to boyhood days
    while each familiar scene,
Recalls life's sweetest memories to
    Captain John McQueen.*
(Chorus)

*In the ancient game of shinty he was
    always to the fore,
His touches were aye pretty and he knew
    well how to score,
A game might be exciting but he'd play
    on fair and clean,
A credit to the grand old game was
    Captain John McQueen.*
(Chorus)

*Skye's great and worthy rivals, the bold
    lads of Argyll,
Wish God-speed to this young son of the
    dear old misty Isle,
They're grieved to see him leaving and
    although oceans intervene,
They will with us often recall the gallant
    John McQueen.*
(Chorus)

*All kindred clubs how join us, our wishes
    are as one,
"May Health, Success, and Happiness and
    Fortune follow John",
We know he's the ambition and where'er
    his footsteps tread,
He'll prove a credit to the Isle where he
    was born and bred.*

(Chorus)

*Personal Then fare thee well my own
    dear pal most happy be thy life,
I trust you soon will meet the girl who'll
    prove to be your wife,
But if you've many troubles methinks
    'twould be a shame,
Did you not teach them all the tricks of
    the good old Shinty game.*
(Chorus)

by John (Kaid) MacLean (from his *Book of Rememberance*) (published by Archd. Sinclair, Celtic Press, Glasgow, 1939)

An unfortunate incident was mentioned in the report at the Annual General Meeting of 1911 which was held in Inverness on Friday 22nd September. Sixteen clubs had taken part in the competition, the final being played at Inverness where Newtonmore defeated Ballachulish by 3 hails to 2. Ballachulish protested against one of the hails and, the protest being sustained, a replay (with Newtonmore playing under protest) took place at Roy Bridge and this resulted in a win for Ballachulish. As a committee had earlier been appointed to revise the constitution and rules of play it was hoped that with the present more clearly expressed rules a similar dispute would not occur in future.

Beauly and Inveraray entered the competition of 1911-12 after a lapse of some years and the final was played at Perth. From a financial point of view it was a disappointment as the gate money amounted to only £18, the smallest sum of money at any final. There was some discussion at the 1912 Annual General

Kingussie — Camanachd Cup Winners, 1914

Meeting as to the best way of improving the financial position which was poorer than usual because of the small sum taken in at the final in Perth. A motion by the Skye Club that all ties in which the Skye Club are drawn first, and have choice of ground, be played at Portree instead of on the mainland was ruled out of order on the ground that the motion was not sent to the Secretary in time under the rules.

Before the arrangements were made for the drawings for the competition of season 1912-13 it was intimated that three new clubs had entered, these being Invereshie, Edinbane and Fort William while Inverness, Laggan and Paisley had dropped out.

A handsome donation towards the funds by Mr Alex. Littlejohn of Strathcarron was reported at a meeting of the Council in February 1913. It had been suggested that a match be played between the winners of the Camanachd Cup and the winners of the Littlejohn Vase for which the university teams compete. In a letter Major Cameron, Inverness, informed the Council that he intended to visit several districts with the view of increasing interest in the game and was to take with him a supply of camans to be loaned to boys. He wished to know if a supply of balls would be provided by the Association and it was agreed to co-operate in this matter.

A suggestion for the better protection of goal lines was made by the Secretary at the Annual General Meeting held on Friday, 19th September, 1913. As spectators tended to encroach on the hail keeper it was agreed that 15 feet from either side of the post should be protected as also 6 feet behind the nets.

Fourteen clubs entered for the cup competition in the season 1913-14. Edinbane, Glasgow Cowal and Newtonmore were not among the entrants which included Aberdeen University and Glasgow Oban and Lorne. Aberdeen University was described as a new club but the minutes show that that club had taken part in the competition in the 1899-1900 season.

At the meeting of the Council in Inverness on 14th February, 1914, the last recorded in the minutes before the outbreak of war in August, arrangements were made for the final which was played on Saturday, 4th April between Kyles and Kingussie at Possil Park, Glasgow. The pitch was described in the report as being a very poor one. About 200 spectators had travelled from Badenoch and Argyll and along with many Highlanders living in Glasgow saw Kingussie win by 6 hails to 1.

The teams, which included some of the most skilful players of the early years of the century, were:

Kingussie — A.G. Mackintosh; William Macpherson; John Mackintosh; C. Mackintosh; A.B. Tolmie; T.J. Macpherson; E.G. Ormiston; William MacGilivray (captain); L.W. Macpherson; F.L. Maclean; A.D. Dallas; J.G. Macpherson.

Kyles — Donald MacFadyen; Celestine Nicolson; Robert Thomson; Neil MacGilp; Allan MacFadyen; William Jamieson; Calum Nicolson; Alex Gemmel (captain); George Nicolson; Charles MacKellar; Duncan Weir; William Brown.

The referee was Mr A. Macpherson, Glasgow Skye.

The office bearers who were elected at the 1911 Annual General Meeting were re-elected in 1912 and again in 1913 and at the outbreak of war were:

Chief: The Right Hon. Lord Lovat, K.C.V.O., C.B., D.S.O., A.D.C.; President: John Macdonald, Esq., Keppoch; Vice Presidents: The Mackintosh of Mackintosh, Sir John A. Dewar, Bart., M.P., Alex. Littlejohn, Esq., of Invercharron, Brigadier General H.L. Malcolm, D.S.O., A.C. Macpherson, Esq., of Cluny, Major E.G. Fraser-Tytler of Aldourie, Captain Colin MacRae, Millport, Dr Campbell, Oban, Colonel Campbell, Kingussie. Members of Council: The Council shall consist of one representative appointed by each club affiliated to the Association. Secretary and Treasurer: Mr William Macdonald Fraser, Inverness, Auditor: Mr George Mackenzie, Clubmaker: Mr John Macpherson, Church Street, Inverness.

Although no competitive shinty was played during the war, it was engaged in from time to time by players serving in France.

Many players fell during these years, the Beauly and Skye clubs respectively losing twenty-five and eighteen killed.

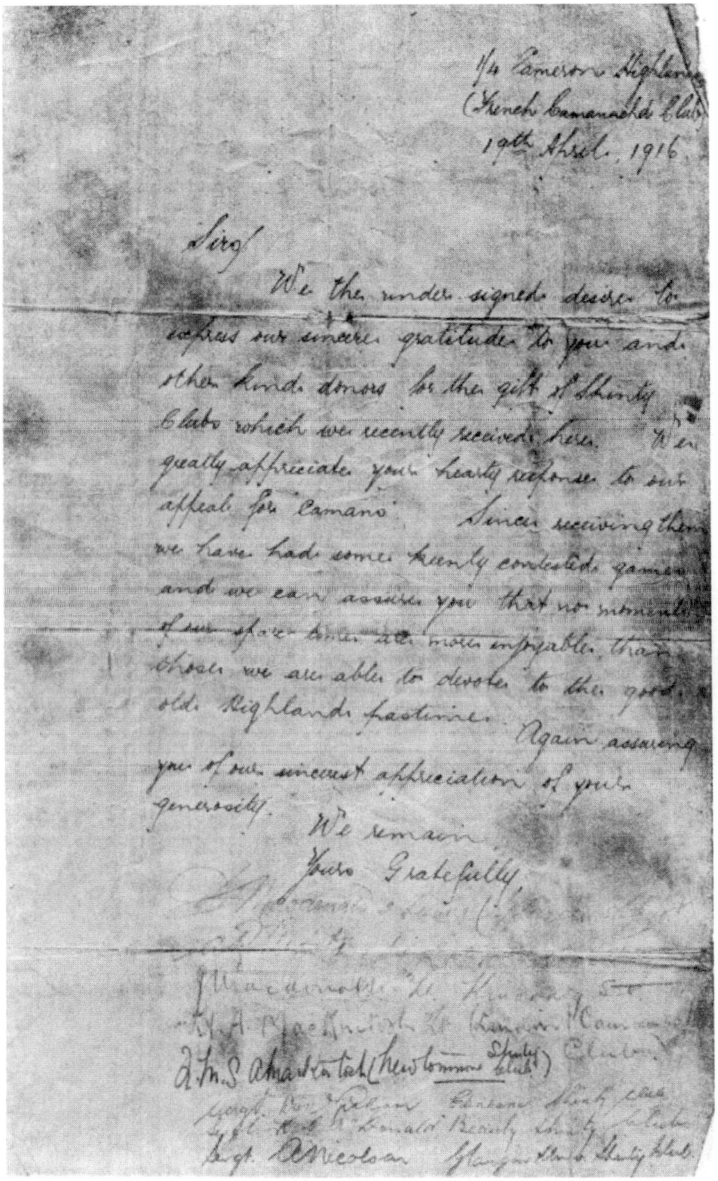

1/4 Cameron Highland
(French Camanachd Club)
19th April, 1916

Sirs,

We the under signed desire to express our sincere gratitude to you and other kind donors for the gift of Shinty Clubs which we recently received here. We greatly appreciate your hearty response to our appeal for camans. Since receiving them we have had some keenly contested games and we can assure you that no moments of our spare time are more enjoyable than those we are able to devote to the good old Highland pastime. Again assuring you of our sincerest appreciation of your generosity.

We remain
Yours Gratefully

Letter from the front.
In May, 1916, Mr John
MacAskill and Mr Roderick
Macleod of the Inverness Club
had several sets of camans and
balls sent to the 4th Battalion
of the Cameron Highlanders

(this and following page): observations on the origins of shinty from the Littlejohn album

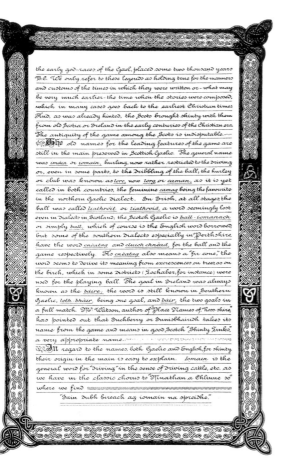

literature practically commences in the 15th century), be traced further back than the beginning of the 17th century. Tradition holds strongly that in pre-Presbyterian days, which means before 1700, the men played shinty to and from the church, and one of the feats of the ubiquitous "minister laidir" was to put a heroic end to this phase of Sabbath-breaking much in the same way as he stopped putting the stone and the other games played in and around the Churchyard. The earliest bardic reference in modern Gaelic is in an elegy on Neil Og of Machrihanish (about 1720) where we are told that beautiful golf devoted shore of Machrihanish was on Neil's death no longer the scene of Camanachd:

"Ho our bhair le deannal cruaidh."
Nor playing shinty in hardy conflict.

The records of presbyteries and synods for the 17th and 18th centuries, so far as published or otherwise known to the writer, have no mention of shinty, even as a Sabbath-breaking game, though it certainly flourished greatly in those times in the semi-pagan Highlands.

The old Statistical Account does not make it a point to speak of sports; they were looked askance at under Presbytery-rule, and, as a matter of fact, the old system of Church holidays and free life had given way by this time to a hard struggle for existence. Shinty as far as the present writer knows, is referred to only once in the volumes of the old Statistical Account, that being in the account of the Parish of Moulin, and the clergyman apologizes for its existence a generation previously; saying it was played now only by boys. Part of the passage is as follows: "At every fair or meeting of the country people, there were contests at racing, wrestling, putting the stone, &c, and on holidays all the males of a district, young and old, met to play at football, but oftener at shinty - a game played with sticks crooked at the end, and balls of wood." As already said, the author of the "Grampians Desolate" refers to shinty and devotes two pages of his poem to a lively description of this game as the prince of Highland sports. Dr Norman Macleod

108

Notes of Interest

This Gift to the University of Aberdeen
has been personally arranged and sympathetically treated by
the Donor.

He wishes here to acknowledge with warmest thanks the
valuable assistance right willingly rendered in various
ways by the following gentlemen:—

The Very Rev⁴ John Marshall Lang, D.D.,
    Vice Chancellor and Principal of the University of Aberdeen
J. E. Crombie, Esq. M.A.(Abdn) Lord Rector's Assessor.
Rev⁴ Angus Bethune, M.A., (Abdn) Rector of Seaham, Co. Durham.
Arthur Anderson Bethune, Esq. (Barrister at Law) London
Alexander MacBain, Esq, LL.D.(Abdn) Inverness
Rev⁴ James Maxwell Joass, M.A., LL.D.,(Abdn.)
    Parish Minister of Golspie
Rev⁴ R. E. Ritchie, Parish Minister of Croick.
A.N.Macaulay, Esq, Solicitor, Golspie, Factor for Invercharron and
John Webster, Esq., M.A. B.L.(Abdn) Law Agent for the Gift.

The Album is bound in silk, the front being of Gordon
tartan representing the County in which the University is
situated, and the back of Mackenzie tartan for the County
of Ross and Cromarty, of which Invercharron is part. On
both sides of the cover forming an edging and protection to
these clan colours is a raised band of Royal Stuart Red
Morocco ornamented with Celtic tracery in gold; in the centre
of these designs on a raised oval of the same leather in Celtic
lettering are hand worked Monograms of the University on
the front and of the Donor on the back.

On the first page is a drawing of Caman and ball
with a riband on which is inscribed one of the best known
Gaelic sayings, indicating best wishes or good luck to the
competing Shinty Clubs. This sketch is designed by the
Rev⁴ D⁴ Joass of Golspie from a Caman belonging to
A.N.Macaulay, Esq; a former Chieftain of Cuideachd Camanachd
Dhunedinn (Edinburgh Shinty-Club) now the premier Shinty-Club

On the frontispiece or title page which faces this sketch
within Celtic Ornament copied from crosses and carvings &
in the Island of Iona, of very great antiquity, are views of

1992 Shinty/Hurling International — pre-match introductions

Scotland v. Ireland — Under-21's
at Inverness

Willie MacRae of Skye (left)
was Man of the Match at the
1990 Camanachd Cup Final
in Fort William
— Skye's first ever win

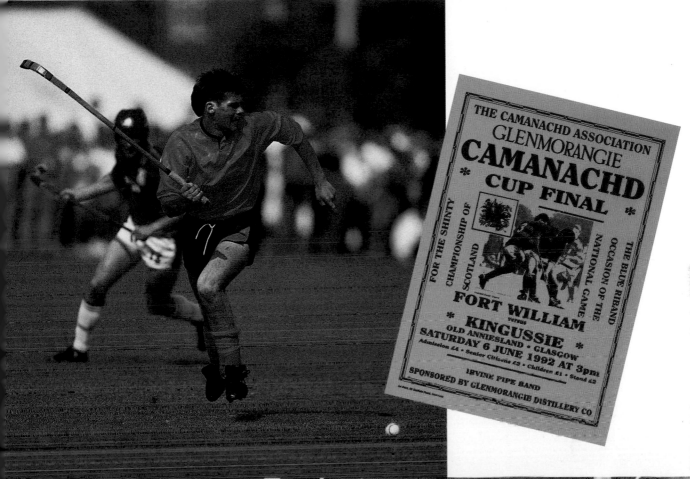

THE CAMANACHD ASSOCIATION
GLENMORANGIE
CAMANACHD
* CUP FINAL *

FOR THE SHINTY CHAMPIONSHIP OF SCOTLAND

THE BLUE RIBAND OCCASION OF THE NATIONAL GAME

FORT WILLIAM
versus
* KINGUSSIE *
OLD ANNIESLAND • GLASGOW
SATURDAY 6 JUNE 1992 AT 3pm

Admission £4 • Senior Citizens £2 • Children £1 • Stand £2

IRVINE PIPE BAND

SPONSORED BY GLENMORANGIE DISTILLERY CO

A famous victory at Glasgow in 1992:
The Camanachd Cup Final:
Fort William 1—Kingussie 0

BETWEEN THE WARS

"They died to save their country and they only saved the world" (G.K.Chesterton)

1914-1918   1939-1945

THE CAMANACHD ASSOCIATION

**In Rememberance
of the Players of Camanachd
who in the
Two Great Wars
Made the Supreme
Sacrifice**

**"In the far corners of the earth,
and in the deep they lie".**

The First World War claimed the lives of many outstanding shinty players and few, if any, Highland communities were left unaffected. Not only did many men not return from the war, but of those who survived, many chose to pursue the rest of their lives in pastures new. Shinty, as with everything else, had to regroup and begin anew.

Some areas suffered worse than most. Of these, Skye arguably felt the ravages of war more than most. As Martin MacDonald details in his history — *Skye Camanachd — A Century Remembered:*

"From the village of Portree alone 26 boys lost their lives, and the losses throughout the rest of the island were proportionate. Among the dead was Billy Ross of Skye Camanachd who had gone to France although exempt because of his age. After the Battle of Festubert (May 16 and 17, 1915) Captain Ronald MacDonald, also from Portree, wrote to his widow: "Every night we patrolled together the long line of trench held by the company until daylight when we used to sit in the shadow of the parapet together, a few Portree boys around us, and have a Gaelic ceilidh, talking over old incidents and looking forward to the future and when we would return home..."

After the agony of war, however, some semblance of normality was restored. Many of those crucial to the game's development in the pre-war years were no more, but their successors endeavoured to pick up the pieces. The first meeting of the Camanachd Association after the dark days of 1914-18 was in September 1919, when an Annual General Meeting

---

Camanachd

Camanachd gur roghadh spòrs e
Am a'gheamhraidh 's tùs an earraich,
ach 'san achadh na gillean greanmhor
an deagh ghleus ri cluich cho annamh'
ach Camanachd bu dual d'ar sinnsir,
ag iomain bhall air Là Callainn,
C'àit eil coimeas ris 's an Eòrpa'
a h-uile fear cho eudmhor ealamh
Dol g' a dhubhlan bhuidhinn tadhail.

Aonghas Moireasdan

Dàin is Orain, 1929

"With a healthy continuity of bloodline, of fraction and reconciliation, shinty slipped into the 20th century...In large parts of those sections of the Highlands and Islands which were, ironically, to become the last redoubt of the language and traditional culture of the Scottish Gael, the game of shinty ceased to be played during the first four decades of the 20th century. It was an inexorable decline".

Roger Hutchison, Camanachd.

was held in Inverness. Lord Lovat presided over the proceedings with Mr W.M. Fraser as Secretary. He intimated his resignation owing to pressure of business and Mr J.C. MacKay was appointed Secretary and Treasurer in his place.

A Roll of Honour of shinty players who fell in the war was drawn up and inserted in the Book of the Constitution of the Association. It was also agreed at this meeting that steps be taken to foster the playing of shinty in Highland schools.

The new Secretary in his first report wrote:

"I have pleasure in stating that the movement for the revival of shinty has met with gratifying response throughout Scotland considering how very seriously camanachd clubs were hit in players being killed during the war.

It will be remembered when Britain declared war in August 1914, camanachd clubs were beginnning to make preparations for the championship competition. Shinty players, who were the most athletically fit of young men, in great numbers joined the

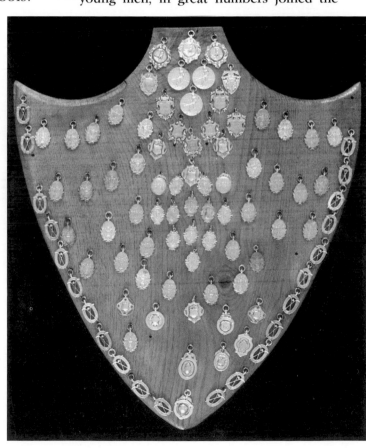

Some of the medals won by the legendary MacKenzies of the famous Caberfeidh teams of the 1930's. It includes, amongst others, 3 Camanachd Cup Winners, 8 Runners-up, over 20 MacTavish medals and a similar number of MacGillivray League medals

colours, and as the Roll of Honour shows, many were killed fighting.

"Now, after five years of war, the Camanachd Association has called upon clubs to resuscitate their forces, and from the numbers that have responded, it is evident that the old national pastime of the Highlands holds as firm a place in the pastimes of the people as it did in pre-war days. Not for many years before the war have teams from Scotland joined so readily or in such large numbers as they have done now."

Eighteen clubs joined the Association in season 1919-20 and one of these was the new Oban and Lorn club. Skye, however were experiencing problems and they asked that any game they played on the mainland be on a Thursday instead of a Friday as laid down in the Rules, the reason being that Skye was only in communication with the mainland on three days a week — from Skye to the mainland on Tuesday, Thursday and Saturday and from the mainland to Skye on Monday, Wednesday and Friday. Skye's plea was granted so that their players could return to the island on the Friday.

The business of arranging Challenge Cup ties continued at the next Council meeting. Colonel John MacRae-Gilstrap of Eilean Donan offered a park at Balliemore for the playing of the semi-final tie between Furnace and Kyles Athletic and this was gratefully received. Also, the Secretary was instructed to thank Alexander MacDonald of the Highland Railway Company for his excellent series of articles on 'Shinty: Historical and Traditional' which had helped in the revival of the games. Mr MacDonald also presented a paper to the Gaelic Society of Inverness on the same subject, published later in Volume XXX of the Society's Transactions.

The same meeting of the Association was told that limbless soldiers were now making shinty balls much superior to the machine-made balls. They heartily approved of shinty clubs helping the industry in every way, including the playing of matches to help discharged soldiers.

Hand-made shinty balls

The Farraline Park School team of 1920-21 epitomised the new enthusiasm amongst young people for the game. A number of the all-conquering Inverness team went on to play Highland league football. The team's vice-captain Charlie Robertson (centre row, second left) died in a road accident shortly after the picture was taken.

At the September AGM, Mr J.C. Mackay, the Secretary, noted that it was gratifying to report that the prospects of the second post-war season for shinty were brighter than those of the previous year, which not only marked a new beginning in the game but a decided advance in its popularity.

He reported that a crowd of over 3,000 had watched the Kyles of Bute Athletic versus Kingussie final played at Inverness,

"In a game in which the finer points were revealed on both sides and which ended in a 0-0 draw. The match was replayed at Glasgow on a pitch that was perhaps not too good, and the match afforded hundreds an opportunity of reviving their interest in the game, which they had known from their youth. Kyles of Bute Athletic had a narrow 2-1 win, but none, not even their brilliant opponents, grudged the Argyllshire team the high honour."

As to the future, Mr MacKay was optimistic:

"The game has made an excellent start and if it is to hold as it should, the first place among amateur games in the Highlands, the key to that position is in the hands of the clubs themselves. Let us hope that the little district jealousies of the pre-war time have gone forever."

Clubs may have heard Mr MacKay, but his pleas had to be repeated by many of the Secretaries and indeed Presidents who followed over the years.

Nine new teams then joined the Association in season 1920-21 from Ross-shire, Inverness-shire, Argyllshire, Glasgow and Paisley. Training of shinty

Edinburgh University Team 1922-23
(back row): JM Anderson, —Mackay, (middle row): A. Fraser, D. McKintosh, A.F. Campbell,
I. Campbell, J. Colquhoun, J. Gray, A.M Ross, K. Mackenzie

players became a priority and it became accepted that if the game was to continue to flourish, teams would have to undergo systematic training; the modern players of the eighties and nineties should not, clearly, think that they have a monopoly on 'modern' methods such as training!

At the September AGM of that season, the Secretary reported in glowing terms on how the game was developing, particularly with regard to youth policy and at senior level. "Not down the centuries have the youth of the Highlands shown more enthusiasm for shinty than at the present time, and what is pleasing to those who are helping to forward the game is the fact that the youth in Highland schools have taken up with eager enthusiasm caman play".

As ever, Rule changes were made, and there was a breakthrough for Skye when, at the meeting mentioned above, the last sentence of Rule 7 was deleted — 'All ties in the Northern District in which the Skye Camanachd Club take part shall be played on the mainland'. Rule 25 was also altered to read: 'A player wilfully disabling an opponent must leave the field when ordered by the referee to do so. Such a player must be reported by the referee to the Association. The referee is also required to report to the Association when the conduct of an official or officials, players or spectators is such as to interfere with the game.'

Despite large scale migration from the Highlands after the war, shinty continued to flourish and season 1921-22 was one of the best between the wars in terms of teams joining the Association. Twenty-nine teams entered for the Challenge Cup with two teams dropping out from the previous year, Glasgow Oban and Lorn and the Ross County team. Six new teams came forward, Caberfeidh, Strathconon, Edinburgh University, Glengarry (after an absence of a year) and Fort Augustus. Mr MacKay also reported the arrival of Mull.

The 1922 AGM was moved from its usual September spot on the calendar to April, to coincide with the Camanachd Cup Final. Not only were clubs continuing to flock to the Association, Mr MacKay reported, but "the early fights in the cup competition were noticeable for brilliancy of play, fleetness of foot and accurate hitting. The old ideas of play, good as they were, are fast disappearing on the field, and the attempts made at combination, method and science, in play are evident in the enthusiasm with which the public support the pastime".

The Secretary also reported that the Final would be contested between Beauly and Kyles of Bute, remarking that a Badenoch team had contested the final every year since 1899, apart from 1913 — "a splendid testimony to their playing ability."

Migration from the Highlands began to take its toll, however, and the numbers playing the game began an inevitable decline, a decline which as Roger Hutchinson eloquently demonstrates in his book *Camanachd*, had its wider implications:

"Apart from the obvious weakening of the spirit of the game which occurs when areas which have known it since the beginning of recorded time cast the sport aside in favour of any other — or in favour of no other — the strength of the material body of shinty has been relentlessly sapped since the start of the 20th century. Once the game of shinty becomes no longer a valid part of that expansive, ecumenical identity then shinty, as well as the Highlander, is the loser. As the 20th century comes to a close, it is as common and regrettable to find two Gaels who cannot, upon meeting, while away an hour or two discussing the memories and merits of shinty teams of the past and the present, as it is to find two Sgiathanaich who cannot carry on a conversation in Gaelic."

Twenty-five teams entered the Camanachd Cup in season 1922-23. Unemployment and the consequent search for work meant that teams such as Kirkhill, Mull, Glencoe, Glengarry, Kincraig, Paisley, Strathconon and Glasgow Kyles all folded. One new team appeared however, Glasgow Islay, and Glasgow Cowal re-joined.

The debate about play at junior level continued with general agreement that there were too many players who were unable to command places in the first teams not being afforded the opportunity to play. After many months' debate at several meetings, it was agreed that a special competition for Juniors be inaugurated. And 1923 saw the introduction of the Sutherland Cup, donated by Sir William Sutherland, M.P. for Argyllshire.

Col. Archibald MacDonald

The first winners of the handsome trophy, which was played for by second division clubs, were Newtonmore from the north, who defeated North Bute from the south at Keppoch by 3-2.

The tragic losses suffered by many clubs during the Great War were still to be seen in many areas but assertions that shinty was dying on its feet as the century progressed are not supported by the evidence contained in the Association's Minutes. The Secretary reported to the Annual General Meeting in 1923 that:

"...the game is now on a more sound and solid foundation than it has ever been and is fast becoming one of the most popular of national pastimes. For almost twenty-seven years the Camanachd Association has done real spade-work in stimulating interest in the pastime, the fruits of which are now very evident. Never have so many of the youth and manhood of the nation indulged in the sport, never have there been so many opportunities to do so and more encouragement given, and what is still more pleasing, the interest of the public is on a larger scale than it has ever been in the long history of the pastime."

The extended patronage which supported the game in the early years of the century is evident from the names listed in the Secretary's report of 1923, as being invaluable: Colonel Archibald W. MacDonald D.S.O. who was in France and had missed his first AGM for "well nigh a score of years"; Duncan MacLeod of Skeabost; Colonel George MacKintosh of Clune; Major MacRae C.B.E.; ex-Provost Skinner of Oban, (grandfather of the current Association Chief Donald Skinner); and Major Davey.

The game is reported to have been advancing in all parts of the country. Players in the west vied in their enthusiasm to excel their comrades in the north, five substantial teams were operating in Glasgow, each of whom would, it was reported, "hold their own against any of the other teams in the Camanachd Cup competition". The Association and the game were heading in one direction, and one only, according to the Secretary — "forward".

The administrative structure of the game was, however, feeling the pace. 1923 had been 'the most strenuous officially since the inception of the Association'. Newtonmore and Furnace contested an historic Cup Final with the Argyll-shire side completing their unique record of having won the trophy without conceding a goal. It is a record which still stands unrepeated and has earned the club a place in the Guinness Book of Records.

The Furnace Shinty Song
by J. Kaid MacLean

*Good old Harry do not tarry, hasten o'er
    the brine,*
*And drop me by the Quarry on the shores
    of dark Lochfyne.*
*From there I shall not wander, nor shall
    I ever stray*
*When I met with Dr Campbell and the
    boys who won the day.*

Chorus:
*The grand old game of camanachd our
    fathers played of yore*
*How can he claim his father's name who
    can't his fame uphold?*
*With neatness, fleetness, stamina and
    keenness to the fore*
*The grand old game of camanachd shall
    live for evermore.*

*In the first round old Oban found that
    they were on the run*
*And after all they saw the ball and that
    was all they won.*
*Ballachulish sons with their great guns
    were next held in the trap*
*The Furnace boys caused a great surprise
    with an easy going "nap".*

*The country cheered when Kyles appeared
    to damp the Furnace roar*
*But there inspired the Furnace fired and
    four times did they score.*

Furnace's record-breaking team of 1923

*T'was very sad if Kyles were had and
    with their great success
The boys went forth up to the north to
    win at Inverness.*

*Now let us sup we've won the cup, we've
    vanquished Newtonmore
With sterling play they won the day we'll
    toast them o'er and o'er.
They've heads with sense in their defence
    I just record the fact
In all their ties with many byes they kept
    their goal intact.*

J. Kaid MacLean, a native of Skye, was a noted caman wielder for his island and a versatile entertainer in Glasgow and Highland circles, as well as one of the main proponents of links with Ireland and the international matches. Indeed he officiated at one of these games at Croke Park, Dublin on August 2, 1924, 'picturesquely attired in the Highland tartan'. The 'international' match may not have caught the imagination at home in

Scotland, but in Ireland it certainly commanded attention:

Irish Times   August 2, 1924

Gaelic Games — The International Match
(By Pat' O)

The International Hurling shinty match will be a distinctive feature of the opening ceremony of the Tailteann Games to-day. The Irish side has been selected after preliminary trials. The Scottish team arrived yesterday and includes all the best players in the Highlands where shinty enjoys the same popularity as hurling does in this country.

The Scottish team is as follows:- D. McLachlan (Argyle), capt., W. Armstrong (Kyles), vice-capt., D. MacFadyen (Kyles), Alex. MacDonald (Glasgow University), A. MacLean (Skye), H. MacGregor (Brae Lochaber), John Gemwell (Cowal), Allan McFadyen (Kyles), Hugh Nicolson (Skye), Andrew Nicolson (Kyles), D. Weir (Kyles), W. Greenshields (Kyles). Substitutes — Colin Murchison (Skye), D. Campbell (Furness). Neil MacCallum (Furness).

So painstaking has the Selection Committee been that for each man picked a player has been selected for the same position as a reserve. The individual members selected have been prominent in League and championship games for some years.

The Nicolsons are of the famous athletic family of whom the veteran 'Tom' won the hammer (Scottish and open styles) and shot putt championship of Scotland recently. How our Irish hurlers will figure against the superior dribbling and shooting of the dour Highlanders will be anxiously anticipated.

The Irish team is selected for individual places irrespective of provinces or counties. The broader blade of the Irish caman will prove of greater service and accuracy overhead. The wider 'pole' on the shinty stick gives the Scots an advantage in ground play. So the Irish twelve will have a tough struggle. The Irish side is as follows:- J. Mahony (Galway), goal; D. Murnane (Limerick), full-back: J. Darcy (Tipperary), right back; M. Dirwan (Galway), left back; D. Rine (Cork) left half; James Walsh (Dublin), right half; James Humphries (Limerick), mid-field; B. Gibbs (Galway), right wing; M. Power (Kilkenny), left wing; Hayes (Tipperary) and Howard (Dublin), forwards.

The material is here for an excellent game. The Scottish side is a powerful, well-trained one, full of steam and a repute of boundless pluck and energy. The game should furnish an engrossing study of the capabilities of the crooked ash as a medium of outdoor sport. The ground will be too short for the Scots; the ball too small and light for the Irish hurlers. So the dice is weighted at both ends, and neither side has a considerable advantage.

I rather favour the visitors, who are fitter and more capable with the little ball. The respective sides are the best available at the moment, and each man has big credentials. To-morrow Irish hurlers meet their American friends. This will be another genuine international test of strength and skill. The American team are capable hurlers. In conversation with them this week I got the impression that they are confident of beating Ireland.

The ground at Croke Park is smoother and truer than the American pitches of rugged, uneven surface and infinitely faster ball pace. The Irish team should win all their games, but

the Americans will beat all other conten-
dants. Some ex-All-Ireland hurlers are included in the Irish side.

Sunday Independent

August 3, 1924

Shinty Men Clash with Hurlers at Croke Park

Novel and Exciting

The novelty of a clash between the Irish
caman and the shinty stick of Scotland made
a tremendous appeal to the thousands present at the opening of Aonach Tailteann in
Croke Park Stadium yesterday. An exciting
contest ended in a victory for the men from
the Highlands by the narrow margin of one
goal in three.

The first change noticeable in the game
when compared with our national pastime of
hurling was the difference in goal posts and
methods of scoring. The 'net' is much nar-
rower than the hurling goal, but higher, and
points, as in hurling, are not counted. The
Irish caman is broader and more useful in
overhead play; the shinty stick is capable of
greater accuracy on the ground. Handling the
ball is not permitted in shinty.

The difference in style was at once apparent. The Irishmen, used to clean, vigorous,
open hurling, were somewhat non-plussed
at the beginning by the brilliant ground work
of their opponents.

The handicap was particularly evident in
the forward line, where, with the possible
exception of Garret Howard and Gleeson,
both Limerick men, the Irish representatives
were outplayed.

Brilliant Defence

In defence and at midfield the hurlers were
supreme, and many a time when the Highlanders swarmed round our goal our hearts
were in our mouths until Murnane, or Dirwan, or 'Builder' Walsh, or Jack Darcy — a
magnificent quartette — rushed in to drive
the ball back to their forward line.

It was fully fifteen minutes before the Irishmen accommodated themselves to the swift
ground play of their opponents. Hence-
forward, however, they could do everything
but score.

Play was in progress twenty minutes when
Weir intercepted a flying shot from Nicholson, and with wonderful dexterity curled it
past Mahony into the Irish net. It was the only
score in the first half.

A chapter of missed chances by our forwards followed, and when the ball went
within the reach of the Scottish custodian he
returned it with some of the wizardry which
we are accustomed to associate with Tom
Daly, the University College keeper.

From the Tee!

In the first half Garrett Howard and Gleeson
tested McFadyen with shots from every angle,
but he was unbeatable. His methods of puck-
ing out, too, evoked considerable amusement, but proved quite as effective as the
high drive from the Irish end. Placing the ball
carefully, and measuring his stroke as in golf,
he invariably sent it well over the half-way
mark.

A slight re-arrangement in the Irish forward line brought a change of fortune soon
after the resumption. Mick Darcy, who was
playing instead of Mattie Power, the brilliant
Kilkenny left winger, sent a long pass to

(left): sections of a shinty stick
(below): Modern shinty and hurling sticks

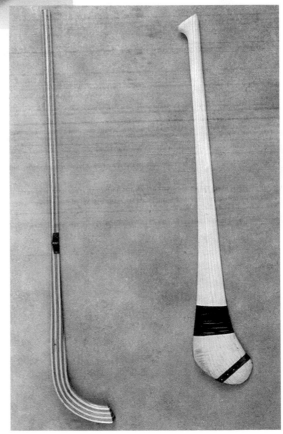

Gleeson. With a rapid glance towards the Scottish goal, the Limerick man sent the ball past McFadyen for the equaliser amidst tremendous cheering.

Faugh a Ballagh

'Builder' Walsh and Hugh Nicholson were then seen in an exciting duel for possession, which ended in the advantage of the Faugh and All Ireland player.

The Highlanders were again active round the Irish goal, and a brilliant piece of combined play by the whole forward line was finished by Greenshields beating O'Mahony and giving Scotland the lead once more.

Fast, high-class play characterised the closing stages, and the long whistle found Scotland winners of a memorable game by two goals to one.

The referee was Mr. J. Kaid MacLean, picturesquely attired in the Highland tartan.

A monument is erected in his memory on Loch Lomondside where he died tragi-

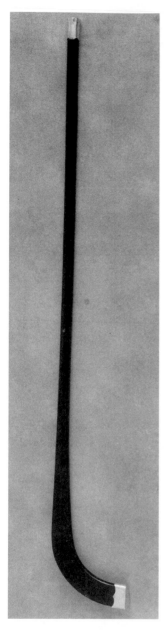

The silver-mounted caman — the most prized individual honour in shinty, presented to the winning captain at Cup Finals since 1896

cally following an accident. The Kaid MacLean Cup, for competition between Skye and Wester Ross teams, was also instituted in his memory.

The advent of the Sutherland Cup was seen as a 'means of stimulating clubs to have a clever second team, where players will be early trained and better qualified for the senior team, thus raising the standard of caman play and making the game more finished and methodical. Shinty is thus, while holding on to all its old time traditions and sportsmanlike qualities, keeping pace with the times — a clean, healthy amateur sport... With the game in such a position it is up to the youth of the country to maintain and stimulate such a healthy amateur game and to hand on the traditions of the game untarnished and unsullied in the years to come'.

Tribute was also paid at this time to significant work being done with young players by the MacTavish Trophy Association in the north with junior cup matches and leagues having been introduced.

The rules of play were, as ever, the source of great debate at the AGM. The Glasgow Skye club, supported by Glasgow Islay, proposed that the curved end of a caman should be standardised so that it would pass through a hole of, say, two inches in diameter. The rule was agreed and still holds. The same meeting agreed to a proposal by the Beauly club that the goalkeeper be allowed to slap the ball with his open hand. After some debate the rule was accepted by 15 votes to 9 and it, too, still pertains.

Twenty-five clubs entered for the Challenge Cup in season 1924-25, with Fort William and Kincraig being absentees. Three new clubs were admitted to the Association however, Argyll Park Battery, Oban, Glasgow University and Strathnairn. There were, as ever, rule changes, the most important being the addition of the off-side rule. 'No attacking player shall be allowed within the ten yards area, unless the ball be within that area'. That rule, having survived several modifications, has stood the test of time and is still a feature of the modern game. It was moved in its original form by Mr J. Malcolm of Inveraray, seconded by the redoubtable Kaid MacLean of Glasgow.

Two more new names appeared in the Association's membership next season — Glasgow Mid-Argyll arising from the Blawarthill club and also Glasgow Invernessshire. In all, twenty-two clubs entered for the Challenge Cup.

At an October meeting of the Association, it was reported that an 'international' match had taken place between Scottish shinty players and a team representing Ireland. The Secretary said that he had had no communication from any responsible person regarding any socalled 'International match'. If such a match had taken place, it was not representative of the Association. It was reported at the February meeting thereafter

that the match had been in fact run under the auspices of the Southern League. The matter of relationships with Ireland was to become a topic of considerable discussion over the next few years.

The optimistic spirit with regard to shinty's fortunes and standing continued. In his report to the 1925 AGM Mr J.C.MacKay claimed that "the traditions of shinty have always been immune from the commercial spirit, and the curse of professionalism has not stained its escutcheon". He further added: "It is now an indubitable fact that never in the history of this pastime has it had a bigger place in the minds of the rising generation. Hardly a rural district is to be found where 'ball play' does not find a place in the itinerary of sport".

Colonel A.MacDonald D.S.O. retired from his position of President and was replaced by Ex-Provost Skinner of Oban. Lord Lovat was elected Chief; and it was decided at this point that after the district finals of the Challenge Cup, the referee in charge of a tie should not belong to either competing club.

Exhortations to maintain the traditions of the game and enhance its standing are, however, indicative of some concern that complacency might be leading to an erosion of the game's position. In his report to the 1925 Council meeting Mr MacKay urged members "to keep the shinty flag flying. It is incumbent on every chief to put aside petty jealousies and work unitedly for the well of a game, which has stood the test of centuries and which has

John MacPherson

been handed to us untarnished and as free as the mountain air''.

The new President added a note of caution when he drew attention to the fact that not enough interest was being taken in the second division by members of Council and seniors generally. He added that unless they had a nursery to prepare youths for senior matches, the pastime was sure to suffer. He mentioned that Mr John MacPherson of the Sporting Stores, Inverness had that day given him a silver-mounted caman to be presented to the captain of Lochside Rovers, winners of the Sir William Sutherland Cup in the previous season.

The minute of the April Council meeting reports that ''The Secretary intimated that he had received a polished hickory club from Mr John MacPherson, Fishing Tackle Maker, Drummond Street, Inverness to be presented to the Captain of the team winning the Camanachd Trophy.'' The club was accepted by the meeting and was much admired. This laid the foundation of a long and beneficial relationship between the Association and the MacPherson family whose contribution to its well-being is remarkable.

At the 1926 AGM, the post of Secretary and Treasurer was divided with Mr William Paterson of Beauly becoming Treasurer and Mr J.C.MacKay remaining as Secretary. At this same meeting, following a proposal by Fort William who had returned to the fray after an absence of three years, it was agreed that 'no player who has committed himself in the

the Inveraray team— Scottish Champions 1924-25

Camanachd, MacTavish or Celtic competition be allowed to take part in the Sutherland Cup since the real object of the latter is to foster the game among younger players and to prepare them to take their place in the senior ranks.'

The distinction between senior and junior levels is one which has exercised the Association and its members ever since, and this rule has, in all probability, been changed more often than any other rule adopted.

Referees too were being criticised, not for any perceived bias, but for the exorbitant fees they were allegedly charging for their services. The Committee also commented on 'the high charges made by persons responsible for the lay-out of fields of play and were of the opinion that such charges should not be paid in future without careful consideration by officials and the Finance Committee'.

Twenty clubs set out to claim the Challenge trophy in the 1926-27 season, but alarm bells began to ring when it was reported that Kingussie, the first ever winners of the trophy and arguably the game's pre-eminent club at that time, were, for the first time in their history, scratching from their first round tie against Stratherrick.

A combined team — the Amalgamation, made up of perhaps the most unlikely

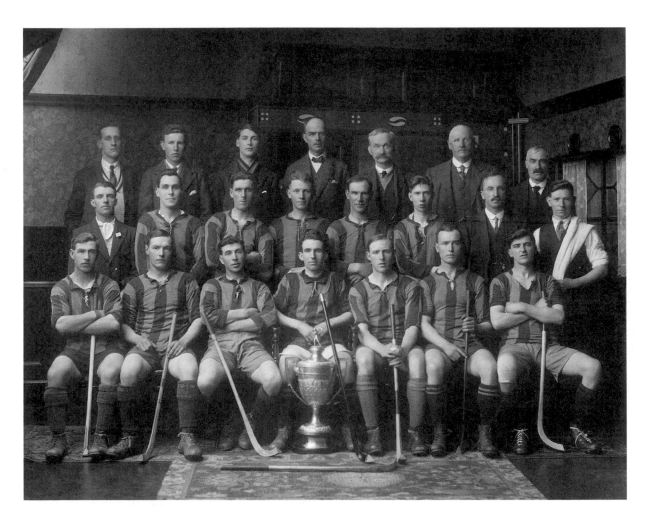

Inveraray — The famous Yellow and Blacks, put their name on shinty's premier trophy for the first time in 1925, defeating Lovat 2-0 at Inverness. They then retained the championship the following season, defeating Spean Bridge at Oban by 3-2

combination in the sport, the traditional rivals of Newtonmore and Kingussie, were to meet Stratherrick in the District Final. The combined Badenoch force was enough to secure victory. Mr MacKay reported: "It is a matter of regret that districts such as Kingussie and Newtonmore, which should certainly be able to each produce as they have done in the past, a team capable of winning the blue riband".

The Association was not, however, completely tied up with legislative matters and the resolution of disputes. It was announced at the 1927 AGM that Mr Duncan Munro, Inverness, a member of the SFA, had approached the President with a view to the Association combining with local football bodies in the town, to raise one thousand guineas for the purpose of endowing a 'sports bed' in the Royal Northern Infirmary. This was agreed in principle and Mr John MacPherson, Inverness suggested that a Badenoch Select versus the North would attract a large gathering. The proposal was eventually placed in the hands of the clubs themselves who were to organise local matches to help with fund-raising.

The Association's membership continued to change. Caberfeidh and Edinburgh University returned to the fray in 1927-28 after an absence of five years; Inveraray, so recently a force to be reckoned with, withdrew; Fort Augustus and Kingussie also returned and the Almagamation in Badenoch, always an uneasy relationship, came to an end. A new club, Boleskine,

an amalgam of the now defunct Stratherrick and Foyers, came into existence. Various significant rule changes were also adopted at this time, including the definition of a penalty hit. The President, on behalf of the Oban club, moved that the following be added to Rule 14: 'For any foul granted by the referee, for an infringement within the ten yard area by a defender, a free hit be given, the ball to be placed twenty-five yards in front of goal, and if a goal is scored from the free hit so granted, it shall count.' After a full discussion, the motion, to which was added 'all players except the goalkeeper to stand aside', was carried by 21 votes to 11.

There was general approval, however, of the operation of the Sutherland Cup competition. Twenty-three teams entered in season 1928-29, compared to twenty the previous year.

North Bute stepped up to senior shinty that year, emulating Caberfeidh who had taken the same decision the previous season. It was reported that the competition "was now fulfilling its object in fitting clubs to take their place in our Senior Competition".

Senior players, with some exceptions, were now debarred from playing in the Sutherland Cup competition, but there was some disquiet about the operation of the 'three year rule'. This prevented players who had played at that level for three years from playing in the junior competition. The rule was changed just two years later to state that only players who had

The Lovat team

played in a previous year's senior competition could be re-instated as juniors.

The appointment of referees by the Association's Council appeared to herald an outbreak of peace and a period of relative calm, but only so far as the officials were concerned.

Inveraray and Oban became embroiled in a dispute which finally saw their District Final replayed.

Mr John C. MacKay was presented with a gold watch by the Association at the AGM in appreciation of his services as Secretary from 1902-04 and thereafter from 1919-27. The assembled company then sang ''For he's a jolly good fellow'',

not a practice which has been repeated all that often at Association AGM's.

The annual expenditure in season 1928-29 remained more or less constant at between £70 and £90 and of this sum, about £20 went towards the administration of the Sutherland Cup.

With regard to the alterations to the Constitution and Rules, it was agreed that London Camanachd Club be allowed to play in next year's Camanachd Cup Competition. Rule 7 of the Rules of play was changed to: ONE hail judge to be appointed by each club in place of TWO. The secretary asked for a definition of Rule 15 of the Rules of play as to 'when is a pitch unplayable.' After discussion, it was agreed that this point be left to the discretion of the referee.

The Secretary, Mr W. Paterson, reported to the October Meeting in 1929 that twenty-four teams were competing for the Challenge Cup and that London were in the draw but with the reservation for this season that they play in Scotland at a venue decided by the Council. Fort William had entered the Sutherland Cup competition but as the majority of their players had played in the senior competitions last season, this was not allowed and they were accordingly entered for the senior competition. At the end of this meeting, Mr W. Paterson tendered his resignation as Secretary/Treasurer because of business commitments. Mr Donald MacLean, Strathpeffer, was appointed interim Secretary until the next AGM.

Below is an extract from a letter written in the 1930s by Rev. Coll A. MacDonald (born Iona 1873, died Logierait, 1954) to his son Alan, by then living in America. The letter is an account of a game of shinty played on Iona, an island not known for its participation, over one hundred years ago:

To you, 1881 is remote, but I was there in my eighth year and while I remember many things that happened before that day, such as the great storm that destroyed the Tay Bridge, 1881 stands out as the year of the last shinty match on New Year's Day. I have seen many interesting contests and you have seen the excited crowds at interna-

*Lochaber —
late 1920's*

tional matches but all these later events pale before the shinty match of 1st January 1881.

Though the match was played one afternoon, it was not a one-day affair as you may think. For weeks, the youth and manhood played shinty, talked shinty, dreamed shinty.

In Iona the winter is never cold. The wind may blow with all the fury of Atlantic gales, but the air is balmy and the ground but rarely frost-bound. There were camans to secure and there was no Lumley or Ivo Anderson to provide them. They came from the hazel woods of the Ross of Mull. If it takes the eye of a sculptor to see in the block of marble a Venus or Apollo, it takes an expert woodsman to see the well-shaped caman in the uncouth block of wood. The skilled makers of clubs were real craftsmen with all the joy of creative art as they shaped the weapons of the young generation.

At noon, the whole male population flocked to the scene of play above Ceann na Creige. What a scene for the Homeric combat! The Atlantic breakers with unhurried, rhythmical swish beat upon the shore where the gravelly beach made a strange musical sound as the pebbles rolled seaward with each receding wave. The southerly goal-posts lay as near the rising ground as possible and the northern goal-posts lay in the hollow beneath the brow of Cnoc na Maoile Buidhe, the hill of the yellow brow.

The teams were only limited by the number of adults and youths of playing capacity. The risk of disturbing the peace by a game on New Year's Day was not to be left out of the reckoning. No-one lost caste however much whisky he consumed on that day. I would not have you infer they were a drunken generation. But on the opening day of the year there was a special licence and men freely indulged who were very abstemious for the rest of the year.

But on 1st Jan 1881 it was a sober crowd that covered the velvety sward above Ceann na Creige. They denied themselves like Grecian athletes who strove for mastery at the Olympic Games. What-

ever may have been the evening potations, the men were temperate in all things in the morning.

The sea was the boundary on one side and the little loch on the other. The players streamed out like the caddies at St. Andrews when the captain of the year plays himself into office. The leaders stood in mid-field and he who won the toss of the coin was asked whether the ball — a wooden one — was to be thrown on the ground or cast in the air. I do not think there was any referee, the ball was in play and the great game began. What racing and chasing of that small ball! There were too many players engaged to make scoring easy. My recollection is that there were neither backs or halves. All were forward and first, but as the too eager combatants tired and rested to recover breath there were cute ones who hung on the wings and made fast runs that thrilled the onlookers. Though more than the half-century has passed, I can still see the two bearded warriors on the sea side of the plain, whose speed filled my boyish eyes with wonder and delight.

Shintys were smashed into splinters and with the stumps only that elusive ball travelled from end to end. They seemed to have no time limit any more than a limit in space. It looked as if the darkness of the short winter day only would end the fight. But big John MacAulay now got possession for your grandfather's side and from mid-field drove a ball with such speed and power that no weapon could stay its flight. Like an arrow it sped between the posts and Sinclair's fortress fell. The great game was ended: it was a draw.

The bottle that was in little demand in the morning journeyed from end to end of the table many times. Tales of great games on Traigh Sanna and Saorphin were heard and we, of immature age, listened spellbound while our seniors related the history of the heroes of their youth, now on Canadian plains or 'neath the Southern Cross. Song and story chased each other to the end of a perfect day.

At the Council Meeting in February 1930, the chairman, Ex-Provost Skinner,

made a fitting reference to the appointment of the Association's late Secre-
tary/Treasurer, Mr W. Paterson, as chief
engineer to the L.M. & S. Railway Company in the North. The interim secretary,
Mr D. MacLean, intimated to the Council
that a protest had been lodged by Fort
William about their match in the first
round of the Camanachd Cup with Fort
Augustus. However, the Council dismissed their protest. He also reported
that applications for re-instatement of
players from senior to junior ranks were
causing a great deal of trouble, and he

*Edinburgh University 1929-30, winners of the Littlejohn Vase — a 'limited entry prize as
curiously valuable as the Calcutta Cup'. Members of the team include Somhairle
MacGill-eain, (front, far-left) who went to find unrequested acknowledgement as Scotland's
greatest Gaelic poet and contributed hugely to the revival and well-being of shinty in
Wester Ross while headmaster of Plockton High School in the 1950's and 1960's; M.C.
MacQueen and W.E. Stuart (rear, third from left — and front, right, respectively). Ellis
Stuart was the first Hon. Secretary of the Schools' Camanachd Association, founded in
November, 1937*

Somhairle MacGill-eain

thought that something had to be done to put the matter of re-instatement on a clearer basis.

The 1930 AGM at Oban ratified Mr D. MacLean as Secretary/Treasurer. The penalty hit rule was changed from twenty-five yards to twenty yards on a motion by Mr W. Paterson, Beauly and seconded by Mr J. Malcolm, Inveraray. The question of re-instatement of players was fully aired at this meeting. It was pointed out that there was no general rule for the re-in-

statement of players, but that the Finance Committee, who ran the Sir William Sutherland Cup competition used their common sense. Generally no player was re-instated, who had played more than three years previously in the senior competitions.

Mr Ferguson, Kyles Athletic, moved that the three year rule be rejected and that in future no player be re-instated except those who have played in the previous year's senior competitions. This was seconded by Mr W. Campbell, Beauly. The President, Ex-Provost Skinner, seconded by the Oban Honorary Secretary, moved an amendment that the present rule be left in force. The matter was then voted on and the motion carried the day by thirteen votes to eight.

The October meeting of that year heard a full discussion about the lodging of protests and a recommendation was drafted which went to the AGM in the following terms: 'That the referee appointed for ties should not have had any previous connection of any kind with either of the competing clubs, and that protests and appeals must be formally intimated to the Referee and captain of the team protested against before they leave the field of play, to be followed in writing to the same parties within one hour of the conclusion of the game.'

At the AGM the motion was changed to semi-final and final ties and then adopted.

The Secretary, Mr D. MacLean in his report to the October meeting regretted that Spean Bridge had dropped out of the Challenge Cup competition but welcomed the admission of two new teams, Glengarry and Oban Celtic. He also told the meeting that the penalty hit was now from twenty yards instead of twenty-five yards, "and from what I have seen in the past I trust the difference of five yards will lead to greater accuracy in the taking of penalty hits." This is a point which is still being debated.

The Secretary at the February meeting of 1931 brought up one matter which was of sufficient importance in his opinion to warrant its being placed on the agenda of the AGM. During Camanachd Cup-ties several players were ordered off. In the Lovat v Inverness tie one was sent off; in the Lovat v Beauly tie three were off and in the Oban v Inveraray tie, one was off. Despite their offences, all these men were able to play the following Saturday without suffering in any way. He continued: "I would propose that every man put off the field should have his case brought before a small committee who would give it their consideration. This committee should have the powers of suspension granted to them by the Council." This went to the AGM and it was agreed that the Finance Committee be empowered to consider these cases for a trial period of one year.

Ex-Provost Skinner retired as President at the 1931 AGM in Inverness and Mr William MacBean, Muir of Ord took over the presidency. The question of injury to referees was raised and the Secretary was instructed to make enquiries as to insuring referees and to have the whole matter discussed by the Finance Committee. Mr William Paterson, Beauly moved that in view of the large amount of correspondence entailed in carrying out the affairs of the Association, the secretary should be authorised to get a second-hand typewriter. This was unanimously agreed.

Invergarry and Skye were missing from the Challenge Cup competition in the following season 1931-32. However, Spean Bridge were back in the fray after an absence of one year. At the October Council Meeting in Inverness, Mr D. MacLean, the Secretary, reported that he had "observed in the Press of late, references to the cleaning of the Game of Shinty which this new Rule is expected to do. Far too much stress is being laid on the Rough Play with which shinty is supposed to be affected. Things are not as bad as that. We certainly have cases of players being put off the field for rough play, but one would think that the game of shinty would come to a terrible pass. My view, which I have always held, is that the Association should have the powers to impose penalties for Rough and Dangerous Play, but we cannot expect Shinty to be a Parlour Game. It is essentially a game for the man of sound and strong constitution."

The February meeting heard of the death of the redoubtable Mr John Kaid MacLean, Glasgow and the death of Ex-Provost Skinner's wife.

The Secretary in his report referred to the pleasing factor that no player was ordered off in the Challenge Cup matches this season so far and that the new Rule made at the last AGM giving powers to the Finance Committee to deal with Rough Play was justified.

The 1932 AGM in Glasgow heard Mr MacLean intimate that in Ross-shire there were three new entries for a local cup from the Kintail district — Kintail, Lochalsh and Glenshiel, the forerunners of the present day club, Kinlochshiel. He further commented, "I would like to say

In memoriam.
This cairn was erected beside the road near Shiel Bridge by friends of Donald Campbell, of Glen Shiel Shinty Club

a word on the sportsman-like attitude of the players in this season's Competition. It is most creditable that not one player was reported for being put off the field of play. At the Camanachd Semi-final in the North and the MacTavish Final it was a treat to watch the clean healthy spirit in which those matches were contested, and I am assured that the matches in the South were conducted in a like manner. I attended, not so long ago, a Football Match for the Scottish Cup and the tactics adopted by the men on both sides would not be tolerated for one moment by this Association. The contrast between the Professional players and our splendid amateurs made me feel prouder than ever of our great game. It should be our aim to keep the game of Shinty as clean as it is possible to keep any game."

Oban competed in the Camanachd Challenge Cup final for the first time ever that year against Newtonmore with the latter winning 1—0.

Little seems to have ensued in the rest of 1932. There was a special meeting held in Glasgow in April of the following year between representatives of the Irish National Association and the Southern Shinty League. Its purpose was to make arrangements for a fixture between an Irish hurling team and the Southern Shinty League select. An advertisement gave the details. There was an appeal: "that the Irish people in Glasgow will give them the support it would receive in Ireland by turning out in large numbers to give the Irish team a hearty welcome and show that the exiles still hold dear the National games of Ireland."

The match was fixd for May 6, 1933 in Shieldhall Park, Hardgate Road, South Govan between a picked hurling team from the constituent University colleges of Dublin, Cork and Galway and a selection from all the clubs in the Glasgow Southern Shinty League who were all of Highland birth and descent. The Irish Provisional selection was J. Flanagan (Galway), J. Hogan (Dublin), G. Gleeson (Cork), T. McCarthy (Dublin), C. Jennings (Galway), J. Lanagan (Galway), M. Cronin (Galway), J. Canning (Dublin), C. McGrath (Cork), M. O'Flaherty (Galway).

The Irish team won by the only goal of the game but:

"the result was of secondary importance to the fact that this essentially Gaelic game was shown to have a large following in the West of Scotland and the possibilities for its development are attractive..."

Under the agenda item 'Alteration to Rules' Mr William Paterson put forward a motion that the duration of each game should be ninety minutes. Teams were to play forty-five minutes each way, with an interval of at least five minutes at half-time. A debate arose as to whether a maximum of two or five minutes' stoppage time should be allowed in each half for injuries etc., and it was agreed to allow two minutes.

After such a stoppage the match should be resumed with a throw-up at the spot where the ball was last in play, unless a previous incident necessitated the award

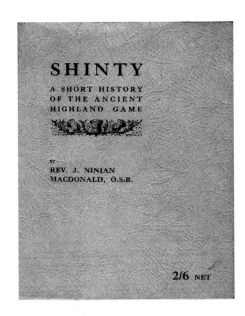

the "excellent book on Shinty"

of a set blow. This motion was carried by the meeting.

The President brought before the Meeting what he called "the excellent book on SHINTY" written by Father Ninian Macdonald, with a foreword by the chief of the Camanachd Association, Lord Lovat.

Twenty-three teams entered the 1932-33 Challenge Cup competition and this was two less than the previous season. The Secretary said, "London, no doubt, in view of the Council's decision that they have to play in Scotland, have not entered, and I have not received any entry from Fort William. In view of the fact that the Mod was held there this year, one would think that a stimulus would have been given to everything Highland, but I am afraid that Shinty was forgotten. Indeed, if An Comunn Gàidhealach did a little more for our pastime, they would be doing a service both to themselves and the cause for which they stand.''

He further added, ''We have a new name on our Vice-Presidents list this year, Miss Farquharson, Coignashee, Newtonmore. This lady has done a great deal for the game of Shinty, and is well worthy of being added to our list.''

With regard to the new rules introduced for this season he explained: ''We have several new rules this year, all of which will be marked in the new Rule Book when published. Stoppages are now limited to two minutes for each stoppage, the additional time to be given in the half in which the stoppage occurred. Any member of the defending side can now send the ball afield after a bye, the goal-

crossed camans

keeper alone being allowed to do formerly. Opposing captains must now meet on the field of play when protests and appeals must be formally intimated. It is hoped that this new rule will do away with the trouble which formerly existed as to the proper time for protests and appeals to be intimated. There are also other changes, and let us hope that all combined will be the means of assisting those who control the ancient game.''

At the February 1933 meeting, Peter M. MacLeod of Glasgow raised the question of having the shinty results broadcast on radio along with the other sports news on Saturday evenings. It was agreed that if it was possible, arrangements would be made to have the shinty results broadcast.

At the 1933 Annual General Meeting, tribute was paid to Lord Lovat KT, Chief of the Association, who had died. The President Mr W. MacBean said: ''Before proceeding with the business, may I be allowed to say how deeply we all felt the death of Lord Lovat, our Chief, of whom it can truly be said that he was the inspiration of the Camanachd Association, which has been the means of placing the old Highland pastime in the high position it occupies today. When steps were taken to revive what was undoubtedly becoming a lost pastime even in the north, Lord Lovat, a keen player in his youth, took a leading part, and since the inception of the Association forty years ago, he has been our worthy head. Indeed, it was on

Lord Lovat's motion that it was agreed to institute the Challenge Trophy — the Final of which has brought us to Lochaber today — a trophy around which hover the memories of great and gallant fights and which has proved a real stimulus to the game.

''It is our duty to record in our minutes our appreciation of Lord Lovat's untiring efforts throughout his life to foster the most manly pastime in our beloved High-

William Paterson, Beauly, 1896-1964, President 1937-48

lands. It was particularly fitting that a Highland Chief should be the leader in re-establishing the game, and I am quite sure every one in the Highlands will agree with me when I say that Lord Lovat's work will be lovingly remembered in the towns and glens wherever shinty is played down the ages. As a sportsman, a landlord, a county legislator, a statesman and a worthy Highlander and soldier, the Chief of the Camanachd Association nobly played his part and he has left behind him a record of service which should be a cherished memory in the Highlands, and an inspiration to those who occupy high stations in life not only in our own day but in the years to come.''

Colonel A. W. MacDonald, D.S.O., was unanimously elected as the new Chief to succeed Lovat. Mr W. Paterson, Beauly moved that a new office be created and that the present Lord Lovat, who was a young man and exceedingly interested in shinty, be elected Vice-Chief.

Sir Colin MacRae of Feoirlinn informed the meeting that the Playing Fields Association would give sympathetic consideration to any club wishing to improve their ground in the form of a grant and he requested that clubs should consider the offer and write to him on the matter.

The Secretary, Mr D. MacLean, read a letter from the Irish National Association requesting an informal meeting with the Camanachd Association to see if the rules of shinty and hurling could be unified. The meeting appointed ex-Provost Skinner, Mr Archibald MacPherson, Mr J.M.MacDonald, Mr Fletcher and Mr W. Paterson to represent the Camanachd Association at the proposed meeting. The gentlemen were not given any powers but were to report back when convenient.

The following October Council meeting heard that report from Ex-Provost Skinner on the talks with the Irish. He remarked that Camanachd Association officials were all agreed that on no account would they agree to change their Rules which had taken forty years to perfect, and this decision he had conveyed to the Hurling representatives. At the same time the Camanachd delegates agreed that Rules on a basis of equality might be agreed on for an international match between the respective Associations.

The delegates then considered the Rules of Shinty and Hurling and agreed on a basis on which an international match might be played. These Rules were being put into 'more concrete form' by Mr Morgan, who acted as Chairman of the Conference and were sent to the Camanachd Association Secretary. He in turn was instructed to send copies of them to clubs when they came to hand.

The Rules were to be considered at the meeting of the Camanachd to be held in Glasgow in February when it was expected an invitation to play an international match in Ireland at Easter would be to hand. Ex-Provost Skinner said that it was made perfectly clear that on no account would the Camanachd Association play a match on a Sunday.

The international match was again debated at the February meeting and it was agreed to play the game under the Rules agreed at Glasgow, but that it could not be played until such time as the Camanachd matches had been completed. Financial arrangements were also discussed. It was thought that the most reasonable arrangement was to pay expenses to the visiting team and then to entertain the visitors. Any surplus would be equally divided between the Associations. However, it was decided to refer the whole affair to the AGM in April.

When it was raised there, a letter recieved from Mr Horgan of the Irish Hurling Association was read to the meeting. It contained an offer to pay the expenses of a Camanachd team to play in Dublin on April 21 or 28. The minimum to be paid was £50 and the gate was to be divided after the hurlers' expenses had been paid.

At this point, the proposals began to look distinctly less attractive. Mr Paterson, the Vice-President, informed the meeting that John MacLennan, Strathconon, Vice-President had made enquiries and the information he had received was that the Association was "anti-British". Ex-Provost Skinner said that he had the opinion of "one in high authority" who said: "Have nothing to do with such a match".

Major Colin MacRae of Feoirlinn also spoke and was of the opinion that the whole matter had a political flavour and advised the meeting to "keep clear".

Oban, who defeated Newtonmore in the Final in April, 1933 at Keppoch, Lochaber, after a drawn game, 1-1 at Corpach, Fort William

The whole matter was then dropped after a vote, on the motion of Mr W. Paterson, seconded by Ex-Provost Skinner.

"With no explanation as to how it had taken the Association 50 years to learn that the GAA (hurling's ruling body) had its origins in the struggle for Irish independence... and apparently with no questioning of the right or the motivation of 'people in high authority' to dictate policy to a small sporting body in the north of Scotland, the Camanachd Association slashed the twine and let the rope bridge fall." (Roger Hutchinson, *Camanachd*)

The Association was to find, however, that it was not that easy to extinguish the moves for closer ties between the two countries and a succession of clubs and Universities continued to ply the Irish sea. In the fifties, the spectre of internationals again raised its head and died a death; in 1964 the Association again pronounced itself to be firmly against any links; its members were asked not to patronise shinty/hurling internationals. It was to be a further ten years before the enlightened few eventually convinced their peers that internationals were a worthwhile pursuit and Scotland and Ireland finally met at Inverness on August 5, 1974.

The Shinty Referee

O sure I'm not sea-faring
But I'll tell you how I felt

When we went o'er to Erin
To meet our brother Celt Ach,

the boat she started tossing
When Dick Cameron said to me
'"Twill be a divil o' a crossing
For the Shinty Referee!"

But sure we're all together
From the castle and the plough
The shamrock and the heather
They are intermingled now
Long may they be in harmony
And rivalry prevail
To show the world our flags unfurled
And we are Clann nan Gaidheal.

But that blooming Irish Ocean
Sure she neither ebbs nor flows
She set me right in motion
From my head down to my toes
Till the big and little fishes
Came up in turns to see
And gave their grateful wishes
To the Shinty Referee!

No longer are we troubling
About the grand old game
Since we have seen in Dublin
Both countries play the same
Those camans told of days of old
Of muscle, brawn and brain
So let us strive to keep alive
Our grand old fathers' game.

As for differentiation
I would never ever dream
Agin Ireland as a nation
We had an ideal team
Yet Ireland said about the Kaid.
Our humble Referee
'"Twas such as him with heart and limb
that set old Ireland free!"

John Kaid MacLean

Martin MacDonald: *Skye Camanachd — A Century Remembered*

Caberfeidh:
(above): KenMacMaster of Caberfeidh (later to be President of the Association) leads his team on to the Winterton for the 1934 Final against Kyles

(right): The first team to win the Camanachd Cup, the MacTavish Cup and the MacGillivray League Cup in the same season

Caberfeidh:
Action from the final.
Alistair MacKenzie
(Caberfeidh); John
Olding (Kyles); Tommy
Hossack (Caberfeidh
goalkeeper — swinging
club); Ken MacMaster
(Caberfeidh); Davy
Thomson (Caberfeidh,
at rear)

Meanwhile on more familiar, and obviously acceptable ground, twenty-five clubs entered the Camanachd Challenge Cup in season 1933-34, with Fort William competing again, along with Edinburgh University.

He also reported, incidentally, that the shinty results were now being broadcast on Saturdays. "I was not always at home when the shinty results were broadcast, but I understand they came through very well," he said. The following February, however, it was reported that "the name Boleskine, which caused the BBC announcer so much trouble, will no longer cause him anxiety as the name is gone, but Foyers, which we can hardly call a new name, takes its place."

Twenty-four teams entered for the trophy in 1934 which was to be a famous year for Caberfeidh. At the AGM that year the President Mr W. MacBean, resigned

and was replaced by Ex-Provost John Dallas, Kingussie.

The February meeting of that season had to deal with some trouble which arose from an incident at the Oban versus Inveraray District Final of the Camanachd Cup. The game had been abandoned some thirteen minutes from the end due to an invasion by spectators. The referee reported that, following some decisions against Oban players, the field had been invaded twice. He had decided to abandon the match.

Oban claimed a replay and Inveraray claimed the tie. Two letters were also read to the meeting from policemen who had been present. After great deliberation, it was agreed to award the tie to Inveraray following a 19-14 vote.

Another letter read to the same meeting requested the Association to take steps to have a Broadcast or "Eye-Witness

Account'' of the final arranged. The Secretary was instructed to write to the BBC with a request for a ten minutes' eye-witness account of the final, and if that reply was favourable, Mr J.W.MacKillop should give the account.

Shinty Final 1934

Give ear, O Lords and ladies gay,
To this, my humble sporting lay.
A rousing camanachd display
You'll see, when Kyles and Cabers play.
Seventh April is the day,
Inveraray is the way;
  Toss thine antlers, Caberfeidh.

Calum MacQueen is referee;
An Edinburgh University Blue is he,
Who knows the game like ABC.
He rules each match with firm decree;
Determined aye fair play to see,
No back-chat will permitted be.
  Toss thine antlers, Caberfeidh.

Eight times champions are Kyles,
Against teams of many different styles.
No club on mainland or in Isles
Knows more of shinty's subtle wiles;
Shall Cabers come one-sixty miles
And beat them? Tighnabruaich smiles!
  Toss thine antlers, Caberfeidh.

Though Nicolsons at last have gone
(Most worthy father, brother, son)
Donald MacFadyen carries on,
Of all hail-keepers Number One;
The forwards dribble, pass and run,
Then shoot with caman as with gun.
  Toss thine antlers, Caberfeidh.

Many a time in days of yore
The final tie saw Newtonmore,

With Doctor Cattanach to the fore
Pile up the hails in mighty score,
Successive triumphs numbering four —
E'en Kyles can boast but three, no more.
  Toss thine antlers, Caberfeidh.

It seemed that history would re-tell
In 1934 as well,
For Kyles and Oban put their spell,
To sound the reigning champions' knell,
But, on Kingussie's famous Dell,
The pride of Badenoch shinty fell.
  Toss thine antlers, Caberfeidh.

Let now Strathpeffer have its say —
Their second final tie today;
Four years ago, their skies were grey,
They lost, near Oban's charming bay.
Now may they bask in Sol's bright ray;
Too often Kyles and Newtonmore held
    sway.
  Toss thine antlers, Caberfeidh.

Though Kyles' great talent none ignore,
Mackenzie, Campbell, Cummings, more
Can carry Cabers to the fore,
And, when they hit the winning score,
A thousand yells will skyward soar,
A thousand throats will wildly roar:
  ''Caberfeidh''

Eric Ros Birkett

The 1935 AGM heard from the retiring Secretary Mr D. MacLean, that the affairs of the Association had not run all that smoothly. ''Protests were frequent, and as is to be expected, the decisions arrived at were not always to the satisfaction of the club protesting. Referees came in for a very rough time, and I repeat what I said in Glasgow, that unless care is taken, and young referees encouraged, the referee question will in a very short time become

(left): Strathdearn, 1930's.
(standing): R. Douglas, W. Kennedy, D. MacKenzie, J. Fraser, D. MacPherson, M. Corr, J. Noble
(kneeling): C. Kennedy, A. MacKenzie, A. Campbell, J. MacDermid, F. MacKinnon

(below): Glasgow, Inverness-shire, late 1930's

serious. As it is, the securing of substitutes when the appointed referees are unable to act, is a very dificult and expensive one.'' Mr MacLean might well have been speaking at any of the Annual General Meetings held in the last decade!

In the 1935-36 season, it was reported that three prominent clubs were missing — Furnace who won the cup in 1923 without conceding a goal, Fort William and Glasgow Cowal.

The Secretary, W. MacPherson, reported that all the Rules remained the same but he wished to comment on two records, one of which the Association could be proud, the other not. ''The former, the record gate for any final, the latter the number of protests and disputes which arose during the season. I trust that this season, things may run more smoothly, and there is incumbent on all of us, players, referees, officials and spectators alike, to do all in our power to keep clean the game of Camanachd, so that this branch of sport may be held up as a shining example to all other sports whether Amateur or Professional.''

He also read a letter from An Comunn Gàidhealach, asking for financial assistance in promoting the game of Camanachd among the children of the Gàidhealtachd. After discussion, the Association decided that whilst they recognised the good intentions of An Comunn, they could not see their way to making a donation, and that it was the opinion of the meeting that these activities should be financed by An Comunn, ''a body sounder financially than the Camanachd Association.''

The 1936 AGM also heard of the death of Vice-President James L. Malcolm, Inveraray. Mr Donald Cattanach, Kingussie was appointed in his place.

The Secretary reported that very few clubs had taken advantage of the offer made by the BBC to broadcast the results. ''This I think is regrettable'' he said, ''since there are many enthusiasts in remote places throughout the Highlands and Islands who would greatly appreciate hearing these results on Saturday evenings.''

It was proposed at this meeting that all the entrants for the 1936-37 Camanachd Cup competition ''be put in a pool together and that the District system be abandoned for one season.'' The Chief, Colonel A.W. MacDonald, who proposed the motion stated that a general balloting of teams would not only lead to a greater interest being aroused for the game throughout the Highlands, but that clubs would also benefit financially. Spectators were growing tired of witnessing the same teams in action.

Ex-Provost Skinner moved an amendment, seconded by Hugh MacLachlan, Spean Bridge, with an impassioned plea based on the costs, he swung the debate away from an open draw and won the vote 18-15. There was to be no open draw for nearly fifty years.

Twenty-three teams entered for the Challenge cup in the season 1936-37 which saw its fair share of controversy. One meeting in February dealt with an incident involving five players who had been ordered off in a match between Inveraray and Oban Celtic on January 23, 1937.

The Rough Play Committee had decided, after full discussion, that, "in the interests of the game, very drastic action must be taken, not only as a warning to players but also to clubs, in view of the increasing evidence that unnecessarily rough play and disgraceful conduct are being introduced to the game, they (would) severely censure and suspend from taking part in any further part in the Cup Competition the five players."

Two were suspended until the start of the 1938-39 season and the rest were suspended for the remainder of the current season. The clubs were also reprimanded in the strongest possible terms and the referee chastised as 'he ought to have acted more firmly.' The Committee re-

Inveraray, 1936

served its full wrath for an official of the Oban Celtic team who was involved in an incident with a Celtic player. The official was 'debarred from further official duties on the field of play for all time.'

Mr H. Dunn, representing the Oban club, stated that they had no wish to appeal, but asked that the matter be at least discussed as Celtic felt they had been unfairly treated. The President, Ex-Provost John Dallas, Kingussie, however, did not allow any discussion on the subject and it was dropped.

The same meeting heard of the death of Lieutenant-Colonel MacRae-Gilstrap, brother of Sir Colin MacRae. Camanachd had lost another great supporter.

The 1937 AGM took place in the dramatic setting of Inverness Castle, and it was reported by the Secretary, Mr MacPherson that "for the first time in the history of the game, part of our Final match is to be broadcast. This will afford great pleasure to many shinty enthusiasts, especially of the older generation, who are unable to travel to witness the match. We hope to make this an annual event." It was the beginning of a long and successful relationship with BBC Scotland whose radio and television broadcasts on the game have been much appreciated over the years.

The Secretary went on: "While we as an Association can congratulate ourselves on our financial position, we must keep in mind that our aim is not to amass wealth but to foster and develop the national game. This, I think, could best be achieved by setting aside a sum of money which could be judicially spent in providing shinty equipment for boys' teams. Any money so spent would be returned tenfold in the interest and enthusiasm aroused in the younger generation. We must not forget that the boys of today will be the men of tomorrow." The meeting agreed to allocate the sum of £20 towards helping young teams.

The money was eventually shared amongst the following bodies: Ross-shire Camanachd Association Juvenile Competition; Matheson Cup competition; Schools Shinty League Association; Lord Lifford Cup competition (Glengarry District); Taynuilt Boys' competition; Inveraray and Furnace District Boys' competition; Lady Margaret MacRae of Feoirlinn Cup competition; and the Tighnabruaich District Medal competition.

The Chief, Colonel MacDonald returned to his attempt to have the Camanachd Cup made on an open-draw basis. Having failed the previous year, he offered this alternative: "That, after the first ties in the Trophy Competition in each district have been decided, the names of the clubs still remaining in the competition be drawn for in one ballot." This attempt to have the open draw introduced failed once again, but there was an indication that the tide of opinion was turning. It was agreed that there should, eventually, be a change in the district format on which the Cup was being run. After a great deal of discussion, it was agreed that from the following season, as an experiment, the semi-finalists would be balloted.

The AGM also returned to a well-worn theme which has pre-occupied the members ever since play and equipment was regularised. The Inverness club made a plea to have experiments carried out with a larger ball, being of the view that play would, as a result, be "more accurate and scientific." Mr John MacPherson, Inverness, stated that it was proposed to conduct trials with such a ball at a forth-coming charity match in the town and the Association gave the proposal its blessing.

1937 was also significant in that it saw the formation of the Schools' Camanachd Association, and its founders were, interestingly, connected with two of the game's strongholds. Ewen A. MacQueen, a teacher of technical subjects and his brother Dr Malcolm C. MacQueen had spent their formative years in the Kyles of Bute. Being interested in all manner of outdoor activities, they had formed a close connection with the Kyles club and when they moved north to Inverness, they quickly took up the game amongst kindred spirits.

It became apparent to Ewen MacQueen, who had returned to the town after a period working in Yorkshire, that there was a pressing need for some organised form of the game in Highland schools and by 1937, he had almost single-handedly planned the formation of the new Association. In the first two years, with the

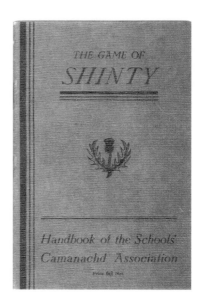

In 1939, the Schools' Camanachd Association produced it first handbook with 'Hints on Playing Shinty'. Ten years ago, the Association was again instrumental in the publication of the first Rules of Play and Coaching Manual

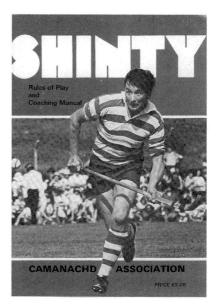

whole-hearted support of the local authorities, interest spread rapidly from the Isle of Skye to Argyll and ultimately as far south as Glasgow. At the outset, the handsome John MacPherson Trophy was put up for annual competition, with teams participating on a league basis.

Kingussie High School were, fittingly perhaps, the first winners in 1938, followed in 1939 by Oban High School.

The founding members of the Schools' Association were Ewen A. MacQueen, Charles MacKintosh and Ellis Stuart, and their contribution to the game in schools was outstanding. Their work and example has been followed over the years by a number of outstanding servants — John MacDonald and Hume Robertson at Tomnacross; John MacQueen, J. Ewan, W.T. Eunson, Kenny Campbell and Roddy MacKinnon at Beauly; W.MacPherson, I.Maclean, J.W.Campbell, Charles MacKintosh and Ellis Stuart themselves in Inverness; Somhairle MacGill-eain and D.R. MacDonald in Plockton and Skye; John MacKinnon and Andy Dunn in Kingussie; John Millar and Donald Finlayson in Newtonmore; Bruce Tulloch in Inverlochy; Alex MacLeod in Caol and Walter Cameron in Banavie.

To select these names is, perhaps unfair, and no slight is intended on those not mentioned, particularly in Argyll where Oban High School have always been to the fore. The Inspectorate and Directors of Education such as Murdo Morrison and Dr J.A. Maclean of Inverness-shire are also worthy of mention for their contribution.

Over the years further competitions have been added to the schools' structure, principally the Wade Cup, donated by Mr Tom Wade of Kingussie and the MacBean Cup presented by William MacBean.

The Association has also been fortunate to have benefited from significant sponsorship from the Bank of Scotland since 1986 and their contribution to a Final, played in conjuction with the Camanachd Cup Final, has ensured that the schoolboys of today are still as important as ever in the overall structure of shinty. It is perhaps significant that Mrs Donella Crawford, President of the Schools' Association became the first woman to sit on the Executive Committee of the Camanachd Association.

The 1937 February Council meeting heard of the deaths of two more stalwarts, Mr Hugh MacCorquodale and Mr James P. MacGillivray. The former had devoted a life-time to the game as referee, player and writer. The latter was a former Secretary of the Association and had donated the most famous of its cups.

It was reported that the season's cup competition had been more open than ever before, with Fort William and Inverness making their first ever semi-final appearances. They were joined in the ballot by Kyles and Oban Camanachd, no strangers to this stage of the competition. The trophy eventually made its way to Oban where Camanachd emerged as 4-2 winners over Inverness. Their day was yet to come.

An t-Earrach — 1937

Air an raon fhada leathann
An ear-thùath air Port-righ,
Shuas air cùl a'bhaile,
Raon mor iomain na Bòrlainn,
Sgioba Sgoilearan Phort-righ:

Gillean mu shia-diag 's mu sheach-diag,
Iad uile deante is sgairteil,
Cruadalach agus tapaidh,
Sgitheanaich, Ratharsaich, agus fear dhiu
Leòdhasach mòr socair laidir.

Latha o chionn lethchiad bliadhna,
Latha grianach ciùin,

Gun snaithnean ceotha air a' Chuilthionn
No air claigeann a' Stòir.

Ach an diugh ceò eile
Air raon mòr na Bòrlainn,
Ceò na lathaichean a dh'fhalbh
Ciar thar na h-òigridh a chaill an òige
Is ochdnar dhen dha-dhiag marbh.

Chaill iad uile an òige
S i'n toiseach mar linn eile,
Ach an ceann dà bhliadhna
Borb le cunnartan a'chogaidh,
Le tinneas, leòintean agùs bàs,
a shearg flùraichean na h-àbhaist
Ged a thàrr a'mhòr-chuid as.

Am bliadhna tha buidheann eile
A cheart cho gleusda 'n Sgoil Phort-righ,
A cheart cho calma ris an sgioba
A bha san t-strì air raon na Bòrlainn

The ingredients of a McKellar ball

The making of a ball —

Cutting the core from a cube of cork

Mun do bharc an leth-cheud bliadhna
Air an linn laidir ud de dh'òigridh.

Somhairle MacGill-Eain

Sorley Maclean's poem is based on the Robertson Cup Final of 1937 when Portree School defeated Sleat to win the trophy for the second time.

Oban was also the venue of the 1938 AGM and the meeting had before it the recommendations of a sub-committee which had been set up to look into the 'reform of the Association and Council of Management.' Forty-five years after its formation, the Association was to take a look at itself, albeit a tentative one.

The AGM unanimously accepted the recommendations of the sub-committee on the motion of Sir Stewart MacPherson, seconded by Donald Cattanach.

The recommendations were:
(a) Vice-Presidents be restricted in number to Twenty.
(b) Representation of Clubs at general Meetings and Council meetings by mandate be abolished, and a re-presentation by specified individuals from each club substituted.
(c) An enlarged Rough Play and Finance Committee be formed, and
(d) The matter be remitted back to the Sub-Committee for further consideration.

The Committee had recommended that:
(a) At the Annual General Meetings or Special General Meetings of the Association Twenty to form a quorum, and that at Council Meetings of the Association Ten to form a quorum.
(b) All members of the Finance and Rough Play Committee be Vice-Presidents of the Association.

Smoothing the cork core of the ball

(c) The duties of the Committee acting under Rule XIX. of the Constitution be undertaken by the Finance and Rough Play Committee.

(d) The Joint Committee be known as the Executive Committee.

(e) It consists of the Chief, Vice-Chief, President, and eight Vice-Presidents. Four to form a quorum. Two Vice-Presidents from each District.

(f) Its duties be:

To give guidance to the Secretary of the Association in regard to the running of the Competition between Meetings of Council.

The Secretary, on points where he requires guidance, shall consult with the President; if they deem it necessary a Meeting of the Executive Committee shall be called. The President and the Secretary, in disposing of matters without a Meeting of the Executive Committee, may consult informally with other members.

To look after the Finances of the Association; to report on financial matters to the Council; to scrutinise Accounts, allocate Gate Monies from Semi-Final and Final Ties.

To deal with rough play, misconduct on the field, and other such breaches of Rules of the Association, with full powers to suspend, caution players, or otherwise dispose of the case. The finding of the Executive Committee shall not be subject to review by the Council or Association, but if, in their opinion, the circumstances of a case warrant further action, they shall call a Special Meeting of the Council.

To investigate and look into Protests, Disputes and other matters, with no authority to award a Tie to a Club, or to order a re-play. The function of the Executive Committee is to consider if the merits of a dispute or protest justify jurisdiction by the Council.

If the merits of a case so demand, a Meeting of the Council shall be called. If, in the opinion of the Executive Committee, the case is trivial, or if the outcome is clearly defined by the Rules of the Association, no Meeting of Council is called, and in consequence the protest is not sustained.

To deal with matters remitted to the Committee by the Council or the Association. Amongst the alterations in the Constitution and Rules were that the advisability of balloting Semi-Finals be considered; that the number of club bearers admitted to the field of play be limited to one; that the first Council Meeting, at present held towards the end of October, be held at an earlier date; that Clubs entering the Camanachd Cup be grouped in two districts, North and South, with the respective winners of the Districts representing the areas in the Final; that a Rough Play Committee be appointed in both north and south districts; that the Annual General Meeting of the Association take place on a day other than Cup Final day, and such a meeting to be held at a place centrally situated for all clubs in the Association.

Most of these recommendations were accepted with little discussion and the new Constitution and Rules were to form the basis for the game's administration for over thirty years. It may have been the first major re-organisation of the game's structure, but it reflected the conservative nature of its administration, a nature which was to remain an integral part of the collective psyche for years to come.

The first ever meeting of the newly formed Executive of the Camanachd Association took place in Fort William on May 10, 1938 and the next was in Inverness in October, immediately before the Council Meeting.

That meeting heard the news of the death of John MacAskill, Tomatin, who had been a Vice-President of the Association for many years. The Secretary Mr MacPherson, in a sombre address detailed

Winding wool over the cork core

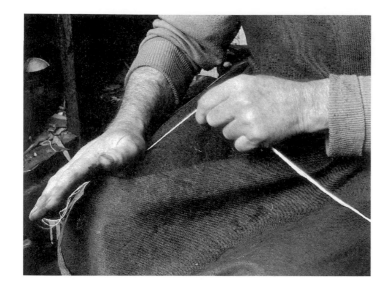

*Making the thread,
which is then waxed*

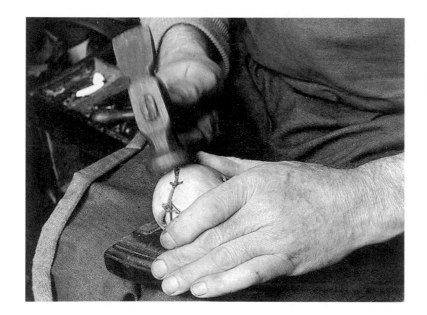

*Stretching the cover into
shape*

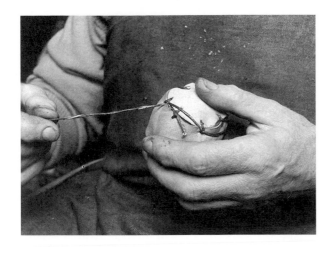

Basting the cover into place before stitching

The making of a McKellar shinty ball, Tighnabruaich

(right): John McKellar starting to sew the seam

Stitching the cover

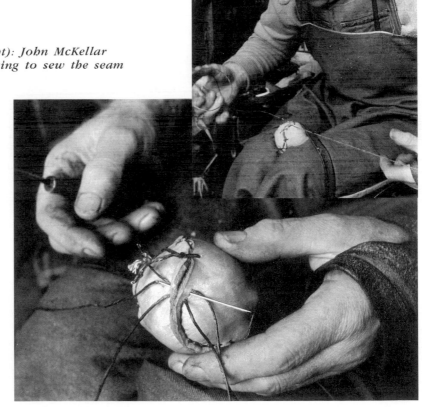

the position the Association found itself in as the face of Europe began to change:

"For a time, during the recent crisis, it seemed doubtful if we were to going to have a Shinty season at all, but, happily our players have not been called upon to take part in the diabolical game of war, but are free once again to return to that manly and peaceful pastime, the game of Camanachd.

"This season nineteen teams have entered for our senior competition. This, unfortunately is three less than last year. Fort Augustus, Spean Bridge and Glasgow University have not entered, while Inveraray has not yet decided to return to the fold. Glasgow University, for some unknown reason, enter a team every alternate year, but it is to be deplored that districts in the heart of the Shinty country and with long and honoured traditions, should fail to come forward. In conclusion, may we have a good sporting competition and may each team strive to give of its best in the matches ahead."

The meeting also adopted the recommendation by the Executive Committee that shinty equipment to the value of £50 be given to juvenile associations.

A plea from the Secretary to bear in mind that the new Executive was looking

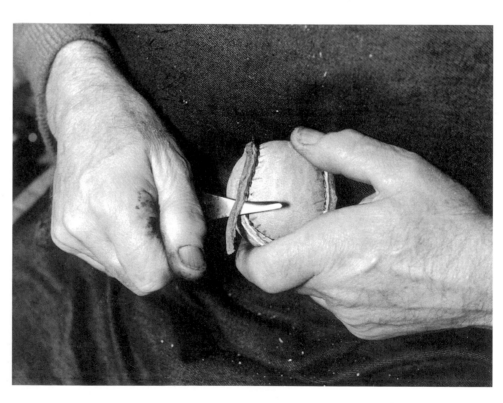

Trimming excess leather from the seam of the ball, after sewing

after the best interests of the game did not lead to an anticipated outbreak of peace and tranquility. In December 1938 Brae-Lochaber lodged a protest relating to their Camanachd Cup second round match at Keppoch on the 10th of that month.

"(a) I am asked by the Brae-Lochaber Club to lodge a Protest against Provost Donald Cattanach's action in influencing the Referee to alter his decision. Shortly before half-time, the Referee ordered two players off the field. At this stage, Provost Cattanach went on to the field of play, and told the Referee to allow the two players to carry on. This is not in accordance with Rule 16, and my Club thinks that the interference by this member of the Executive Committee had a bearing on the Referee's decisions for the rest of the game.

(b) The second hail scored by Kingussie was definitely kicked into the net. The Referee consulted the Hail-judge (Alex. Mackintosh, a referee of long standing), who told him that the ball was kicked. This hail was allowed to stand. The Captain of my Club intimated the Protest to the Referee, and, when time was up, he called the two Captains to the middle of the field, in accordance with Rule 17. The Kingussie Captain took no notice of the Referee's orders, after blowing his whistle three times. My Club feels that this game was not conducted according to the Rules, and that we are entitled to a replay."

At the outset, the President, Mr Paterson pointed out that certain technicalities in connection with the protest had not been observed by both clubs. In the first place, the captain of the Kingussie club had not gone to the centre of the field at the conclusion of the game, and secondly the Brae-Lochaber Club did not send copies of their protest to the Kingussie Club or to the Referee in accordance with

Rule 18 of the Camanachd Trophy. It was unanimously agreed that these breaches of technicalities be overlooked.

Then statements were read from the Referee, Mr John MacLeod, Fort William; from the clubs concerned; from the Hail-judge and from the two players who were ordered off by the referee; and also from Provost Cattanach. It was also agreed that a hail scored direct from a hit-in now be allowed. After great deliberation, Provost Cattanach was exonerated of the charge of interfering with the Referee.

It was also agreed that the Referee had shown incompetence with regard to one incident in that he had ordered off William Dallas of Kingussie and James Toal of Brae-Lochaber and that he had allowed them to resume contrary to Rule 16. The meeting's decision was that Mr MacLeod be deleted from the list of officials and that the game be re-played. The two players who had been ordered off were censured and warned as to their future conduct.

That was far from being the end of the matter, however, and at the next Executive meeting in Glasgow on February 10, 1939 Provost Cattanach of Kingussie tendered his resignation "owing to the lack of confidence shown by the President and others in Inverness, in connection with the Lochaber incident prior to the Meeting of Council being called." His resignation was accepted with regret.

Kingussie as a club also made representations to the meeting, appealing against the findings of the Council at their meeting of December 27, 1938. The secretary, after consultations with the President replied that the decision could only be reviewed at a Special meeting of the Association under Rule IX(a) and X(e) of the Constitution. It was the first of many wrangles at Executive level which would have tested the diligence and ingenuity of a Philadelphia lawyer. It was not to be the last.

Mr John MacPherson, Inverness, was given authority to have a new 'die' made for casting the Camanachd Cup and Sutherland Cup medals at this point.

"There are qualities in Shinty which appeal to the primitive and scientific natures of man.

That renowned African traveller, Major C. Court Treatt, F.R.G.S., relates in his book, *Out of the Beaten Track*, how his party were amused to see a crowd of Dinka boys apparently playing a ferocious game of hockey with crooked sticks cut from the bush and a ball consisting of a Dom palm nut. "An English

The indomitable spirit which had seen many Highland heroes through the First World War also re-surfaced between 1939-45. Teams were formed in various POW camps and teams of wood-cutters sent to cut down natural bends to make camans. These pictures, provided by Roddy MacPherson of Glenelg, were taken at Stalag 9C

referee," he writes, "would have turned them all off the field for fighting and deliberate shin-cracking! However a hullaballoo of shrill laughter clearly indicated their keen enjoyment. These boys must have been playing Shinty."

The changing face of the Association was meeting with general approval however, the Secretary reported in 1939:

"I make bold to say that the game of shinty is in as flourishing a condition as it has ever been, and clubs and players throughout the country are taking a very keen interest in the game, as is evident from the large number of proposed alterations to the Constitution and Rules put forward for consideration at this meeting. Besides the Camanachd Association, other Associations are doing valiant work in promoting and developing the game of Shinty. A special word of praise is due to the youngest body, the Schools' Camanachd Association, for the very excellent work it is doing among the juveniles. Not only has it increased interest among the younger generation in districts where the game is thoroughly established, but, what is more important, it has aroused interest in districts where the wielding of the caman has become a long lost art."

"'S ged a sgaoileadh am mòd-s'
Tha rud gu tighinn oirnn,
Nollaig le ròic thaining i;

'S bheir a' Challainn di'n cleòc,
'S bidh gillean gu leòr
Ag iomain 's an t-seòl a b' àbhaisd
doibh."

(Transactions of The Gaelic Society of Inverness, Vol XXX, p.35)

Having developed the taste for change and tinkering with the Constitution, the members then proceeded to address a number of other changes including the establishment of a list of referees and the need for a two-thirds majority at AGMs in order to effect changes to the Constitution, Rules of Play or Rules of the Camanachd Trophy.

Events elsewhere were, however, to interrupt proceedings and the Association did not meet again until Friday, August 30, 1946.

"Let us therefore brace ourselves to our duties, and so bear ourselves that, if the British Empire and its Commonwealth last for a thousand years, men will not say: "This was their finest hour"

(Winston Churchill, June 18, 1940, in a speech delivered in the House of Commons)

Rinn sinn an cruinneachadh fann,
S cha b'ann gu cluich air a'bhall;
A'spionadh nan corp as an fhang,
An gniomh a bh'ann bu sgràthail e.

1991 — Roddy MacPherson of Glenelg reminisces with Gregor McBain of Kincraig about their time in Stalag 9C

Latha Foghair

'S mi air an t-slios ud latha foghair,
na sligean a'sianail mu m' chluasan
agus sianar marbh ri mo ghualainn,
rag-marbh — is reòta mur b'e 'n teas —
mar gum b'ann a'fuireach ri fios.

Nuair thàinig an sgriach
a mach as a' ghrèin,
à buille 's bualadh do-fhaicsinn,
leum an lasair agus streap an ceathach
agus bhàrc e gacha rathad:
dalladh nan sùl, sgoltadh claistinn.

'S 'na dhèidh, an sianar marbh,
fad an latha;
am miosg nan sligean 'san t-strannraich
anns a'mhadainn,
agus a rithist aig meadhon-latha
agus 'san fheasgar.

Ris a'ghrèin 's i cho coma'
cho geal cràiteach;
air a'ghainmhich 's i cho tìorail
socair bàidheil;
agus fo reultan Africa 's iad leugach
    àlainn.

Ghabh aon Taghadh iadsan
's cha d' ghabh e mise,
gun fhoighneachd dhinn
cò b'fheàrr no bu mhiosa:
ar liom, cho diabhlaidh coma
ris na sligean

Sianar marbh ri mo ghualainn,
Latha foghair.

Somhairle MacGill-Eain

An Autumn Day

On that slope on an Autumn day,
the shells soughing about my ears
and six men dead at my shoulder,
dead and stiff — and frozen were it not
    for the heat —
as if they were waiting for a message.

When the screech
came out of the sun,
out of an invisible throbbing;
the flame leapt and the smoke climbed
and surged every way:
blinding of eyes, splitting of hearing.

And after it, six men were dead
the whole day:
among the shells snoring
in the morning,
and again at midday
and in the evening.

In the sun, which was so indifferent,
so white and painful;
on the sand which was so comfortable
easy and kindly;
and under the stars of Africa,
jewelled and beautiful.

One Election took them
and did not take me,
without asking us
which was better or worse:
it seemed as devilishly indifferent
as the shells.

Six men dead at my shoulder
and an Autumn day

Sorley MacLean

Foyers

FROM RENAISSANCE TO TERRIBLE PAROCHIALISM

"The great dark clouds raised by the war, that over four years devastated civilisation, are rolling by, and once more the sun of peace brightens the view." (*Alexander MacDonald*, Transactions of the Gaelic Society of Inverness, *Vol. XXX p.56*)

"At the outset the President expressed his pleasure at seeing so many shinty enthusiasts gathered together. Now that the years of trials and tribulations had passed he felt that the time had come to get competitive shinty going again. The chief difficulty at the moment was the supply of camans, balls and equipment, but he was confident that with the traditional Celtic spirit they could surmount these difficulties."

And on that optimistic note following the years of war in which many shinty players lost their lives, the Secretary recorded the resumption of organised shinty.

There was an immediate desire to pick up the pieces and it was unanimously agreed that entries for the Camanachd Cup be received by October 1, 1946.

The "traditional Celtic spirit" immediately shone through and had never, in fact, been extinguished.

In the summer of 1946, when I was twelve years old, Ally Fraser was my sporting hero. He didn't play for one of Scotland's great football teams nor was his name known beyond the parish boundaries of Glenshiel and Kintail, a remote but beautiful corner of Wester Ross. The district, now easily access–ible by fine roads, was in these far-off days, little known to the outside world and little changed in the economic and social life of the people in the previous three or four generations.

Camanachd had not been played during the war years and was unknown to children of my age. But in the summer of 1946, the demobilisation and the return of young men to their homeland re-awakened interest and teams were formed in each parish, with old rivalries being re-kindled.

Our new team was named "Kintail and Glenshiel" or vice-versa. Time has clouded the memory, but at the time the precedence caused some controversy. We children were not concerned with such matters and a severe bout of "shinty fever" swept through the one classroom Shiel Public School.

An assortment of ash, rowan and alder branches, some of them resembling shinty sticks, appeared in the hands of every boy from infants upwards, and there were many bruised shins and knuckles caused by the inexpert wielding of these makeshift sporting implements...

....The sights and sounds of that day are indelibly printed in my memory; the sharp clatter of the camans, the skirl of the bagpipes and shouts of spectators and players.

It is the smells though which are unforgettable — newly mown grass; dubbin on boots brought from a five-year hang-up; linseed oil from the camans and a faint whiff of linament from suspect knees and ankles. Now, almost fifty years on, these memories are as vivid as the day itself."

(Tom MacMillan, "Balmacara post-war heroes revived", Shinty Yearbook 1992-93)

And gradually normal service was resumed. Members at the meeting agreed that a special meeting be held on October 11 at which the draw would be made for the Camanachd Cup. It was also raised that some change could be made to the traditional dates for the competition in order to take advantage of more favourable weather.

At the October 11 meeting, tribute was paid by a packed attendance to those who lost their lives during the war, and specific reference was made to the passing of the Chief, Colonel A.W.MacDonald, D.S.O.

"Today we must also remember the many fine lads who laid aside their camans and marched off to battle and did not return. No more will they strike the ball upon the shinty field, but we as an Association can discharge though in very small measure, the debt we owe them, by keeping alive the game of Shinty, the game they loved to play."

(Association Minutes, October 11, 1946)

It was intimated at the meeting that 16 teams had entered for the Camanachd Cup — "taking everything into consideration... a very satisfactory entry". It was also agreed that the pool of Clothing Coupons held by the Association be

1947 Balmacara school stars

(below): Arguably the biggest crowd ever to witness a shinty match saw the "Pots and Pans" match of 1947 at the Edinburgh Highland Games at Murrayfield. The teams were (8-a-side) Ballachulish and Newtonmore. Far left are Gabriel Fraser (Newtonmore) and Alex MacKenzie (Ballachulish). The players were presented with commemorative pots and pans after the match. Their amateur status was therefore intact — Sandy Russell of Newtonmore claims he still has his set!

(above): Kilmallie, MacTavish Juvenile Cup winners, 1946. This was the first time they had won the trophy and it was a sign of things to come, with the club going on to win the Sutherland Cup two years later; the MacGillivray Senior League championship in 1959 and the Camanachd Cup in 1964.

divided equally among the Clubs competing in the Camanachd and Sutherland Competitions.

Once competitive play got under way, there was general satisfaction with the way events were unfolding. It was reported that an interesting feature of the first round ties was the high scoring, with no fewer than seventy-two goals scored in eight matches. "Whether this is due to faulty tactics in defence or to the fact that the present day forwards have developed more craft and deadlier finishing, is a debatable point."

Before the close of business the Vice-Chief Duncan MacLeod intimated he was gifting the sum of 250 guineas to be used to promote the game. It was felt that the best use of the money would be to use it in the promotion of juvenile shinty, the development of which was being hampered by the lack of finance.

Severe weather disrupted the first season's play but it was generally felt that the standard of play was remarkably high despite the fact that "the camans were relics from pre-war years or have been fashioned locally from home-grown material".

During the season the new touch rule had been in operation, replacing the old rule in which the ball was taken in 16 yards and thrown up between two opposing players. It was eventually agreed that the 1948 A.G.M would discuss the possible re-introduction of the old throw-up for a 'touch'.

Incidentally, heading the ball, made illegal at the 1992 AGM, was withdrawn from a list of actions — running, kicking, catching and throwing which were to be outlawed.

Gradually, the supply of camans was regularised with ash camans being reasonably easy to come by, but with a shortage of hickory remaining a particular problem. The shortage of petrol was also causing some concern and a strongly worded letter was sent to the Minister of Fuel and Power pointing out the effect restrictions on supply would have on the game. The support of Highland MPs was also to be sought on the matter, and this wasn't the last time their assistance was asked for, and received on matters relating to the game.

A more modern approach to the requirements of the game at this stage is to be detected in the approach made to the Norwich & Union Insurance Company which led to their offer to insure a team of twelve players for £5.12s per annum. The game was also granted an Exemption Certificate from Tax by the Commissioners of Inland Revenue which covered matches for the whole season.

Mrs Flora MacAulay, the visionary editor of the post-Second World War *Oban Times*, recognising that there was little competition for clubs after the completion of the Sir William Sutherland Cup and the Camanachd Cup — the final

The famous Kennedy brothers who represented Glengarry post-war, pictured at the Bught Park, 1948. They were the backbone of the Glen team. Fort Augustus also had a team at this point and were trying to tempt the Kennedys to play for them. The solution was an amalgamation of the two clubs into one team, Inveroich

Links with Ireland continued at club level immediately after the war, and the Association was again to try to come to terms with the situation before the end of the fifties. Edinburgh University was amongst the most enthusiastic supporters of links across the sea, and played in Belfast in 1952.

(right — Back row): D. Lamont, I. Gourlay, J. Couper, D. Millar, I. MacPherson, C. MacAllister, S. MacGee. Front: S. MacKenzie, H. MacDonald, D. MacDonald, D.N. Nicolson, I. Michie, A. MacKinnon, G. Menzies.

being played in April at that time — presented a fine silver trophy for competition amongst "all the Senior Shinty Clubs of Scotland". The first round of the competition was to be played in June and the Final in July.

In December, 1946, the MacAulay Cup Association held its first meeting with Archie MacInnes, Oban's Town Clerk and a former Ballachulish player, as President and Donald Cameron, the advertising manager of the *Oban Times* as secretary. The founding committee members were: Major Harry Dunn, Archie Gillespie (both of whom died within a week of each other in October, 1992), Bob MacLachlan and Walter Paterson.

The competition was advertised in the *Oban Times* on January 11, 1947 and twenty-one clubs had entered by the closing date of February 15.

The largest crowd which had attended a match at Mossfield Park, Oban up to that date, some 4,000, attended the first final which was between Ballachulish and Newtonmore. The north team won by 4-1. Their team was: D. MacDonald, J. MacDonald, L. MacQueen, J. MacKintosh, G. Sellar, A. Bain, A. Russell, G. Fraser, C. Kennedy, A. MacDonald, A. Anderson (capt) and J. Campbell.

The MacAulay Cup competition, currently sponsored by builders Keyline, still flourishes, being run by the Mac–Aulay Cup committee. It is one of the elements of the modern Grand Slam of senior shinty trophies and the Final is still held at Oban, as is the south Semi-Final. The current Chairman is Alastair Clark, headmaster of Rockfield Primary School, Oban.

Kingussie are the record holders of the trophy with nineteen wins including 1992; Newtonmore have nine wins, Kyles Athletic nine, Oban Celtic five and Oban Camanachd three. Seven of Kingussie's wins have come in the period since 1980 when they have been the game's dominant force.

The Camanachd Association suffered a great loss which was reported to the Council Meeting in February, 1948. Mr John MacPherson, a Vice-President and member of the Executive Committee and official Club and Ball Maker had died and fulsome praise was made of his exceptional contribution to the sport.

Post-War, there was clearly a feeling of renaissance abroad. The Secretary reported:

"At no time in the past has the popularity of the game been at a higher level, which was evident from the record crowds which attended the northern semi-final and replay."

Players were also, incidentally, prohibited from wearing tackets in their boots at this stage!

A new President took up the reins early in 1949, Mr J.W. MacKillop, who was congratulated on having received the honour of C.B.E. One of his first tasks was to pay tribute to the late Vice-Chief Duncan MacLeod, Skeabost who had made an out-

(above):
The legendary MacKenzie brothers, a formidable part of the Lovat team in the early fifties. (left to right): Addie, Charlie and John 'Horky'

(right):
A beaming Ashie MacRae on his way to polish (fill?) the trophies

Lovat's supporters certainly travelled in style. Bob Kennedy (in belted raincoat), bus and disciples

standing contribution to the game. The customary minute's silence was held as a mark of respect for his passing.

The Association returned to Glasgow for the first time in seventeen years for the Annual General Meeting and once again it was remarked that the game's affairs seemed to be proceeding in the right direction. The financial position was also much improved and the Secretary's emolument was increased from £35 to £50 per annum. Rules were drawn up during this period for six-a-side competitions and the rule regarding hit-in's changed to make a player take the hit with both feet square to the side line. Only one opportunity was allowed.

Later that year other famous names connected with the game passed away — Sir William Sutherland, donor of the junior championship trophy which carries his name and Sir Stewart MacPherson, a Vice-President of the Association.

As the fifties beckoned, the spirit of renaissance continued: "The public generally have become 'shinty conscious' and clubs are looking forward to bigger gate-drawings to offset the ever increasing costs of travelling and equipment. The game has surmounted many difficulties in the post-war years and this reflects the greatest credit on Club committees, espe-

Lovat: Lovat team and committee, 1953 (back row —left to right): A. Reid, W. Harrison, G. Ross, T. Pirrie, W. MacLean, J. Fraser, D. Bruce. (third row —left to right): R. Cameron, D. MacKenzie, C. MacRae, A. Grant, T. Fraser (goal), J. Morrison, L. MacLaren, A. MacRae, R. Fraser. (second row —left to right): D. Thow, G. Anderson, A. MacLaren, A. MacKinnon, D. Kirkwood, A. MacKenzie, W. Cowie, C. MacKenzie. (front row —left to right): S. MacRae, D. Campbell, A. Thow, W. MacLean

It was to be Lovat's most succesful period in their history and their team which swept the boards was exceptional

cially those in sparsely populated districts who have kept their clubs functioning year after year"

Sheas mi car tamuill
Le ioghnadh gun smalan'
a'coimhead nam fearaibh
Le'n camain chruaidh ùr;
Gaoth tuath is clach-mheallain
'Gam bualadh 's 'gan dalladh;
Bha 'chuideachd cho dannair
'S nach aithnicht' orr mùth'.

Laoich chalma le 'n camain
'Gan dearbhadh 's gach bealach,
Laoich eutrom 's na caraibh
Mar cheathach nan stùc;
Cur ball anns an athair
Le luathas na dealain,
'Nuair gheibh i ri spealladh
Ri talamh 'toirt cùil.

Gur bòidheach an treud iad

Air faiche le chèile,
'S iad ruith mar na fèidh
Air slèibh nam beann àrd;
A rèir cumha an fhèidhe
Bha mactalla ag èigheach;
Sud 'nis, òlaich threubhach,
Nach gèilleadh gu bràth.

O'n dualas a lean ribh
O ghuaillibh 'ur seanir,
Bhiodh cruadalachd daingeann
Nis leanachd ri 'n àl;
Ard-inntinneach fearail,
Foinnidh, fuasgailte, fallainn;
Bhiodh suathadh de 'n fhallus
Mu'n mhal' air an tràigh.

Transactions of the Gaelic Society of Inverness, Vol XXX.

The fifties started on a high note for the island of Skye with the Sutherland Cup being taken to the Misty Isle for the first time in 1950. The Sgiathanaich did that with arguably their best and cohesive forward line ever, despite the individual brilliance of earlier players and it was the island team's first shinty trophy for over fifty years. Sadly though, within a year at least six of the players had to leave Skye to continue their careers elsewhere.

Another twenty five years were to pass before the prevailing economic climate allowed Skye to retain enough players of quality to challenge for honours and they won the John MacRae Cup, the MacGillivray League Division Three championship. Further, greater, honours were to follow, however.

Skye were not the only relatively new name to feature on the roll of honour in the fifties and the decade will be remembered on the field of play at least, for the dramatic victories of Inverness in 1952 when they won their first and to date only Camanachd Cup; the hugely successful Lovat team of 1953, the first team to complete the unique 'Grand Slam' of all the available senior trophies including the Celtic Society Cup; and the emergence of Kilmallie as a force to be reckoned with.

The difficulties with supply of equipment which plagued the Association in the immediate post-war years showed no signs of improvement and various attempts were made to facilitate an improved supply of, for example, hickory. The Board of Trade were approached and travel expenses began to feature once again in the list of obstacles being faced by clubs.

It is to their credit, however, that the fifties produced players and teams of such high quality. The balance of power on the field at least seems to have swung firmly in the direction of the north and in the ten years between 1950 and 1960, only three south teams took the Blue Riband — Oban Celtic (in 1954); Kyles Athletic (in 1956) and Oban Celtic again (in 1960).

Difficulties with the Association's finances led to the refusal of a request for £50 assistance from the Schools'

The prized Camanachd Cup Medal in use in the fifties

Camanachd Association towards the cost of making an "Instructional Film on Shinty". The Association's view was that their hard-pressed finances would be "more usefully employed in purchasing camans". But £100 was given towards the supply of equipment to the Juvenile Association.

The Association did, however, consider it worthwhile affiliating with An Comunn Gàidhealach, although the relationship was strained from the outset, especially as An Comunn insisted on the representative of the Association on An Comunn's Executive being a member of

Ewan Ormiston, Camanachd Association, 1954-57, succeeding Archibald MacPherson of Skye who had served as President from 1951 after the death of J.W. MacKillop, C.B.E.

An Comunn. The condition was not well received by the Association, and the relationship has not, over the years, been as fruitful for either body as it might have been.

The Council Meeting of September, 1954 mourned the passing of Ex-Provost D. MacDonald Skinner of Oban, affectionately recalled by the meeting as 'The Grand Old Man of Shinty'. Mr Skinner had been actively connected with the Association since 1895 and had been President between 1925-31. The meeting agreed that "no man had done more for the Association or the game and would go down in history as one of the greatest shinty enthusiasts of all time".

The Skinner family connection with the Association has, of course, been maintained by the splendid service rendered by Mr Skinner's grandson Donald as President of the Association (1976-82) and as Chief since 1986.

Throughout the fifties reference is also made frequently to difficulties arising from the continuation of National Service, particularly for clubs fielding both junior and senior sides. It was also in the mid-fifties (1955) that it was permitted to score a goal direct from a hit-in. And during this period too Walter Cameron of Banavie, a hugely influential figure in the Association for the next two decades, began to make his mark. His first contribution was a memorandum to the Executive Committee on shinty in schools and at juvenile level, a field in which he

Inverness Royal Academy was amongst the schools very active at this juncture and they also knew how to assemble their teams for official photographs.

(right): The 1955 Inverness Royal Academy side, with teacher Ellis Stuart.

(left): Inverness Royal Academy, 1961, with teacher Rob Cameron who was later to be heavily involved with Kilmallie and the Camanachd Association's coaching committee. Rob is, in fact, sitting on the extreme left of the 1955 picture (above) as a pupil.

emerged as one of the game's truly great figures in following years.

That same AGM agreed that a joint disciplinary committee be formed to have jurisdiction over all players playing in games governed by the Association, but only for a trial period of one year.

Another thorny issue which raised its head once again towards the end of the decade was the relationship with Ireland and the possibility of playing an international match. The President Harry Dunn informed the Executive in August, 1957 that he intended to visit Dublin "in the very near future" and offered to get in touch personally with the Irish Hurling Association. The Secretary was later asked to make a formal approach to the Irish with a view to reviving the shinty-hurling internationals. The matter was to be brought to the attention of the Executive again and again before its eventual resolution.

Publication of a Schools' Camanachd Association Handbook also caused considerable difficulty for the Executive at this time and an attempt by Walter Cameron to have 3,000 copies printed at a cost of £68 failed to find adequate support. It had been suggested that the Camanachd Association would take over the cost of the publication but Mr Dunn informed the meeting that "the finances of the Association could not meet the cost of publication".

Ken MacMaster of Strathpeffer (a long-term supporter of schools shinty and still an active coach in his eighties) suggested that instead of postponing the publication indefinitely, each senior club be approached and invited to subscribe the sum of £3 towards the Publication Fund. This proposal was eventually agreed, and it was reported at the February meeting, 1958, that £34.10s had been received as donations following the appeal, with a further £12 being received "from other clubs".

(left): Walter P. Cameron, President, Camanachd Association, 1961-66. Mr Cameron was appointed headmaster of Banavie Primary School near Fort William in 1938 and his pioneering work in the school led directly to Kilmallie's emergence as a powerful force in the late fifties and their eventual Camanachd Cup triumph in 1964. Mr Cameron became Chief of the Association in 1974.

(left): Willie MacPherson served in various offices and made a remarkable contribution to the administration of the game. He was Secretary and Treasurer of the Association from 1935 until 1962, continuing his contribution to the well-being of the game in various capacities until he retired as secretary of the North Disciplinary Committee in 1982. In recognition of his contribution during thirty years as a player and nearly fifty as an administrator, Willie received a special presentation at the AGM of the Association in June, 1982.

Ken MacMaster, (second left) another of the game's greats continued coaching his beloved youngsters at Fodderty school until well into his eighties. The highest point in his playing career was leading Caberfeidh to victory in the 1934 Camanachd Cup Final. He then went on to hold virtually every office in the administration of north shinty and was elected as President of the Association in 1970. His son David has maintained the family link with Caberfeidh and served as Chairman of the club. The Ken MacMaster Trophy for Under-14 players was played for in 1992 for the first time. Caberfeidh were the winners!

(above): Littlejohn Vase medal, 1950's

(right): Edinburgh University in the '50's, who had a successful decade and took a lead in fostering links with the Irish. Team captain Ian Michie is sitting immediately behind the Littlejohn Vase.

Financial matters were well to the fore as ever as the fifties drew to a close and it was reported that the lack of finance would be one of the difficulties to be overcome if the relationship with the Irish was to be pursued. It was made quite clear at this point that the Association "was in no position to commit themselves financially", but were "willing that negotiations be continued". The Secretary was again instructed "to explore further the position regarding the proposed Hurling v Shinty international at the end of the season". He in turn was to report at the February Council meeting the following year that he "was still awaiting a reply to his last letter of 27th October".

In April, 1959 the whole matter of an international match with Ireland was dropped as the negotiations with the Irish "appeared to be going nowhere", although Mr A.H. Cameron of Glasgow agreed to make personal contact with Irish officials when he visited Dublin later that summer.

The start of what was to become eventually the Swinging Sixties found shinty still grappling with age-old problems — lack of finance; an apparent decline of the game in areas such as Ballachulish; referees' shortages and the minutiae of the Rules of Play.

The Council Meeting of April, 1961 heard of the death of the President Angus Cameron of Glasgow, who had been elected the previous year. The meeting marked his passing with appropriate tributes and in a tradition which is still maintained, observed a minute's silence. Walter Cameron, who was to succeed Mr Cameron as president, paid handsome tribute to Mr Cameron's contribution to shinty. He had, Walter Cameron said, undertaken outstanding work for the game as a player, official and administrator.

While Kingussie have been regarded as the modern shinty team *par excellence* it is often forgotten that it is only in the last fifteen to twenty years that they have really dominated the game. It is in that

"Kilmallie's (first) day of glory" —

(above right): Mr W. MacGillivray, Glastullich, a nephew of the donor, presents the MacGillivray League Cup to Derek Fraser, Kilmallie captain

(above left): MacTavish Cup and MacGillivray League Cup winners, 1959. This squad laid the foundation for the club's Camanachd Cup victory in 1964

(left): One P.T teacher who made his mark was David Cargill of Lochaber High School, (second from left) who was instrumental in preparing the Kilmallie team of the late fifties for their finest hour, the MacGillivray League Final of 1959

Kingussie's Camanachd Cup winning team of 1961. Two members of the team, Iain Ross (front left, kneeling) and Donnie Grant (standing, immediately behind the cup) were to take the initiative and revitalise the club with modern training and coaching methods which led to unprecedented success in the eighties and nineties.

period, for example, that most of their MacAulay Cup triumphs have been secured. That is not to say that they were strangers to success up to that point, but the foundations for their modern success may well have been lain in the Camanachd Cup victory of 1961.

In the forty years before that, the Camanachd Cup's only trips to Badenoch had been to Newtonmore, but in 1961 the famine finally came to an end with a 2-1 victory over Oban Celtic at Fort William.

It is worth noting that at this point the Association's financial position was said to be improving and the Secretary reported in 1961 that the balance was £114.18.5 The Association now has an annual turnover in excess of £50,000.

The Association still held on to its traditional structure and any suggestions of an overhaul of the way the game was being run were, at best, tentative.

A new trophy joined the Association's list of competitions in 1963, the Grampian Cup. Now played for between the North and South at under-21 level, the first competition was held in Oban on May 18, 1963 involving four teams representing the Camanachd competition districts — one from the MacAulay Association, one from the Southern League and two from the North of Scotland Shinty Association.

In the same year, it was agreed that the Camanachd Cup Final be played in successive years at Inverness, Glasgow, Lochaber and Oban and the Spring-Autumn meetings of the Association were changed in line with this.

With regard to another attempt to resurrect the links with Ireland in 1964, it was noted that as the match was due to be played on Sunday, "in the circumstances it was decided not to attend". Mr L. Grout of Oban succeeded Mr D.W. Campbell as Association secretary.

In 1966 the Association suffered another great loss with the death of Captain Duncan MacRae of Balliemore. A new President was also elected that year, Hume D. Robertson.

Secretary Leslie Grout reported at the AGM of 1966 that attendances at matches were continuing to fall. He wasn't the first Secretary to warn that "continuation of this state of affairs is not a bright future for our ancient game and a remedy must be found before it is too late", nor will he likely be the last.

A new item appeared on the Association balance sheet that year — Association ties, specially commissioned for winners of the Camanachd Cup. It was reported that Kingussie, the first winners of the trophy in 1896, were "again first in the field for those ties".

The AGM also considered a proposal for the introduction of substitutes for an injured goalkeeper and one injured outfield player during the first half only. The Rule was accepted, but subject to review at the following AGM.

A new date for the start of the playing season was also set — September 15, of each year. That date has more or less re-

(above): The Caol Cup Medal, presented to Willie Batchen

(right): Caberfeidh, winners of the 1963 MacGillivray Cup, defeating Kingussie 2-0 in the Final at Bught Park, Inverness

mained the same since, with play now starting on the first Saturday of the same month.

As part of the Association's deliberations on its own well-being, the 1968 AGM invited representatives of the "Other Shinty Associations" to the meeting, with a view to discussing their proposed affiliation to the Association.

A delegation from the "others" met with the Executive and after discussion, it was recommended to the AGM that all Shinty Associations should affiliate to the Camanachd Association.

It was further agreed that the Associations concerned be informed of the following decisions:

1 All Shinty Associations to affiliate to the Camanachd Association.
2 That the Annual Affiliation Fee be £1.1s.
3 That each Association shall have two representatives at AGMs' and one representative at Council meetings.
4 The Camanachd Association reserved the right to examine the Bye-Laws and rules of competitions of the individual Associations.

It may have been something of a cosmetic exercise, but the drawing together of all the bodies administering the game was an

Arguably the most famous people to have attended a shinty Cup Final arrived at Strachur in 1964 and were spectators at the Sutherland Cup Final between Boleskine and Kyles. The Russian Foreign Secretary Gromyko, Prime Minister Kosygin and Kruschev's son, editor of the newspaper Pravda *at the time, were house guests of Sir Fitzroy MacLean, MP for North Argyll and Bute, on whose field the match was being played.*
The visiting party (left to right) Mr Julian Amery (in cape), Kosygin, Sir Fitzroy MacLean. Kruschev's son and bodyguard enjoyed themselves immensely, although the weather was somewhat inhospitable. Camans were taken back to Russia, where the game is understood not to have caught on!

(above): In 1966, following the sad loss of Captain Duncan MacRae as President, the Camanachd Association appointed Hume D. Robertson, (1966-69)

(above right): The Murchison Cup, donated by Dr John Murchison (President, 1969-70) has always been one of the most prized trophies at schoolboy level. One of the most famous victories in the competition was that of the Inverness Royal Academy side of 1965, coached by John Willie Campbell, himself later to be President of the Association (1982-85)

important step, although it was soon to become clear that old habits died very hard, and there were occasions when the self-interest of individual Associations still held sway when decisions were to be made at full Association level.

Some minor adjustments were also made to the organisation of the Camanachd Cup in 1969, with play being in two districts, North and South, with the proviso that in the South, two Argyll-shire teams would be included in the first round draw with the Southern League Clubs.

The game's finances remained in a precarious state and falling attendances began to take their toll. The Secretary reported in May, 1968 that there had been a decrease of £13.13s.2d, the first since 1963. He reported that this was largely due to the Cup Final share being down by £85.15s.3d which was a normal expectation given that the Final had been held in Glasgow. He appealed to the Association to consider the position before the 1971 Final, also due in the city.

The subject of city Finals has for some time vexed members of the Association

One of the names which disappeared off the Camanachd Association's list of clubs — Glasgow Kelvin, photographed here at Garscadden, Glasgow, February, 1969
Back Row (Left to right): Finlay MacRae, John A. MacGregor, John MacLeod, John Campbell, Dr J.D. Murchison (President of the Camanachd Association), Donald Buchanan, Andrew Dunn
Front (Left to Right): Archie Fraser, Murdo MacKenzie, Alistair Clark, Allan Hoey, Gregor Denoon, Allan MacPherson

but they are still held there, with the 1992 match, held in blazing sunshine at Old Anniesland, being a triumph of organisation for the local committee, and an historic occasion for the Fort William club who won their first Camanachd Cup.

The late sixties were a sad period for the Association in many ways, given the apparent low morale and despondency about the state of the game. There also appeared to be a disproportionately large number of stalwarts lost to the game whilst contributing a great deal. The Secretary, Leslie

Grout of Oban, passed away whilst still in office in November, 1969, having been Secretary for seven years from 1962. He had been a Vice-President of the Association since season 1956-57.

Less than a year later, in March 1970, Association members were mourning the loss of the President, Dr J.D. Murchison. Tribute was paid to his work for the Association and also his contribution as a player and referee. It was agreed that the silver-mounted caman due to Dr Murchison (all former Presidents receive one), be ordered for presentation to Mrs Murchison.

The 1970 AGM of the Association, held at Kingussie, the game's historical home, was one of the best attended for some time, with a voting strength of fifty-nine. The meeting made one significant Rule change, altering the hit-in Rule thus: "If the player taking the hit misses the ball entirely, he is at liberty to re-take his stroke".

A letter from Mid Argyll was fully discussed by the AGM and referred back to the Executive for their consideration and it re-surfaced on the Agenda of the Executive meeting of June 26, 1970 as "Commission for Shinty". After a lengthy discussion, it was agreed that a deputation comprising Walter Cameron, Willie Batchen, Donald Skinner and John Campbell approach the Scottish Council for Physical Recreation (SCPR) for guidance.

The deputation duly met with the SCPR and the up-shot was that at the next Executive meeting it was agreed to apply for a grant to the Scottish Education Department "with a view to improve our administrative structure, and also forward a letter to the Sports Council for their views on a Commission for Shinty."

The meeting also heard from Walter Cameron that he had been approached for a match between Ireland and the Camanachd Association and would contact the Secretary when he received further information.

"The meeting agreed that we consider this match closely, but that the question of a Sunday match was off".

Then in September of the same year, the Association heard of the death of Mr W. MacBean, President between 1931 and 1934. In 1971 the Chief Mr Ian MacLeod also died.

As well as being the end of the decade, this period, in fact marked the end of an era with the loss of so many great figures associated with the game.

The Executive continued to discuss the proposed Commission for some time, and

The origin of this badge, now used as a kilt buckle, is not known. It came into the possession of Donnie Grant, Kingussie, when he was around twelve years of age, receiving it from Donald MacKintosh, Leault, near Kincraig

advice was sought from Mr Robb of the SCPR.

An interesting aside from the Minutes of the Secretary's report of May, 1971 reports that "even during the postal strike our "bush" communications were of the highest order".

A new Award was made for play at the highest level, the Albert Smith Memorial Medal, presented to the Association by Victor Smith of Fort William. The medal, to be awarded to the Man of the Match in the Camanachd Cup Final, was presented in memory of Victor's father Albert. A sum

of money was donated to invest to buy the individual medal for the player selected. The Albert Smith Medal has been won by some of the most famous names in shinty:

1972 John Cambell, Newtonmore
1973 Kenny MacNiven, Glasgow Mid Argyll
1974 Tommy Nicolson, Kyles
1975 Duncan MacNeil, Kyles
1976 Neil Blair, Kyles
1977 John MacKenzie, Newtonmore
1978 Hugh Chisholm, Newtonmore
1979 David Cheyne, Newtonmore
1980 George Nicolson, Kyles
1981 Ricky Ross, Newtonmore

Significant improvements were made in terms of coaching for younger players as the '70's progressed and Kingussie's Donnie Grant, (left) eventually to be the Camanachd Association's Coaching Convener, assisted by John Willie Campbell did sterling work in the Inverness area.

The Albert Smith Medal has been won by some of the most famous names in shinty —

(above right): Born in 1888, Albert Smith was born and brought up in Lochuanagan near Fort Augustus and shortly after the First World War he moved to Fort William where he worked as a joiner. In 1929, he married a local girl, Annie Carmichael.

(above left): Victor Smith (standing left) was their only son

(right): His son, also Victor, taking an interest from an early age, has represented Fort William in two Camanachd Cup Finals and is an Under-21 internationalist

1982 John Fraser, Newtonmore
1983 Ewen Paterson, Strachur
1984 John Russell, Newtonmore
1985 Norman MacArthur, Newtonmore
1986 Dougie MacIntyre, Oban Camanachd
1987 David Anderson, Kingussie
1988 Ali MacKintosh, Glenurquhart
1989 Hugh Chisholm, Newtonmore
1990 Willie MacRae, Skye Camanachd
1991 Rory Fraser, Kingussie
1992 Willie MacDonald, Fort William

Gradually, the initiatives with the SPRC and the SED began to pay off and in October 1971, the Association received a grant of £500 towards "administration, coaching, travelling, insurance — to be used in Scotland only".

It was also agreed at this point to print 4,000 copies of the 'Game of Shinty' booklet, which would include the Rules of Play and a diagram of the field of play.

This meeting of the Executive, incidentally, which had also considered the introduction of the 'Cooler' system as an experiment to deal with indiscipline, closed with the rejoinder from the Secretary that at 1am (it had started at 7pm), the meeting "must have been the longest in the history of the Camanachd Association!"

It was agreed to shelve the 'Cooler' system at the next meeting of the Executive, due to opposition from the North. It was also agreed at the same meeting that it was now hoped to hold an international match with Ireland at the Bught Park, Inverness on August 5, 1972. An Comunn Gàidhealach also offered the Association a position on their Executive and John Willie Campbell the only Gaelic speaker on the Association's ruling body, was appointed.

1971 also marked the publication of the first ever Shinty Yearbook. Produced independently of the Camanachd Association on a voluntary basis by a hard-working committee, the Yearbook has since gone from strength to strength, building on the work done by a number of visionaries who came together in November, 1970.

The first Shinty Yearbook. The Yearbook has gone on to develop into one of the best publications of its kind and is the envy of many other sporting organisations

"The need was recognised for a medium in which the great fund of shinty lore and contemporary statistics on the game could be recorded and in which ideas on the future planning of our ancient game could be aired."

Peter English, Editor, 1971

Planning for the 1972 International — "the great event"— continued apace. No assistance was received from the Highlands and Islands Development Board, but Inverness District Council hosted a civic reception for both teams and officials after the game.

Willie Batchen (after some debate about his selection) was appointed to officiate at the match and the Scottish team took the field under the supervision of Jock Paul MacIntosh and Ian Cameron.

At the end of the day, officials of both ruling bodies, the Camanachd Association and the Gaelic Athletic Association expressed themselves well pleased with this first attempt at the hybrid game at such a level. Pat Fanning, the Irish President and a great friend of shinty, expressed the wish that the games continue and that the special friendship engendered in Inverness would be built on in years to come. Thanks to a great deal of effort by a relatively small number of people on both sides of the Irish Sea, that friendship has, indeed, developed and it is significant perhaps that the Association's Centenary Year celebrations should see the resumption of full-scale internationals, which had lapsed for a few years, and had been

SHINTY-HURLING INTERNATIONAL

SCOTLAND
v.
IRELAND

Bught Park, Inverness

Saturday, 5th August

Throw-up 7 p.m.

Admission 30p   Stand 20p extra

In attendance the Pipes and Drums of the
7th GURKHA RIFLES
by kind permission of the Commanding Officer
Lieutenant Colonel I. M. ELLIOT

*(above): The medal received by players at the international match, Scotland v Ireland, 1972.
Result:
Scotland 4 goals 5 points;
Ireland 6 goals 4 points.
The game looked to be all over in favour of the Irish in the early stages with their aerial hitting and superior fitness. But the Scots were to emerge eventually with great credit and in goalkeeper Hugh Chisholm of Newtonmore had arguably the best player on the field*

(right): The 1973 medal presented to players in the shinty/hurling international

most successfully replaced by a series of matches played at Under-21 level.

There is little doubt, however, that without the considerable efforts of people such as Jack Richmond, Douglas MacKintosh, Donnie Grant and Ken Thompson that the international series might well have died the death.

Scotland's best result in the full internationals was in 1976 when they held the Irish to a 5-5 draw at Glasgow in a stirring contest and it was left to the under-21's to make the historic breakthrough, end-

It was the wettest Cup Final ever, and it was an historic occasion with Glasgow Mid Argyll defeating Kingussie at Claggan Park, Fort William for their first ever championship in 1973

ing a 60-year wait for victory over the Irish, with a win at Inverness in 1990.

All of a sudden, developments took place which were to significantly increase shinty's profile. Apart from the international which attracted a great deal of media attention, a 16-team indoor tournament was planned for the Bell Sports centre in Perth. The tournament and its eventual successor, the Highland Queen/Glenmorangie Sixes at Aviemore, added a new dimension to the game, which also attracted significant media interest. Indeed the Aviemore event has gone on to become the largest social gathering of shinty followers after the Camanachd Cup Final, and is a very highly regarded event run very efficiently by a small committee of enthusiasts, independently of the Camanachd Association.

A shinty team was also formed in Cumbernauld with Glasgow Mid Argyll providing the first opposition.

There were also significant advances in terms of coaching although it was to be nearly ten years before a fully-fledged coaching committee was to take formal responsibility for development.

There was, however, a groundswell of opinion forming that matters had to be taken in hand and that the future of the game should be constructively discussed. The May Executive meeting in 1973 had before it a letter from Gabriel Fraser and Jack Richmond of Newtonmore regarding a "talk-in" they proposed to hold on the game. Their initiative, which was warmly welcomed and received the backing of

(above): Tom MacKenzie, Inverness, President of the Camanachd Association 1973-76

(below): Douglas Mackintosh, President 1985-90

the committee, was eventually to lead to the historic Shinty Forum in Newtonmore a year later.

The shinty community was, as Roger Hutchinson describes it, now "grappling with its identity and role in the modern sporting world". The Forum eventually attracted 60 delegates from 19 clubs and they were, understandably perhaps, divided on the state of the game. Sandy Russell of Newtonmore was to argue that it was "in a healthier state than ever it was", and Iain Cameron of Glasgow (of whom much more later) was to insist: "We play as ineffectually, and accepting a low standard, as we do in organising the game". The blame for that he laid squarely at the door of the Camanachd Association.

George Fraser of Newtonmore and Nigel Evans of Oban Camanachd race for the ball in the 1981 Camanachd Cup Final at Glasgow

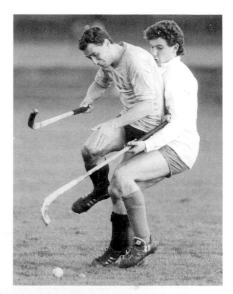

(right): close encounters

(below): timely intervention — Skye's John MacKenzie (left) attempts to clear in the Camanachd semi-final against Kyles at Spean Bridge

200

The Camanachd Association

courtesy Guinness Book of Records

'74

SHINTY FORUM and **EXHIBITION**

in the Balavil Arms Hotel Newtonmore 26-28 April 1974

EXHIBITION open to the Public
Friday,   26th April - 3 p.m. to 10 p.m.
Saturday, 27th April - 10 a.m. to 10 p.m.
Admission Charge 20p

BECAUSE OF SPACE — Attendance at the Forum will be limited

Particulars may be obtained from the Secretary :

Jack Richmond, Badenoch Hotel, Newtonmore.   'phone 246

THE SHINTY FORUM AND THEREAFTER

MAKING A SHINDY ABOUT SHINTY

1973: Memorandum to the Camanachd Association

Re: Conference "Talk-In" on Shinty

We, Jack Richmond and Gabriel Fraser, have, for some time, talked over the possibility of a chance being given for an in-depth discussion among people who really care about the present and future health of shinty. We have asked the Newtonmore Camanachd Club if they would be willing to act as hosts for this and if they would put our proposal to your executive committee to enlist your sponsorship.

We know that, since the game was first put on an organised basis, succeeding enthusiasts have given their time selflessly to the administration of the sport and this is as true today, as with yourselves, as it ever was. Nonetheless, the competing pressures of modern life are such that shinty is, we think, at a crisis point and some opportunity, such as we suggest, for as wide as possible views on what can be done to help the game to survive and prosper is necessary.

We would like an invitation given to all who care about shinty to attend the conference and a special effort made to see that those particular individuals, known to have influential views, were there. We think representatives from the Sports Council, The Gaelic Athletic Association of Ireland, An Comunn, the Highlands and Islands Development Board, county councils, the press and broadcasting authorities should be in-

The 1974 Forum was the brainchild of Jack Richmond (right) and Gabriel Fraser of Newtonmore

vited. We had in mind that a small exhibition be staged about shinty with photographs, interesting press cuttings, trophies and equipment, including sticks and balls of different manufacturers, and that films and colour transparencies be shown.

We would envisage the discussion ranging over the organisation of the game and whether one totally embracing administrative body would be in its best interest, the arrangement of leagues and cup draws, training of referees, coaching, encouragement of young players, revision of rules, the composite shinty/hurling ones, improvement of pitches and review of the venues for finals, design and manufacture of equipment, contact with the Sports Council and other fund-providing bodies, publicity through the press and other media.

If you were agreeable to the idea, a suitable location for housing the get-together we know could be found in Newtonmore but a date and duration would have to be fixed on and some financial provision made for the modest cost involved. For this purpose a justified approach might be made to the Highlands and Islands Development Board and the Sports Council for Scotland.

With that impassioned plea, Jack Richmond and Gabriel Fraser of Newtonmore crystalised the views of many within the game and articulated a growing sense of frustration amongst those connected with the game about its apparent decline.

The memorandum was well received by the executive council of the Association meeting which met in Fort William on May 11, 1973. The eventual outcome was the Shinty Forum which was held in the Balavil Hotel, Newtonmore on the first weekend of March, the following year.

The concern about the state of the game expressed in the original memorandum may have been understood by those who appreciated the game's frailties and apparent lack of progress, but the ensuing media reaction could hardly have been predicted.

"Players of a game reputed to be one of the fastest and most ferocious team sports in Europe are appealing to Scottish MP's, education authorities and tourist board officials to ensure that the clash of the shinty stick remains one of the distinctive sounds of the Highlands,"

Gillian Linscott in *The Guardian*.

Headline writers had a field day. *"Danger of shinty extinction"* one screamed; *"Support shinty or it's dead"* threatened the *Daily Express*, whilst *"Making a shindy about shinty"*.

Martin MacDonald's slightly more perceptive and balanced view of the situation was that the Forum was designed to give shinty 'the highly skilled sport of Gaels that Lowlanders love to regard as legalised mayhem' a sporting chance. The game was, quite simply, he said, in a financial strait-jacket which threatened to strangle it completely. The dramatic impact of social change was leading to the death of the game.

Even *The Times' Diary* got in on the act, blaming the crisis in the game on "the competing pressures of modern life."

Opening of the Forum — The Forum was opened by Rev John Sellar of Culbokie, a native of Newtonmore, and a member of 1907 Camanachd Cup winning team from the village. Interestingly, perhaps, the only women at the Forum in their capacity as club officials were Gillian Clark of Kingussie (their treasurer) and secretary and Mrs Julia MacAdie of Newtonmore (also their secretary)

And so it was that the great and the good connected with the game, and some who were not, assembled in the game's heartland to discuss the future. Armed with the formidable list of challenges outlined in their original memorandum, Messrs Richmond and Fraser had drawn together, for the first time since the previous luke-warm attempt at reorganising the game in the late thirties, an assembled company who, given the situation and the dire warning expressed through the media, were expected to overhaul the game and its structure.

The programme of discussion for the Forum, which lasted over two days, tackled almost every topic imaginable from shinty and the law to its place in the surgery; the game's administration and its connections with Ireland; shinty's potential as a tourist attraction; its place in schools and the need for coaching. That and much more besides.

The referee's badge

The Forum's aim was to arrive at constructive conclusions about its continued well-being. Clearly, however, if that was to be achieved, it was to be no mean feat. Martin MacDonald's summary of the task in hand neatly summed up nagging concern which persists amongst those, even now some twenty years later, still trying to alter the way the game is played and administered:

"Shinty is as much a tradition as a sport, and it tends to be shackled by its past. A number of those present at Newtonmore forum can recall playing in competitions as far back as the turn of the century. Their loyalty to the game is absolute and undying, but the ethos created does not encourage revolutionary change."

Those assembled by the organisers, amongst whom were some of the foremost individuals involved in the game at the time — and some of its most innovative thinkers — came representing the myriad of disparate entities involved in the administration of shinty at the time. To have achieved the laudable aims of the Forum — the 'constructive conclusions towards its continued well-being' would have been nothing short of miraculous. But the Forum was the best chance of delivering a radical re-structuring of the game since a tentative bid failed in the late thirties.

The deliberations and conclusions of the Forum were, however, to be bound by its 'advisory' nature, as the chairman, Camanachd Association Chief, Walter Cameron pointed out.

Action from one of the many epic clashes between Kyles and Newtonmore. Camanachd Cup Final, Inverness, May, 1976

There is little doubt but that the addresses delivered and discussions which followed were authoritative, constructive and of the highest order. They included several highlights, notably a spirited plea for more thought to be given to the place of youth in shinty by James Finlayson, formerly of Newtonmore and Kingussie High School.

Opinions regarding the success of the Forum are divided. There is no doubt that it altered the course of thinking on the game. Its conclusions, representing one of the most searching analysis ever of the game's ills did not, however, carry the weight of the constitution and were left hanging hopefully.

It may be too early yet to properly assess the historical significance of the Forum, but from its deliberations clearly arose, eventually, a more stream-lined organisation for the game, the Referees' As-

Dave "Tarzan" Ritchie holds the Glenmorangie Camanachd Cup aloft after Newtonmore's victory in Glasgow. The sponsors' product awaits and company representatives Peter Cullen and David MacDonald look on

sociation and a more clearly defined agenda for the debate on the future of the sport.

Constructive criticism was delivered by Iain Russell of the Sports Council whose connection with the game has been invaluable in a formal and informal capacity for the next twenty five years; and the "Young Turks" made their mark. Shinty was to hear much more from the likes of Donald Skinner, Iain Cameron and their peers in the years to come as they tackled the regionalisation which led to poor communication against a background of lack of finance. North and South teams hardly met and standards were plummeting.

At the end of the day, or more accurately two days' deliberation, the question was asked openly more than once: "Was this just another talking shop, or this time will we do some good for the game?" (Jim Innes, *West Highland Free Press*, May 3, 1974).

As Innes himself remarked, shinty's administrators of the day were more noted for their realism than their romanticism. As Donald Skinner and Iain Cameron pointed out at the Forum, there was no such thing as "they" to be blamed. All the "theys" were in the Balavil Hotel, and there was agreement that the buck had stopped. When the response to calls for more power to delegates was that changes would be "unconstitutional", Iain Russell's telling rejoinder was that "perhaps the constitution needs changing".

Jim Innes' assessment of the Forum went as follows: "Whether it will be an important event in the history of shinty, or whether it will be quietly forgotten remains to be seen. If it is forgotten, then the delegates can only blame themselves. Two men who cannot be blamed are Jack Richmond and Gabriel Fraser of Newtonmore, the men who set up the first ever Forum. In handling such a massive job they have already done more than their share — now it's up to the rest of us.''

Perusal of a summary of the Forum's findings makes very interesting reading. Amongst the ideas ''harvested'' at the Forum were:

The value of preserving records ('The rock from which we are hewn').
The need for a long, cool look at the game's administration.
The possibility of a full-time Executive officer.
The desirability of improving local pitches and the venues and arrangements for big games.
The benefit which coaching can have at all levels of play and the influence this can exert on public interest.

The requirement of more sustained competition throughout the season in schools' shinty.
The importance of supporting the authority of referees and encouraging their recruitment.
The urgency of obtaining a more rational situation in the supply of sticks and balls.
The necessity of finding people, both inside and outside shinty, to take part in the basic running of individual clubs
The reorganisation of the season and competitions to ensure the best player and spectator enthusiasm.
The prospect of a joint approach with other amateur sports towards tax relief.
The exploration of sponsorship and tourist interest with a full realisation of the dangers involved.
The great concern to enlist the interest of the Press and broadcasting media.

And so the Executive of the Association agreed to take on board many of these recommendations and a number of sub-committees were appointed in September of the same year to endeavour to bring about the brave new world — Coaching

In all, Newtonmore have won the Blue Riband of shinty a remarkable twenty-eight times. Their record is second to none although they have, perhaps significantly, not won the Sutherland Cup, the junior championship, since 1959

Kyles and Newtonmore— Kyles and Newtonmore (above) dominated the seventies. Kyles were victorious in 1976 at Inverness, but Newtonmore then gained revenge at Glasgow, Fort William and Oban in successive years

and Development; Administration and Constitution; Structure and Rules; Facilities and Equipment; Communication and Publicity.

In October, at a meeting of a referees' conference held in the Masonic Hall, Fort William, on the motion of Jack Asher, Glasgow, seconded by Douglas MacKintosh, Newtonmore, the Referees' Association was born. Another part of the slowly developing new world fell into place.

The Forum may have achieved a great deal, but it was not long before disquiet with the pace of change surfaced. "I think it would be fair to say that shinty has survived in spite of its past administrators, not because of them," said Iain Cameron, who was by now the coach to the Scottish international team, a year later (*North* 7, November/December 1978).

Much more was to be heard of Iain Cameron and the changing face of the

*Kyles Athletic in
the seventies*

game in subsequent years, but administrative wrangling was accompanied by rationalisation and some extraordinary events on the field of play. The plethora of autonomous league and cup competitions were eventually combined under the auspices of North and South Associations and shinty flourished in hitherto unknown areas — Livingston, Cumbernauld, Grangemouth and Perth.

And the links with Ireland were eventually re-established, some fifty years after Kaid MacLean's exploits in Dublin were dismissed out of hand.

The seventies will, however, be remembered more as the decade of domination by two clubs in particular, Newtonmore and Kyles Athletic, arguably the two greatest names in shinty. Newtonmore's domination of the decade was almost complete and their feats are unlikely to be repeated. They contested nine Camanachd Cup Finals between the years 1970 and 1980 (inclusive), winning seven of them, and losing two.

Their losses came to Kyles who won a total of three finals in the same period, while contesting nine.

Newtonmore also, remarkably, won the MacTavish Cup, the north senior championship every year from 1970 to 1980 inclusive and took the first five MacGillivray League championships from season 1974-75.

Had Newtonmore's domination not been so complete, the odds are that Kyles themselves would have won everything. They shared the league championship in the south in the inaugural season of 1974-75 (with Glasgow Mid Argyll) and then went on to win it every year until Oban Camanachd broke the sequence in 1988-89.

It was only in 1983 when the Camanachd Cup shook off the shackles of the great north/south divide, that the domination of shinty's Old Firm began to be threatened. But by then, the game had experienced another agonising burst of self-examination which threatened to undo most, if not all the good and collective will which had been engendered at the Forum.

The five sub-committees initiated to stream-line the organisation (which carried some twenty Vice-Presidents) of the game after 1974 had proceeded to tackle the matters in hand, but clearly some were operating better than others. Some, quite obviously, were receiving more backing than others from clubs. And it was his particular dis-satisfaction with the progress being made on the coaching front which led Iain Cameron of Glasgow to resign his post as chairman of the coaching committee and as a member of the Executive of the Association.

He was not alone in expressing the view that there was a lack of progress following the Forum. As Willie Batchen stated in his sixth Report to the Association (April 16, 1975) "I wonder are we not too often inclined to put trivialities before our game".

Iain Cameron's dis-satisfaction centred not on trivialities but a lack of co-operation from clubs and led eventually to his prognosis in 1979 that a 'terrible parochialism' was stifling the game.

"Shinty, which has been played now in an organised form for over one hundred years, has failed to respond to the challenge it faces with the introduction of other popular sports into areas which, until recently, knew only the traditional Highland game. With very few exceptions, areas from which shinty drew its former strength are now continually losing young players to football, rugby, golf and other sports which can offer them much greater opportunities for competitive play."

(Iain Cameron, *North* 7, No 36, November/December, 1979)

The six separate autonomous bodies still involved in the running of shinty were directly to blame for the exodus from shinty, and the failure to work together towards a common objective was endangering the whole future of shinty.

And it was this parochialism, evidenced by a lack of concern at falling standards and resistance to change, which prompted Mr Cameron to take a public swing at his fellow administrators who had just five years earlier prophesied their desire to move things along at a quicker pace.

"The next few years are critical to shinty. In that time, those of us who are involved in the administration of the game must decide if we are promoting a modern sport or preserving an aspect of Highland culture. If we decide we are engaged in the latter, then shinty will follow the same course of decline as the language and traditional industries of the Highlands. If, on the other hand, we are sufficiently ambitious to demonstrate to the rest of the country that the sport of the Gael is a skilful and exciting spectacle which can be enjoyed by all lovers of sport, then the future is assured."

Iain Cameron's resignation came at a time when a new Chief and President were to be chosen. He himself was one of the Association's army of twenty Vice-Presidents. Meanwhile there was continued angst about suggestions that a new premier league should be established to bring the cream of the north and south together on a regular basis.

There is little doubt but that Iain Cameron's views attracted considerable support both inside and outside the higher echelons of the Association. The columns of the press paid glowing testimony to his contribution as one of the game's foremost thinkers. The Association's loss was Mid Argyll's gain, but as several people pointed out in letters to the press, the Association could ill afford to lose a man of his calibre.

Shinty, however, as a sport drawing so heavily on the cameraderie, enthusiasm

Willie Batchen of Foyers, one of the game's greatest referees, Secretary/treasurer of the Association for twelve years and latterly the Association's Referees' Development Officer

and labours of love of its supporters, was not prepared to move at the same pace, or in the same direction.

Much of the responsibility for nudging the game in the right direction, at the pace it was prepared to accept, fell then to John Willie Campbell who replaced Donald Skinner as President, (he being elevated to the position of Chief).

By now shinty was benefiting to the tune of £2,000 per annum from the munificence of MacDonald and Muir through their sponsorship of schools' camans.

Iain Cameron had not, however, gone away and at the beginning of 1980 was to be found, in his capacity as a Director of the Celtic Society, convening a meeting to be held in Newtonmore on March 8, to

John Willie Campbell, President, Camanachd Association, 1982-85. Mr Campbell was also the BBC's Voice of Shinty on radio for over twenty years until his retirement three years ago

discuss "Preparing shinty for the 21st century".

Those involved in the administration of the game were clearly, as shinty accelerated towards the 21st century, grappling with the best interests of the game in their own individual ways. Never before had the game been subject to such close scrutiny. Media interest and exposure, by now part and parcel of the game and greater than ever, heightened the tension. As Iain Cameron moved towards the next century at a pace with which his colleagues found it difficult to cope, they had the earnest pleas of Secretary Willie Batchen ringing in their ears. Speaking at the 1979 AGM in Oban, he finished his report thus: "I must say that I feel somewhat perturbed at our standard of shinty at Senior Level. Can we all give that wee bit more to our Great Game and not be blinded so often by the colour of a jersey? Have we got our priorities right? Number One — Our Game. That is why we are here. Let us leave this meeting determined to give our great amateur game what it deserves — that means you and me."

Willie Batchen's exhortations were not that different from many delivered by a number of other Secretaries over the last hundred years and it is perhaps ironic that it was as a result of moves by the Celtic Society, with Iain Cameron at their head, the crisis regarding the game's future came to a head.

It was with the dangers in mind of facing the game in years to come that the

Two of the outstanding personalities connected with shinty in the post-war era were the legendary Jock Paul MacIntosh of Newtonmore and Celly Paterson of Kyles Athletic. Pictured here as Chieftains of two of the game's most famous clubs leading their teams on to the re-furbished Eilan, Newtonmore in 1979, Celly (front, right) and Jock Paul (left) were two of the best-known and highly respected individuals in the game.

Both were noted players of their day and Celly's reputation as a song writer went far and wide. He was also a referee and had been a professional footballer with Crystal Palace in London.

Their comradeship and competitive nature, with no quarter given or asked, summed up all that is best in shinty. They died within six months of each other in 1986.

"Now whenever shinty is played
We who are left can surely relate
We knew and admired a Shinty Great."
(Tom MacDonald)

Glenmorangie have been the game's main sponsors for over a decade. The relationship between the Association and the company began in 1977 and has embraced all forms of the sport, indoors and out, ever since

Society convened a meeting to discuss the topic 'Preparing shinty for the 21st century'. The North and South Associations were invited, the Camanachd Association itself, the MacAulay Association and the Schools' Camanachd Association.

The principal speakers were to be John Fraser of Newtonmore, amongst the finest players of his generation, who was to speak on 'The playing side of the game'; Iain Cameron who would speak on 'Organisation and Administration'; and Dr Peter English on 'Promotion of the Game'.

The North Association was the first of shinty's independent ruling bodies to accept the Celtic Society's invitation. They did so with an alacrity only matched by the ferocity of the opposition expressed about the proposed conference by the Camanachd Association itself.

Jack Richmond of Newtonmore, joint organiser of the 1974 Shinty Forum and Chairman of the Future of Shinty Committee

The Referees' Association had also accepted the invitation; the South of Scotland, MacAulay Association and Schools' Associations did not reply. Six years after the Shinty Forum and despite Willie Batchen's earnest pleas, the traditional divisions within the game had surfaced again and were in danger, arguably of bringing the game into disrepute.

Iain Cameron was branded a ''shinty rebel'' in the media, and the Association's opposition to the Newtonmore meeting (the Executive voted 7-5 to reject the invitation) killed it stone dead. The Association's reasoning was that the Celtic Society had gone about the arrangements in the wrong way and had failed to consult the ruling body.

Frustrated by the lack of progress being made, Iain Cameron's dreams of dragging the game into the next century were put on the back burner. There was, however, an increasing realisation that the unwieldy administrative structure of the game was inhibiting progress. Donald Skinner, caught in this embarrassing scenario wearing two hats as President of the Camanachd Association and Senior Vice-President of the Celtic Society, pointed the way forward, but with a caveat, bearing in mind that the North and South Associations were now considering becoming area committees of the Association: ''This is something that has to be done in stages, and not overnight''.

Iain MacInnes, President of the Celtic Society agreed. It would take at least twenty years, he said, and the Celtic

The legendary Dave 'Tarzan' Ritchie, one of the finest competitors of his day and one of the most sporting players ever to wield a caman. Joint record holder of the greatest number of Camanachd Cup winning medals (12) along with the great Hugh Chisholm, also of Newtonmore

Society bowed to pressure calling off their own meeting and promising to support a similar initiative "when the Camanachd Association chose to arrange it".

And eventually (but perhaps sooner than might have been the case had the Celtic Society not galvanised everyone into action) a further period of self-examination began. Its eventual conclusion was a two-day meeting at Taynuilt which arose from a proposal made by the North Association at their AGM in August 1980.

A small steering committee was set up by the Association and following preliminary meetings at St Catherine's and Aviemore, a committee of nineteen was chosen with Jack Richmond of Newtonmore as Chairman. Their deliberations were eventually to lead to the Future of Shinty Report.

The Committee's mandate was "to examine the game of shinty and to arrive at proposals for its continued well-being".

The Report's introduction sums up the seriousness with which the task in hand was undertaken:

"The discussion, for more than twenty hours, by the Committee is certainly the longest, sustained consideration there has ever been about shinty as an organised game. A particular attempt was made to relate the present to the past in terms of the history of the game back to the formation of the Camanachd Association in 1893 and the earlier efforts towards administration of standardised rules. There was keen awareness by all concerned that what they were doing could easily produce more harm than good.

They knew that the game, an important part of Gaelic society for many hundreds of years, has strong traditions and to tamper with these could offend. Nonetheless, the pressure for the enquiry had come from a mounting conviction that the sport of shinty must examine itself to see how it stands in the modern world for the sake of its own continuing existence. It was agreed that any changes suggested should, if possible, command wide acceptance from those involved in playing, administering and following the game. The final judgement in the proposals arrived at, however, was always made on the primary consideration that they would maintain shinty as one of the world's outstanding team sports."

Mr Peter Cullen of Glenmorangie (left, pictured here with president Douglas MacKintosh before the 1989 Camanachd Cup Final), along with his wife Sydena, have become well-known and highly respected figures in shinty circles. Mr Cullen is a Patron of the Association. Glenmorangie and the Camanachd Association share a common centenary in 1993

Eight sub-committees then set about producing the most radical suggestions to date on the future of the game — Finance, Fixtures, Youth, Coaching, Referees, Equipment, Development and Publicity.

And they eventually produced a formula which would, it was hoped, lead to the "more dynamic" and stream-lined administration which Iain Cameron and those of a like mind felt was required to ensure shinty's survival and development.

The twenty hours of deliberation eventually produced the following proposals:

* The unification of all the independent bodies under the collective umbrella of the Camanachd Association.
* A revised three-level administration of the Camanachd Association: Executive Committee, Council of Management, North and South Area Committees.
* The eventual aim of further District Committees.
* Six elected Executive members appointed by open ballot.
* Eighteen similarly elected Council of Management members.
* The establishment of sub-committees responsible for Finance, Fixtures, Youth, Coaching, Referees, Equipment, Development and Publicity.
* The date of the Annual General Meeting of the Association to be altered.
* A new National Disciplinary Committee.
* An increased financial contribution from Clubs.
* Revenue Grant benefit to be sought from the Scottish Sports Council.
* Aid to be obtained, where possible, from other public bodies.
* A greater income from the Camanachd Cup Final to be investigated.
* The present harmonious sponsorship arrangement to be sustained and augmented as appropriate.

* A finite playing season be imposed.
* A national league and completely revised playing structure be introduced.
* Emphasis be placed on an effective system of schools and youth fixtures.
* The introduction of inter-district representative games at all age levels.
* The desirability of continuing the shinty/hurling international matches, without detriment to the resources of the Association.
* An overall progressive coaching system be progressively pursued.
* The importance is recognised of a sufficient body of respected referees, with discipline in the game properly supported.
* An objective study is carried through into the provision of equipment.
* The rules of the game are constantly re-assessed.
* Effective publicity is given proper attention.

The proposals were accompanied in the Report by the following exhortation, when asking for approval for implementation by asking the AGM of the Association to call a Special General Meeting.

"Those who will be involved in the making of the decisions are asked to fully consider all the implications and desirably with the widest previous discussion at club level. The easiest course of action is, of course, to take no action at all but the Committee has every trust that the game at large, when it comes to a democratic resolve, will have thought collectively and resolutely about the best interests of the game."

Although some felt the Report had not gone far enough, its findings represented proposals for the most dramatic overhaul of the game ever. It was with that in mind that the debate started at 11 am on Saturday September 11, 1981 in the Milton Hotel, Fort William.

And it was a debate conducted in the presence of only thirteen of the Association's clubs out of almost fifty. Those present however agreed to the proposals to streamline the Association, unifying the disparate bodies under the umbrella of the Camanachd Association in the favoured three-tier level of administration. The national league was, however, given the thumbs down as was the hoary old chestnut of summer shinty. A finite playing season was, however, agreed, with play commencing on the first Saturday of September and concluding with the Camanachd Cup Final on the first Saturday of June.

As shinty gradually grappled with its changing circumstances in the seventies and eighties, there is little doubt but that sponsorship played a key role in developing the game.

Whilst it is perhaps widely understood to be a 'modern' phenomenon, shinty has clearly benefited from a considerable degree of transferred support (financial and otherwise) over the years.

The game's relationship with its various benefactors was succinctly explained by Jack Richmond in the 1989 Shinty Yearbook. As he outlined there, sponsorship in shinty is, in fact 'an old story' in shinty:

"In the distant past it (support) undoubtedly was the consequence of the clan chiefs which underpinned the great occasions. The annual 'Ball Play' at Cluny Castle on Old Christmas Day under the patronage of the Chiefs of Clan Macpherson, persisted on into this century as a special gathering of shinty followers in Badenoch. The two famous matches between Glenurquhart and Strathglass in the 1880's owed much to the commanding influence of Captain Chisholm of Glassburn. Bodies like the Club of True Highlanders mounted events as far distant as London. The gift of trophies was obviously of effect, especially endowed, as in the Littlejohn Vase and, again, the Balliemore Cup from Captain Duncan MacRae whose munificence at shinty celebrations is still a rosy glow in the minds of some of our veterans. At a closer level, the local proprietors and innkeepers gave, and indeed have continued to give, their support over many generations. The ultimate in shared costs was probably the 'sixpenny' days, like those at the Eilan of Banchor when everyone helped to pay for the barrel of beer and the bannocks and cheese which sustained the effort and excitement of the players and spectators."

This support in its many and varied forms was eventually superceded in shinty, as in other sports, by the gradual introduction of paid admission. That too, however, failed to sustain the modern shinty clubs faced with spiralling costs. The advent of financial contributions from commercial sources then became a feature of modern shinty and the game can safely be said to have been amongst the most adventurous and successful when it comes to securing sponsorship.

The catalyst for shinty's entry into one of the most long-standing and beneficial financial arrangement of any sport, the relationship between shinty and the Glenmorangie Company, was Donald Skinner,

Marine Harvest International Ltd, the world's largest salmon farming operation and a vital influence on many areas of the Highlands in employment terms, were soon hooked on shinty and became sponsors of the national leagues

S·H·I·N·T·Y
SILVER JUBILEE
2 ⊠ 5
GRAMPIAN
TELEVISION
PROGRAMME

THE DELL, KINGUSSIE
SATURDAY 20th JUNE 1987

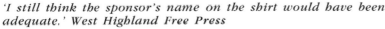

'I still think the sponsor's name on the shirt would have been adequate.' West Highland Free Press

the current Chief of the Association and a successful businessman in his own right.

He led negotiations with David MacDonald, the Chairman of MacDonald & Muir, in the name of Glenmorangie which resulted in 1977 in the first agreement relating to national cup competitions. The four figure sum received from the company then has now become an annual contribution of over £20,000 in cash, and much more besides in kind. Shinty owes a great debt to Glenmorangie, makers of the leading single malt whisky in Scotland, and also the visionaries who had the foresight to enter into the relationship.

Jack Richmond summed up the relationship thus: "It remains a classic model of good match-making in these matters", although it took some time before the company's name was to sit comfortably alongside the hitherto unattached name of the Camanachd Cup (the traditionalists fought a long and hard campaign to have the Championship Trophy's name remain intact).

The next major step the Camanachd Association took in terms of sponsorship was the arrangement reached with the Weatherseal double-glazing company. Their financial injection and the inception of the National League Cup Final were important cogs in the financial wheel which began to spin with a regularity and beneficial effect which made shinty the envy of many allegedly more powerful sports.

With the league and cup competitions on a sound financial basis, it was left to the Bank of Scotland to step in and fill the void left in cup terms. They have recently been sponsors of shinty's North and South Cup competitions, as well as being major benefactors of schools' shinty, with their sponsorship manager at the time Alan Gammie (a rugby man who saw the light!) now a Patron of the Association.

Other sponsors have also come and gone, but amongst the most faithful have been Grampian Television whose Cup has been played for in varying competitions since 1963.

Apart from commercial sponsorship, which has been the life-blood of many clubs at local levels, the main benefactors currently involved in the game are the Scottish Sports Council, through their funding of the Association's part-time paid official and many other grants to clubs, particularly in terms of ground improvements, one of the most major being the £50,000 capital grant which led to the building of a grandstand at An Aird, Fort William. Shinty has come a long way in a very short time and there is little doubt but that sposnorship changed the face of the game for ever.

The first note of the finances of the Association on 21 September 1894 is:

"The Secretary and Treasurer reported that the Income for the year amounted to £6 and the Expenditure to £2 leaving a balance at

There aren't many people who can recall, from first hand, the experience of playing shinty in Uist at the turn of the century. Murdo MacLennan was one and he was a guest of honour of the Camanachd Association at the 1992 Camanachd Cup Final in Glasgow. Murdo, (second from the right) originally from Carnan celebrated his 98th birthday the following day

credit of £4. The Secretary further reported that at the present time there were 15 clubs in the Association of which 12 had paid their subscription of 10 shillings. These were simpler times. Would we want to go back? Is our game better for all the bread on our water now? Who can say for sure? The one thing certain is that no sport can continue to exist in modern times without this commercial form of the old patronage.''

Shinty Yearbook, 1989

One hundred years later, shinty (or more accurately, the Camanachd Association,) is benefiting from commercial sponsor-

After the titanic clash of 1985 at the Dell, John Russell, Newtonmore's winning captain, presented the Trophy to Miss Christina Cattanach, one of the team's most fervent supporters. Born in the first year of the century, Miss Cattanach was a member of a celebrated local family and had five brothers who played for the club

ship to the tune of some £30,000 per annum. The real value of sponsorship is much more. The game has come a long way, but there is no room for complacency. The current economic climate does not augur well for sponsorship in general. Companies are constantly changing their fiscal policy and there are no guarantees as to the future. Sponsorship is rarely played on a level playing field and it is shinty's great fortune that they have had able negotiators such as Donald Skinner, Ken Thomson, Sandy Cameron

When Neil Reid (Kingussie) raised the Camanachd Cup aloft, he was mistaken for the then Secretary of State, Malcolm Rifkind. A letter to The Scotsman *newspaper pointed out the striking similarity*

and Jack Richmond to call on when developing the relationship with outside agencies. In a world of escalating costs shinty's future is no more secure than that of any other sport on which the most severe demands are made, particularly at local level.

The fragile basis on which the game is built would be in jeopardy were it not for the munificence of a few and the single-mindedness of others. There is no doubt, for example that shinty has often come close to having lost some of its most valued benefactors. There is no doubt too, that there was a significant and powerful body of opinion within the game, absolutely opposed to the introduction of outside funding, and particularly commercial sponsorship. That the situation has developed into one of mutual benefit to the Association and a small, but crucial number of companies, is due obviously to various factors, amongst which happenstance and accidents of history are but two, and perseverance and diligence are others.

As the tills kept ringing — and shinty appeared to be awash with money at this stage, to the detached observer, no less than £200,000 was spent upgrading three of the main venues for the Camanachd Cup Final: the Bught Park, Inverness, An Aird, Fort William and Mossfield Park, Oban — a rapidly changing infrastructure was accompanied by a dramatic swing in the balance of power on the field of play.

The epic clashes of the seventies between the formidable talents of Kyles Athletic and Newtonmore, who peaked at the same time with a barrow-load of the finest players of their generation, were to cease, largely due to the decision taken in 1983 to make the Camanachd Cup, at last, an open draw.

The traditional finals between north and south representatives were to be no more and the decision heralded a period of north domination of the Challenge Trophy, and it has to be said, virtually every other competition throughout the eighties and into the nineties. It is perhaps ironic that given the supremacy of north clubs in the years to follow, the first open draw Final was contested by two teams from the south, but it will come as no surprise that the destination of the trophy on that occasion was Tighnabruaich, home of Kyles.

The eighties will be remembered on the field of play as the Badenoch decade. If

(above & below): No stranger to celebrating, Kingussie's Kevin Thain was captain of the 1991 side and Marine Harvest National Player of the Year

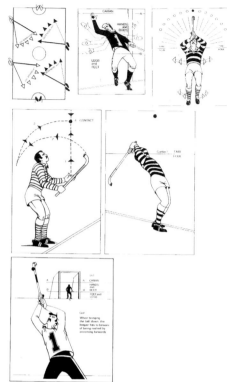

(above): The Schools' Camanachd Association has continued to contribute towards the well-being of the game and in the mid-eighties produced an up-dated version of the Rules of Play and a coaching manual. It was the first serious attempt to produce a tool which could be used by the uninitiated, which came to fruition, explaining the Rules as they stood at the time, and how various aspects of the game could be taught

(right): although not in the rule book, 'Tarzan' demonstrates one rather exotic tactic, Ian MacIntyre pleads innocence

Newtonmore had made the seventies their own, Kingussie were to nudge them from their pedestal and make their own significant claims to be the Kings of Shinty.

The open draw was, perhaps predictably, followed by the first-ever all-Badenoch Camanachd Cup Final. Oban was the venue for the titanic struggle, Kingussie the eventual home for the trophy, as it was for every other piece of silverware available to a brilliant squad.

The Boys of the Eilan, however, allowed the situation to pertain for but one year and in another classic final the following year, the first meeting of the big two at the Dell, they rubbed salt in Kingussie's wounds by removing the trophy from its temporary home, depositing it once again three miles down the road in the Balavil Hotel.

The Camanachd Cup Final — 1985

Remember the road to Damascus...
Shining brightly in biblical lore...?
Behold, now, the road to Kingussie —
Blazing brilliantly through Newtonmore!

Now, hark to that Sassenach tourist —
"What's that game, there, they play?!"
*   hear him yell...*
"It looks like their own he-man hockey —
These are not fairies down in the Dell...."

The Camanachd Cup Final threw up
As the scorching heat made the Dell boil...
Kingussie brought on so much Dallas,
That J.R. wants to drill there for oil!

John Fraser, who lost his golf title,
In remorse, scored with one of his
*   sloshes —*
He led Newtonmore's other scorers —
Ricky Ross and then two MacIntoshes!

Garry Dallas got one for Kingussie
As the tension and heat took a grip...
Ian MacIntosh needed a bottle...
And the referee took a wee sip...!

This wee Yorkshire terrier, Bonnie,
Spoke to me at half-time — right enough!
I asked his opinion of shinty —
From his stand seat, he answered,
*   "Rough! Rough!"*

Though Anderson scored for Kingussie,
Still their troubles were up to their necks..
When Newtonmore swung an old Tarzan,
Gosh! They brought on Neil Reid wearing
*   specs!*

But Neil couldn't see his team winning...

Newtonmore won the Camanachd Cup!
They taste now the sweet wine of triumph
That the sport's ancient glory brews up...

When yon archaeologists plundered
In the Tomb of the great Tutankhamen...
They found he knew shinty's rich
*   glories!—*
For the old boy was holding his caman!

Jimmy Black

Since that titanic collision, however, Kingussie have dominated the game with an awesome performance of athletic play,

In shinty's first 100 years as an organised sport, the great and the good have all been privileged to have been involved in the game. From Royalty to Russian politicians, leading sportsmen to the completely uninitiated. Even Miss World has got her hands on a caman. No less a personality than Cindy Breakspeare, Miss World 1976. Not to be outdone, shinty put up one of its own beauties when she made a visit to Scotland — the reigning Kyles Shinty Queen, Freda Smith (left)

Not content with dominating shinty at home, Skye Camanachd and Kingussie, who built up a very special relationship founded on some epic clashes at the beginning of the nineties, set off to Cape Breton in 1991, where they took the island by storm. A party of 69, ranging from a twelve week old girl to a 79-year old grandfather of astonishing stamina, helped to re-introduce the game to Canada's Maritime Region after an absence of 150 years. The players are pictured here taking part in the Grand March at the Antigonish Highland Games

based on the benchmark carved out at Oban in 1984. Newtonmore temporarily upset the best-laid plans of Donnie Grant and Ian Ross who had single-mindedly re-built the Kingussie club with tremendous assistance from hard-working committee members.

The club was eventually to feature in a remarkable series of matches and trophy aquisitions which will see this period go down in the history of the game as one of remarkable domination.

The senior squad were to string to-gether a remarkable series of sixty-three unbeaten matches in a barnstorming run which was eventually brought to a halt, perhaps predictably, by Kyles Athletic in the 1989 MacAulay Cup Final at Oban.

Taking our sport, language, music, and art from the Scottish Highlands to Nova Scotia (4-18 July 1991)

The Government Of
The Province Nova Scotia
Welcomes
The Visiting Shinty Teams
From Kingussie
And
The Isle Of Skye

The national league title was virtually Kingussie's to keep for the first ten years since its inception. The club featured in nine of the eleven finals up to, and including 1992. They won eight of them.

Their strength in depth has been confirmed by an astonishing period of success for the club's second string which has seen them go undefeated for a remarkable five years and one hundred matches. They have made the Scottish Junior Championship (and nearly every other trophy for which they were eligible) their own, winning the Sutherland Cup each year since 1989.

Few sports have ever seen such a period of domination, but like any other sports, success in shinty is nobody's to keep. There will always be the romantic and the unpredictable which makes this game the unique combination of culture and sport which it is — Glenurquhart's (almost) fairy-tale appearance in the Camanachd Cup Final of 1988, Skye Camanachd's astonishing charge to the championship in 1990, when they rolled along on a huge tide of support, the like of which the island has never seen.

These, then, are but some of the elements which prompt the likes of Roger Hutchinson, a shinty man by adoption rather than birth, to sum the game up thus: "Highland shinty players are capable of elevating their native game to a spectacle so fast, thrilling and skilful that the most dispassionate observer must be moved and entertained".

(above): Caley MacLean, captain of the first Skye team to become champions of Scotland. (below): They put the lights out on Skye and the island eventually celebrated as never before when the triumphant team returned home in the early hours of Sunday morning. A crowd of thousands greeted them, and the West Highland Free Press ran an extra 1,000 copies and a supplement to mark the event

"As long as the boys (and girls!) get shinty...."

"I have a vivid memory of Willie Dula running to the lines at the end of interval, barefoot, with the end of his big toe flapping up and down.

My father, George Ross, was headmaster then and my admiration for the way in which he encouraged shinty and clearly my pride in following Lochcarron's fortunes must have gone very deep.

One of my first thoughts when I got my own school at Uig was that I hoped I could start the boys playing shinty as soon as possible. It seemed a great pity that primary shinty on Skye was confined to Portree. Nobody in the rural areas was promoting it at all at that time, though good work had been done in the past.

I wanted to see camans behind my classroom door again, the way they had been when Peter Gordon and Duncan MacDougall had been in my Primary 5 class in Portree."

Morag Henriksen, Uig Primary School. Shinty Yearbook, 1991/92.

BP National Team Sport Festival, North Inch, Perth, May 1992
Shinty's first ever shinty co-ordinator Allan MacMillan (second from left)
organising young players from throughout Scotland.
Shinty has been one of the most successful sports included in the Team
Sport Scotland initiative which was launched by the Scottish Sports
Council in 1991

THE FUTURE

Pride of the Summer

I still hear the snares in the square
   Colours ablaze in the evening
   The air was still
   Down the stormy hill
   It's good to be young and daring.

I still see the blood on the knees
   The camans swing without warning
   The lads in white
   At the speed of light
   It's good to be young and daring.

Across the bay I still hear the strains
   The two-step loud and blare-ing
   We walked hand in hand
   To the accordion band
   It's good to be young and daring.

She was the pride of my summer that year
   She was my sweetheart, my lady
   We walked the black rock

And we stopped by the loch
   It's good to be young and daring.

Beat the drum
   Beat the drum
   Like a heartbeat
   Lonely and strong
   Beat the drum.

Words by Calum and Rory MacDonald.
By courtesy of Runrig,
The Cutter and the Clan

"Shinty has no divine right to an assured future. If all in the game, however, adopt a fiery cross approach, we will all go on having, and deserving, a sport second to none in the world."
(Donald Skinner, President, Camanachd Association, 1980.)

With these words of warning and exhortation, Donald Skinner crystalised and articulated the new pragmatic, but dynamic, approach being adopted by shinty's administrators as the game prepared itself for the challenges ahead.

As Chapter 5 detailed, the self-examination which a remarkable eighteen sessions of formalised debate had entailed, left shinty facing the second millennium and its own second century as an organised sport, with as many questions as had been answered.

That shinty and its related aspects of Highland culture have survived the ravages of two World Wars at all is remarkable; to have survived the further ravages of increasing economic depression where decisions taken in the United States by chiefs of multi-national oil companies have an increasing bearing on the for-

tunes of the game, is testimony to the resilience of the Gael and the total commitment of groups of individuals in some of the most rural areas of Scotland, and, one should not forget, the cities of the Central Belt and London.

Shinty's fortunes, and those of its guiding spirit the Camanachd Association, have fluctuated wildly in its first hundred years as an organised sport. The two World Wars have had a dramatic effect; from the dizzy heights of the formative years, through the Argyll-shire dominated 1920's; to the seemingly inevitable decline after the Inverness and Lovat-dominated fifties, through to the dramatic resurgence of a game in the last twenty five years where the dominance on the

(left): Camanachd Association Executive Council, Annual Conference, August, 1992

(below): With all the talking, when someone's false teeth flew out they carried on speaking by themselves

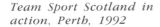

Team Sport Scotland in action, Perth, 1992

field has returned to what is arguably the game's heartland, Badenoch.

There is no doubt that shinty enters its second century as an organised sport firmly established as one of Scotland's national games. It is only twenty years or less, however, since the game faced the charge that it was being strangled by a 'terrible parochialism' which had seen the spirit of renaissance more or less extinguished.

In 1980 when Donald Skinner was, along with many more of kindred spirit, undergoing the game's most extended and intense period of navel-gazing, the Camanachd Association's financial resources totalled £700 in a current account and £1,000 on deposit. Twelve years and, thanks to the injection of major sponsors such as Glenmorangie, Marine Harvest and Bank of Scotland, many thousands of pounds of sponsors' cash later, the game has dragged itself (sometimes kicking and screaming) more or less into the next century. Some of the topics under discussion at the seminal

Forum of 1974 and thereafter are still contentious issues, but there is no doubt that a new spirit of professionalism has been nurtured, a new image of organisation and efficiency presented.

The game is now a small business in its own right with a turnover of £50,000 per annum and increasing. There is, though, a stark realisation that sponsors' largesse cannot and must not be taken for granted. There is, quite simply, no infinite pot of gold, particlarly in these dark economic times.

There have been, and always will be, glitches. It is apparently in the nature of the Gael that if these do not occur naturally, they will be created, perhaps subconsciously. But the game has always approached these fluctuating fortunes with a pragmatism which has seen it sur-

Will the greater use of safety equipment prove to be a passing fad, or will fundamental changes in attitudes take place as equipment developed for other sports is adapted for use in shinty? The game cannot be isolated from developments in other sports, but the debate about equipment is nothing new — witness the raging arguments detailed before the formation of the Association about the efficacy of knickerbockers as opposed to kilts!

"Shinty does not require blood and broken bones to prove its character. I am convinced that improving safety can only enhance the game, prevent the loss of players through injury and make it attractive to others who do not yet play it".

Dr Colin Fettes, Highland Sports Medicine Centre, Inverness. Shinty Yearbook, 1992-93.

vive, despite every debilitating influence imaginable.

Shinty as an organised sport has progressed significantly in the last twenty-five years in particular, but that progress has, arguably, not been achieved at the pace it could have been. Witness the accusations of 'terrible parochialism' levelled at the game just five years after the 1974 Forum.

There is now, however, a more active and possibly productive debate than ever before about the game's current standing and its future. Close ties have been developed with the Scottish Sports Council, the body charged with the supervision of sports development throughout the country. The establishment of shinty's first ever full-time shinty co-ordinator, under the Team Sport Scotland initiative, ensures that the game will be seen to be in

the vanguard of changes taking place across the spectrum of sport in Scotland.

There is only one place for shinty to be, according to Duncan Cameron, the Camanachd Association's Development Convenor.

"The new ideas developed in Barcelona '92 are unlikely to take place in Ballachulish or Boleskine in '93. However, through the network of governing bodies in sport and national sports promotion councils, we are likely to see their influence have greater and more immediate impact on shinty in the future. This is already evidenced in the increasing use of professionals trained in the latest techniques working with club volunteers in the field of coaching, introducing new ideas, many developed in other sports, and questioning traditional values. We have now recognised the need to open up the game to all young people who wish to participate, irrespective of the potential they

One of the most recent clubs to be formed, Lochbroom in Wester Ross, who played their first match in September, 1992, at Lochcarron. (Courtesy: West Highland Free Press)

show at an early age. Everybody has the potential to make some contribution to the game in whatever capacity — playing, coaching, training, field preparation or administration.''

There is also a greater degree of understanding of many of the influences which now, irreversibly, affect the nature of sport in general and shinty in particular. The increasing awareness of safety issues, amongst parents in particular, has led to the Schools' Association in particular taking the bull by the horns; the dramatic changes taking place in the educational system are also affecting sport and the part which schools played in the game; the very nature of local government is about to change again; the falling birthrate too, is presenting shinty clubs in many rural areas with difficulties their predecessors thought would never arise again.

Decisions taken by multi-national oil executives and the Admirals of foreign navies are affecting the game's future as surely as the large-scale migration in pursuit of work which blighted the Highlands in the early years of the century. The fortunes of teams such as Col Glen and Lochcarron, to name but two, were, and are, inextricably bound up with decisions over which they have absolutely no control.

The oil boom which brought prosperity and full employment to many areas in the seventies and eighties is no more, the American navy will do as it pleases, but shinty, given its apparently indomitable

Action from the 1989 Under-21 Shinty/Hurling Internationals

spirit, has survived, and will continue to do so, assuming Donald Skinner's exhortations are adhered to.

There may well be fewer shinty clubs in future, but it should be remembered that shinty clubs have always come and gone. The fascinating list of over two hundred clubs admirably researched by Hugh Barron, reproduced at the end of this book, is evidence of the way the game's fortunes have fluctuated. It is not the end of the world if a shinty club folds. What is important is that the consequences of that sad event are suitably dealt with, and that some form of re-generation takes place.

Relationships with other and kindred sports have also developed apace. The full-scale internationals with Ireland which died a thousand deaths before they were eventually formalised in the seventies, some fifty years after they were dismissed out of hand, are once again beckoning, with the two codes' finest young players now firmly established as the greatest of friends and fiercest competitors.

The Camanachd Association has acknowledged the many influences, direct and otherwise, which are conditioning the future of the game. There have always been exclamations deploring the stand-

(above): Dublin airport— Under-21 stars heading for Dublin in 1989 being piped off by Duncan MacGillivray

(right): Action from the 1992 International at Inverness

Drawings by Mairi Hedderwick from the Dublin International

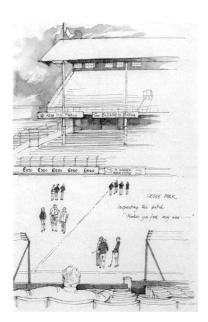

ard of play and calling for an improvement. The modern game is no exception. Centenary Year, however, sees the publication of shinty's first long-term development plan, designed to achieve that single aim.

The highest standards of play are dependent on a commensurate improvement in the standard of playing surface. Few, if any, clubs have bowling-greens as shinty pitches. Relatively few are doing much about it, although the Camanachd Association, with assistance from local authorities such as Highland Regional Council, are now addressing the problem constructively.

The Camanachd Association has not, as yet, discovered a means of controlling the intemperate climate, but there is an acceptance that meaningful changes have to be undertaken to facilitate the best possible combination of playing conditions which will make shinty as attractive, or more attractive, than any other sport. Regular play on suitable pitches with decent ancillary facilities must be one of the game's priorities as it meets the challenges ahead.

Indoor play has become an integral and highly developed and popular part of the game. Play on artificial surfaces may not be all that far off. Summer shinty as a norm (or at the very worst, extended winter breaks) may too be one of the inevitable conclusions to be drawn from the current debate about the game's future.

Duncan Cameron is confident change will come, but realistic enough to accept that it will have to be in stages, and with the willing participation of the member clubs. He says:

"Experience tells us that shinty is likely to opt for gradual and conservative change. It is not part of the Celtic psyche to vote for radical solutions. The Camanachd Association have the responsibility of leading clubs through the complex inter-related issues that contribute to improvements in the standard of play. The Association's committee structure allows all aspects of the game to be examined and solutions included in its development plan. With the help of professional expertise, clubs are already responding to new ideas in coaching, training and the treatment of injuries. It is the way forward, of that I am absolutely sure."

It is no over-simplification to say that the dilemma facing shinty and its administrators is whether to promote a modern game, or preserve an aspect of Highland

(above): Crying shame — the trials and tribulations of a shinty goal-keeper. Roddy MacLennan of Strathglass toiling against Kingussie — but he made a splendid recovery!

(right): Keith MacIntyre pursued hotly by Damien Geoghan during the Dublin International match

culture. It should not be beyond the wisdom and ingenuity of those involved, be they members of the Executive Council, or humble players, to engineer a satisfactory solution to the problem.

Shinty may well always have to survive on the strength of the commitment and drive of relatively few. 'Petty jealousies' attacked in the twenties, the thirties and through to the eighties and nineties as one of the blights halting progress, will always be there. The difference between a 'petty jealousy' and 'defending one's corner' is often a fine one.

Administrative wrangles and debacles have been part and parcel of the game. That is not to say they should be actively engineered, and there appears to be a collective will abroad which should enable shinty to make the most of many of the opportunities currently being offered. Technological advances will give the game a greater platform than ever before; the support of sponsors and other agencies, (which cannot be taken for granted, especially at times of deepening economic recession), must be sought and cultivated; the vision of a few must be realised, for example in terms of an overall national league system, but realistically, at a pace in which the stars of the game and the lesser lights can both be accommodated.

There is no room for complacency. The Camanachd Association has collectively come a long way in its first hundred years and has now rationalised itself into a shape which will bear comparison with the ruling bodies of all other sports.

For life-force and continuing success, the game must continue to aspire to skill and spectacle at the highest level. If these remain the ideals of the greatest game in the world, and as long as the unique enduring comradeship 'after battle' can be maintained, then shinty will maintain the traditions which were founded thousands of years ago and have stood the test of time. It will also remain one of Scotland's truly national assets.

Skye's future lies in good hands — action from the Club's centenary week, June 1992

'Canada 91': A sixty-nine strong party of players and friends
from Kingussie and Skye Camanachd, re-introduced shinty to Cape Breton

Scotland

Ireland

Barry Egan (*left*)
was sàr-chluicheadair
(Man of the Match)
in the 1992
Under-21's International;
with him is Allan Campbell,
Director of Medal Donors,
Comunn na Gàidhlig

The 1992 Scott Oswald
Under-21 International,
Scotland 3 — Ireland 6,
Bught Park, Inverness

SCOTT OSWALD
INTERNATIONAL
SHINTY/HURLING
MATCH

The Gaelic Athletic Association of Ireland

The Camanachd Association of Scotland

SCOTLAND v IRELAND
under 21
BUGHT PARK, INVERNESS
Saturday 25 July 1992 at 3pm
Admission £2.50; Senior Citizens £1.50; Children 50p
Sponsored by
SCOTT OSWALD & CO., Chartered Accountants

More action from Bught Park, Inverness,
in the 1992 International

Scotland v. Ireland, Croke Park, Dublin 1989

Scotland's victorious young lions,
Inverness 1990 — victory after 60 years.
Sir Robert Cowan presenting the
Cowan Quaich.

Glenmorangie Camanachd Cup Final 1991 at
Bught Park, Inverness: Fort William v. Kingussie

1988 Camanachd Cup Final—
Kingussie's Dave Anderson *(left)* **with Man of the Match,**
Ali Mackintosh, Glenurquhart, in hot pursuit

'On the turf, as under the turf: all men are equal'

THE SHINTY CLUBS AND WHERE THEY PLAY

1 Aberdeen University
2 Appin
3 Ballachulish
4 Beauly
5 Boleskine
6 Bute
7 Caberfeidh
8 Col-Glen
9 Edinburgh University
10 Fort William

11 Glasgow Highland
12 Glasgow Mid-Argyll
13 Glasgow University
14 Strathclyde Police
15 Glengarry
16 Glenorchy
17 Glenurquhart
18 Inveraray
19 Inverness
20 Kilmallie

21 Kilmory
22 Furnace
23 Kincraig
24 Kingussie
25 Kinlochshiel
26 Kintyre
27 Kyles Athletic
28 Lochaber Camanachd
29 Lochcarron
30 London Camanachd

31 Lovat
32 Newtonmore
33 Oban Camanachd
34 Oban Celtic
35 Skye Camanachd
36 St Andrews University
37 Strachur
38 Strathglass
39 Tayforth
40 Taynuilt

A HISTORY OF THE CLUBS

RABBIE'S TRIP AROUND THE SHINTY COUNTRY — accompanied by a 'Lad frae the Kyle'

Last night I dreamed a pleasant dream
    — it thrilled me to the core,
I dreamed our National Bard had come
    again tae Scotia' shore,
I rubbed my eyes of sleepiness then sat
    upright in bed
And shouted out "Guid grief, it's Rab but
    lang syne ye've been dead."
But Rabbie sang in cheerful voice, "Ah've
    just a quick trip hame
And ah've always been enraptured wi'
    oor grand old Highland game.

Noo, in ma day ah held the ploo amang
    the fields o' Ayr,
I was always keen on shinty but I'm oot
    o' touch yince mair,
So I've come doon frae up abune tae ask
    some help frae you,
Tae tak' me roon ye'r Hielan folks and
    introduce a few.
Oor transport will be Tam's mare Meg,
    oor track lies up the West,
So just climb up ahint me and forget the
    "breathing test."

I really felt quite honoured as we rode
    on thro' the night,
The COL-GLEN team were training at the
    Clachan by flood-light,
And near the Creggans at Strachur, Rab
    says "noo, who's tae blame —
There's the "Manager" and "Mister Niall"
    still struggling tae get hame,"
But as I explained tae Rabbie, shinty
    training's no sae silly,
Especially up at "Louis" — coached by
    Donald and wee Billy.

I wondered as we galloped on the road
    going round Loch Fyne,
Aboot the INVERARAY welcome Burns
    received in lang, lang syne
Is "Hielan' pride and hunger" scrawl
    aboot the Ducal Town,
I telt him things are different noo —
    Argyll won't raise a frown.
The folks have a "Blythe-spirit" noo —
    MacKay aye keeps the heid,
Hamish Stewart he has used the "loaf" —
    Milanda's shinty "breed".

Whilst climbing up t'wards Claddich Hill
   poor Meg was getting slow.
We rested by the monument tae that
   weel-kent Neil Munro.
When heading thro' Lochawe side — to
   the right stands Donnchadh Bn —
We come into Dalmally where they're
   working on a plan,
GLENORCHY play on Market Field — Jack
   Kennedy keeps on raving,
Tommy Gibson's taking monkey gland
   and MacDougall's started shaving.

Thro' the lovely Pass of Brander, doon
   the Bonnie Corran Brae,
We reached a shinty strong-hold there by
   bonnie Oban Bay.
There's CAMANACHD in red and black,
   the CELTIC white and green
And Cooper says, "Ye'll squeeze an orange
   — but LORNE are tangerine!"
Jock Douglas says, "this is the law",
   Duncan Cameron says, "Don't try"
But Slater says "you can't decide 'till you
   consult G.Y."

I introduced oor Rabbie tae some men
   who'd made their mark —
Some stalwarts who with caman skill
   had graced old Mossfield Park —
Turnbull, Currie, MacIntyre, Millar,
   Dougie, Mick,
MacInnes, Watt, MacCallum — hardy
   handlers of the stick.
Says Rab, "I met nae lasses here wi' a'
   this shinty whirl,"
I says, "ye widna stand a chance we
   Larry and Lachie Birrell."

Then back we went tae Connel Bridge
   and cantered o'er free,
Next stop was BALLACHULISH and that
   spot — the Jubilee.
Relived memories of some battles wi' the
   lads who worked the slate —

The hardy boys in red and blue were very
   hard tae bate,
McLachlan, Dalston, Donnie Rose, as
   hard as their ain quarry,
Carmichael, Hugh Buchanan, and that
   hard man Seedy Lawrie.

The ferry's off — the Brig's no built —
   oor Meg could care no less,
She sprouted wings and wi' mighty leap
   came doon in Inverness.
Then galloped on up tae the FORT and
   MacMillan heard oor wrath,
He didn't see a shinty match but had tae
   tak' a bath,
He says, "We play at Claggan noo — oor
   Council did the planning,
Oor civic heads are a' the big shots —
   oor Provost is a "Canon.""

Then we headed tae KILMALLIE-land tae
   Corpach, Banavie,
And there I introduced the Bard tae oor
   Chief — Walter P. —
Resplendent in his Cameron kilt he's lost
   a lot o' weight,
His interest in Scout movement noo is
   surely oot a' date.
The youngsters there within his care with
   caman skill afire,
Teenagers Derek, Fatty and the "babe" —
   Shep MacIntyre.

Then on we went right thro' the night
   and Meg wis fairly fleein,
We waved tae Donald Kennedy as we
   approached the SPEAN.
Tae Fort Augustus, Invergarry where oor
   game's been on the wane
But I think there'll be a revival here after
   that summer game.
We cantered o'er the hill tae Cluanie on
   twisted roads sae narrow
And reached the home o' KINLOCHSHIEL
   — a nice place Balmacara.

A late licence there in Kintail Lodge we
*   had a dram or two,*
And there I met a Fraser — a wee full
*   back — Ian Dubh.*
He said, "The team's been scoring goals
*   for that we have a "Grant,"*
My son is with me in the team so what
*   more could I want.*
The shinty talent's glistening right along
*   the Ross-shire roads.*
Success just breeds encouragement, well,
*   just ask Albert Loades!"*

Noo time wis scarce — we left oor freens
*   and galloped on tae Kyle,*
We caught the ferry o'er tae Skye tae
*   blether for a while,*
The shinty scene is "Taylor made" and
*   Hume still has his fling,*
While Col. Jock MacDonald says "In Skye
*   I'm still the King."*
But in this age of Aquarius emerges one
*   new star —*
The MacDonald clan has gifted Skye a
*   fella called D.R.*

It's back tae Kyle and up the coast tae
*   country side sae barren,*
Tae Kishorn and Drambuie tae that
*   stronghold called LOCHCARRON,*
It's ther we met the Doctor — he wis
*   fairly in a frenzy.*
He wis trying tae transplant the heid of
*   Calum of Mackenzie,*
While in Maclennan's butcher's shop the
*   folks had caused a rammy,*
For Tex had sawed a sheep's heid all
*   bedecked wi' Calum's tammy.*

Now on we rode thro' the night tae
*   Strathpeffer on the way,*
At Castle Leod the call wis "Toss thine
*   antlers Caberfeidh".*
MacMaster says the "Skye Blues" were the
*   best you've ever seen.*
By the time we got to BEAULY, Campbell
*   says the colour's green.*
For Dingwall rocks and Lovat Rocks we
*   treat them with disdain,*
The only rocks that interest us, is Ronnie
*   "Rox" MacLean.*

And right on to Kiltarlity we went right
to Balgate,
Then Colin spied oor old freen Rab he
says, "Ye've met yer fate,"
There's Murdo here a mainstay up in
Glen Affric Hotel,
Johnnie Gordon, Tommy Fraser noo are
doing really well.
But this womens' liberation noo are
working oot a plan —
The Lovat team is now controlled — by
one called Mary Anne.

Frae there it's up to Kerrow Brae, where
Meg just proved her class,
There Jimmac showed his colours of the
Glen up at STRATHGLASS,
And over tae GLEN URQUHART, Danny
Shewglie's daein swell.
He has tae keep a Dolly bird, as well as
Alan Bell.
For Jan and Alan's come frae Islay —
they're in the SNP scene,
They've even chased the "English" man a'
the way tae Aberdeen.

Away doon there along Loch Ness tae the
Bught Park sae weel kent,
We met up wi' MacPherson and
Mackenzie — President,
Noo Willie's back in training noo since
he gave up at the school,
But Tommy's noo back on the rails —
he's got tae work tae rule,
And Duncan's taken o'er the team — it
does nae gie them solace.
He's handcuffed them tae their shinty
sticks — the Manager frae the Polis.

So back we rode thro' East Loch Ness —
oor mare wid take some catchin,
Until we came tae Foyers toon and fell in
wi' Willie Batchen,
This lad wha runs the shinty scene thro
Highland climes sae braw,

He's got tae watch Boleskine and the
ither teams and a',
Then back we rode tae Inverness and
went tae the A9.
Tae this new team o'er at KINCRAIG —
Donnie Ross is lookin' fine.

And then on towards KINGUSSIE where
the shinty's going swell.
MacGregor had his gathering wi' the
stalwarts o' the Dell,
Jimmie Murchie's noo stopped poachin'
while "Rossie" had a transplant,
Kingussie noo have changed a "fuse" and
Donnie's had a Grant.
But Rab says tae me, "The red and blue
will surely make their mark —
But I fancy their wee Secretary — Mrs
Gillian Clark."

We rode on tae the Eilan tae that
stronghold NEWTONMORE,
We met Ally and Gaby Fraser — blue and
white men tae the core.
Jack Richmond's shinty Forum, Johnnie
Campbell, Kenny Smith,
Fraser, Stewart, Ralph, MacKenzie —
those names are no a myth,
But I said tae Rab, "Here meet Jock Paul"
— they had a right good blether —
Sae weel they might because we know
they started the game the gether.

So oer the Lecht we cantered thro' the
countryside sae green,
Twa teams support the shinty in the toon
o Aiberdeen,
There are Englishmen and Irishmen
competing for their "blues,"
Even Lewismen and Sgiathanachs and
Australian "Kangaroos,"
A conglomerate of nations, ye could ca' it
a real "Hotch Potch" —
Why even Peter English has tae prove that
he is Scotch.

Then we headed for ST ANDREWS tae oor exiled Heilan folks,
We were asked tae form a six-a-side by the "Sassenach" Gerry Stokes.
Then on we went to TAYFORTH thro' country road and lane,
Tae meet up wi' that Irishman — the charming Hugh O'Kane.
And we'd have made "Auld Reekie" tae meet up wi' the creeds,
Or even tae Northallerton — but Richard Tulloch wis in Leeds.

So back we rode tae Glasgow and oor Meg fair galloped on,
It wis there we met MacInnes, Donald Skinner, Iain Cameron,
All the boys frae Glesca Uni' and the Polis Force and a',
Jack Asher even took oor names while Lachie gied a "Blaw".
Where wis Beaton, Bobby Nicolson, I says "Trouble is afoot,"
So with Harvey Smith salutation, we steered oor steed tae BUTE.

While on the Isle oor Rabbie says tae me, "This is nae braggin,
I couldnae noo contest the skill o' that yin Escacraggan."
John MacDonald, Jimmy Duncan and Jock Hunter — they mean Bute,
Why then even Billy Crawford has come on as substitute.
It's grand tae see oor grand old game being fostered in the Isles.
But time was really precious as we headed for the KYLES.

So it's back tae Tighnabruaich — that place I hold so dear.
I showed tae Rab the Scottish Cup that we had won last year.

We have wee Tam and Chic Jamieson and big Barney for the fray,
But noo we have the Vice Chief of the Caman — D. MacRae.
Rab says tae me, "I've heard yer talk aboot yer caman wiles,
But after a' I've seen the night, I've got tae think on Kyles."

Noo after all oor travels right thro' Scotland thro' the night
I awakened in the morning in a really sorry plight,
My body pained with saddle sores — I couldnae shake a leg,
Tae think that I'd toured Scotland on the back of oor mare Meg!
The wife just shook me in the bed and said, "That's Burns away,"
And I realised I'd got tae rise and start another day.

Rabbie's companion on this epic journey, first published in the 1974-75 Shinty Yearbook, was anonymous — principally, it is understood for fear of recriminations by the "polis" on various sensitive issues such as excessive loading of Old Meg, creating scarcities of Stag's Breath at their various ports of call, overstepping the 300 mile maximum journey on a mare allowed by the Ministry of Transport, etc.

Rab's companion was, however, a native of Tighnabruaich who gave outstanding and skilled service to the Kyles team over a long period — latterly as a goalkeeper after his epic journey on Meg had greatly hampered his mobility as an outfield player. The gentleman was at the time a staunch member of the Kyles committee and a Vice President of the Camanachd Association.

The students of Aberdeen have a legitimate claim to have been the first to lay down a properly documented set of Rules with a Constitution, in 1861, almost ten years before Edinburgh Camanachd, which traditionally laid claims to have been the elder statesman of the game.

The club played its first match in 1889. Prior to 1910, the club had been dormant for five or six years and in 1913 entered the Camanachd Cup for the first time. For twenty years before 1949 the club played no competitive games against north teams although they regularly took part in the Littlejohn Vase competition which was played for by the Universities.

One of the club's most successful periods was in the 1970's when they captured the Sutherland Cup, the Scottish Junior championship, for the first time. The trophy was retained in the following year.

Dr Peter English, a stalwart player in the teams of the 1950's is well known as a frequent contributor to the pages of the Shinty

The first page of the Rules and Constitution of Aberdeen University Shinty Club. There were 38 members in the club when first constituted.

(above): 1973 Sutherland Cup winners. The team also won the Strathdearn Cup and the Morrison Cup in that year
(below): Aberdeen University, 1954-55 with the Littlejohn Vase

Yearbook and was instrumental in its foundation. He was also prominent in the founding of Aberdeen Camanachd in 1968. Dr W.J. MacPherson, a son of Thomas J. MacPherson who was for many years a prominent figure in north shinty was a captain in the immediate post-war period and later as Honorary president, served as coach until he left to take up a lecturing post at Cambridge University in season 1955-56.

Ken Thomson, President of the Camanachd Association in its centenary year is a former player of the club and another former player, Burton Morrison, went on to distinguish himself as an international player, becoming a coach to the Under-21 side.

The Club played at senior level in its most successful period during the seventies, and now fields a side in Division Four of the North League.

APPIN SHINTY CLUB

The club was originally formed in the 1930's. It was re-formed in 1946 and continued until 1956 when it was disbanded because of a shortage of players. Following some success at primary school level, the club was re-started in its present form and entered competitions in the season 1988-89.

There are about sixteen players in the club.

Home matches are played on a local farmer's field during the winter months and in spring and autumn at Taynuilt or Ballachulish. Since re-starting, the club has played in the same field at Inverfolla. Plans are afoot to have a new pitch.

The club had some success in the 1950's, winning the Bullough Cup in 1950, 1952, 1953 and 1954. During this period the Munro Shield, the Campbell Cup and Smith Cup were also won. In 1954, Appin reached the final of the Sutherland Cup.

The most outstanding personality in the club was the late Archie Lawrie ("Baldy"). Despite being disabled and in poor health, he re-started the club in 1988. His dedication, hard work and passionate belief in fair play were undoubtedly an inspiration to all connected with the club at the present time and in the early 1950's. His loss to the club was great but his spirit lives on.

The late Archie Lawrie who was instrumental in reviving Appin shinty club in 1988

BALLACHULISH CAMANACHD CLUB

The Ballachulish Shinty Song

Have you seen the Ballachulish,
Have you seen the boys in red,
They're the greatest team in shinty,
From A to B to Z.
They have played at Inveraray,
They have played in Mossfield Park,
But the greatest game of shinty,
Is played in the Jubilee Park.
It's the home of famous people,
Whose praises I must sing,
Hughie Lawrie and the Honda,
Edmund, Jimac and the King.
Andy Dunn and Peter Carter,
Pongo, David and MacPhee,
And the most famous of them all,
Dochan and Nagee.
And when all my days have ended,
And when death has made its mark,
May they scatter all my ashes,
In the middle of the Jubilee Park,
Up in Heaven with the angels,
Up in Heaven in the Glen,
I'll be happy and contented,
When Ballachulish win again.

Ballachulish Shinty Club share a common centenary with the Camanachd Association in 1993. They are one of the most famous members of that Association, having competed at the highest level for many periods of the Association's first hundred years.

In their early years, Ballachulish were a major force within the game, achieving four Camanachd Cup wins in 1899, 1901, 1911 and 1912.

There were also three Bullough Cup wins at the turn of the century.

The outbreak of War in 1914 undoubtedly cost Ballachulish greater success. After the War they were unable to return to the previously high standards they had set, mostly due to the war, but also to a little local difficulty between the villagers of East and West Laroch. Their differences were gradually overcome, however, and by 1938 a strong team had been created, strong enough to beat the much fancied Caberfeidh team in the MacTavish Cup Final of that year.

Ballachulish were Camanachd Cup winners in 1912
(back row): James Skinner, Alistair Cameron, Hugh Livingston, Alex Rankin, Donald Turner, James MacDonald, John MacDonald, Donald Lawrie, Duncan MacColl; (front row): Alan MacLachlan, Willie Lawrie, Duncan McTaggart, Donald MacLachlan

Willie MacDonald — one of Ballachulish's better players of recent years — was Man of the Match in the 1992 Camanachd Cup Final, playing for Fort William

Sadly, for the second time in thirty years, the outbreak of war was to deny the club a more lengthy period of success.

In the years following the Second World War, however, a truly great Ballachulish team was to emerge to reach the Camanachd Cup Final in 1948. After a titanic struggle at Inverness, they lost 4-2 to Newtonmore. The week after the Final, however, Ballachulish confirmed their ability by defeating the same team 2-0 in the Final of the MacTavish Cup.

This team went on to compete at the highest level for many years with further success in the Celtic, Sutherland and Dunn Cups. Unfortunately, after this period, interest in the game waned and by the mid-fif-ties, Ballachulish were no longer the force they once were.

Efforts to revive interest in the game (including a challenge match between Kyles Athletic and Glasgow Mid Argyll at the Jubilee Park) were to prove worthwhile and by the mid-sixties, Ballachulish produced a team that went on to dominate junior shinty for a number of years.

Between 1965 and 1971 they competed in five Sutherland Cup Finals, although they won only once, defeating Skye 2-0 at the Bught Park in 1971. This consistent run confirmed the strength of the game in the area once more.

Since then Ballachulish have achieved only sporadic success in the junior game and have failed to produce a team capable of matching their former glories.

The reasons for this as similar to the experiences of many years ago — lack of interest, lack of dedication and a certain lack of discipline. It can also be said that the loss of players to other, larger and more successful clubs, or to the many varied interests of the modern world have also had a detrimental effect on the Ballachulish game.

Although currently undergoing a fairly lengthy re-building process, the present Ballachulish team is younger and stronger than it has been for some time and indeed rekindles memories of the great Ballachulish team. Listing names like MacMillan, MacPhee, Rankin, MacLachlan, MacDonald and MacKenzie on the team sheet again gives the club every hope for a brighter future.

*'S e mo dhùrachd gum bi camanachd
Fada beò ann an Gleann Baile Chaol*

BEAULY CAMANACHD

Shinty has been played in various places in the vicinity of Beauly from early times, the only regular times when play was held being Christmas Day and New Year's Day. By 1887 a Beauly team was playing teams such as Lochcarron and Strathglass, and a club was constituted in 1892. It was represented at the Annual General Meeting of the Camanachd Association in 1895 by Mr John Nicolson and Mr J.A. Cameron. A Chieftain of the club about this time was Mr D. MacInnes of the Lovat Arms Hotel and Mr Roderick MacRae, Gladstone House, was President.

At present about fifty players are involved and teams at senior, junior, juvenile and boys level can be fielded. Games are now played at Braeview Park, an Inverness District Council complex completed in 1986. Changing rooms and showers are available. Before this the club's last venue was Ferry Park and in earlier times any available farm field was used at places such as Balblair, Dunballoch, Taewig, Wellhouse and Groam. The club's colours have always been green and white. Since its inception the club has not folded or merged with any other.

Beauly entered the initial competition for the Camanachd Cup in 1895-96 and in the following season beat Brae Lochaber 6—0 in the final at Inverness. This cup was again won by Beauly, acclaimed as "Champions of the World", in 1898 when Inveraray were beaten 2—1, again in Inverness. At this time Beauly travelled to London and played in an exhibition game against London Camanachd.

The MacTavish Cup was won in 1899 and also in 1905. It was again won in 1913 in

(above): sent back from the trenches in the First World War, probably composed in honour of 1913 Cup victory

(left): Centenary Year, 1992

which year the Camanachd Cup was also won when Kyles Athletic were beaten 3—1 at Kingussie.

After the war of 1914-18, in which it lost twenty-five players, the club was again prominent, reaching the Camanachd Cup Final in 1922, the last occasion on which this was achieved. The years up to the outbreak of war in 1939 saw little success. In the early 1950's the club had assumed junior status and at this level succeeded in winning the Sutherland Cup in 1952, 1954, 1956 and 1957 and the Strathdearn Cup in 1952, 1954, 1955 and 1956.

By the early 1960's the club was again playing as a senior team and in 1966 reached the semi-final of the Camanachd Cup. A notable success was that over Newtonmore in 1972-73 to win the MacGillivray Senior League. The MacGillivray Junior League was won in the same season.

Another trophy which has been won from time to time is the Lovat Cup which was donated by Lord Lovat in 1904 and is contested annually, formerly at Christmas and since the 1950's at New Year, by Beauly and Lovat.

The minutes of the Camanachd Association show that in its early years Beauly was represented at meetings by such as Mr John MacRae, Mr John Forbes, Mr William Chalmers, Mr Donald Morrison and Mr Thomas Fraser.

Mr William Paterson, who had played for the club as did his two older brothers who were killed in the 1914-18 war, became Secretary of the Camanachd Association in 1929 and was President from 1937 to 1948.

BOLESKINE CAMANACHD

Willie Batchen

Boleskine Camanachd, one of several formed on the east side of Loch Ness, has had a chequered history. The Stratherrick club was formed by 1890, and in 1898, some years after the British Aluminium Company established its factory at Foyers, a club was formed there.

In September, 1927, these clubs combined to form BOLESKINE which entered for the Camanachd Cup and other competitions in 1927-28. Office Bearers at this time were: William Robertson, President; K.J. MacPherson, Vice President; Donald Maclean, Secretary; others were Robert MacDonald, J.Forbes, Tim Pow, Colonel Laughton, J. MacDonald and M.J. MacLennan.

A break-away team under the name of Foyers entered competitions as Stratherrick

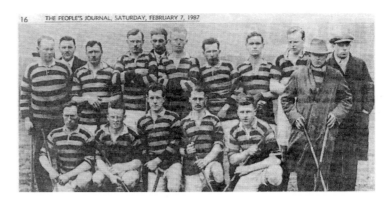

The team of Boleskine Shinty Club, who reached the Camanachd Final for the only time in their first year, 1928

in 1933-34, and Boleskine ceased to exist. On the resumption of shinty in 1946-47 the Foyers club re-formed and Stratherrick combined with Strathnairn (which had last played in the early 1930's) to form Straths Athletic, which continued up to 1951-52. In September, 1953 a meeting was held to re-form Boleskine which has, with some interruptions, continued up to the present time with some notable successes.

The club has generally survived with a complement of up to twenty players, and their base is the Factory Field at Foyers where they have a wooden pavilion. The team play in black and gold.

In its first season, 1927-28, Boleskine were beaten by Kyles Athletic in Glasgow in the Camanachd Cup Final, the club's finest hour. In 1930, 1931 and 1932, the club reached the final of the MacGillivray League before folding in 1934.

Following the re-formation in 1934, Boleskine reached the final of the Strathdearn Cup in 1956 and 1959. In 1964, after winning the Strathdearn Cup, Boleskine defeated Kyles Athletic in the Sir William Sutherland Cup Final at Strachur.

Kyles Athletic were again defeated in the final of the Sutherland Cup in 1966 and Boleskine also accounted for Lochaber in the final of the MacGillivray Junior League competition.

The closure of the British Aluminium factory at Foyers in March, 1967, was a serious blow to life in the district and there was no team in 1967-68 as several players had left home to seek employment. This happened at a time when the club had been showing signs of considerable promise and had been expected to have achieved further honours.

During these years the club owed a great deal to the enthusiasm of Mr William Batchen, Secretary and Treasurer and Mr Kenneth Ross, President. Mr Batchen was a legend in his own lifetime having been Secretary and Treasurer of the Camanachd Association for thirteen years. He was also one of the game's most noted and respected match officials.

Boleskine were re-formed for season 1968-69 but no team was fielded in the following year. In 1971, however, the club was again among the honours, winning the Dewar Shield and they have also reached the finals of the Strathdearn and Glenmhor competitions, winning the Glenmhor successively in 1990 and 1991.

There was, perhaps, no keener supporter of the Boleskine Club than Duncan Mac-Donald ''Birchfield'', or ''Birch'' as he was better known locally. No mean player himself, he was captain of the Strathdearn Cup winning team of 1912-13. Apart from being a sportsman, he was also a poet of note. It must have been after a particularly heavy defeat that he composed the following post-mortem on Boleskine performances on and off the field.

The Burial of Foyers Shinty Club

I strolled along the country road,
And viewed the scenery so gay,
I gazed enraptured on the scene,
As I sauntered up the Bungalow brae.

Soon my thoughts were turned aside,
From all the beauty I could see,
For on the road not far away,
A funeral was approaching me.

I stood aside and bared my head.
In honour of the passing dead,
But when the sacred coach drew nigh,
No human form I could espy.

Alas, all huddled in a heap,
All battled scarred with many a chip,
Saw twisted clubs without a shroud,
Behind them walked the mourning crowd.

I turned around, retraced my steps,
My happy thoughts were now reverse,
It smote my heart with heavy grief,
To see the Foyers club in a hearse.

And when we reached the hallowed
*   ground,*
Where young and old began to pray,
A voice within the sacred coach,
In awesome tones to me did say:

''Good old ''Has-beens'', we know you yet
And we will never leave you so,
Although our bodies they entomb,
They cannot put our souls below.''

Good old ''Has-beens'' if you could last,
This sorry fate was never ours,
You kept us swinging on the field,
You never let us nourish flowers.

In Victory after Victory,
Now the ''Has-beens'' did us wield,
Before the present youngsters grew,
When their sires were on the field.

How the ''Has-beens'' we have fought,
And conquered foes so fierce and stern,
Now we, the Hussey Cup brought back,
And wrenched another from Strathdearn.

That day you knew no wintergreen,
Or embrocation on your skin,
A week-old whisker on your chin was
*   more in your line,*
Than flowing locks round your scalps in
*   brilliantine.*

No more we'll swing upon the field,
With vigour and perfection,
For the Shinty Spirit passed away,
With no signs of resurrection.

And when the day of Union comes,
We'll meet you in the evergreens,
And think upon the happy days,
When we were ''Nows'' and not
*   ''Has-beens''.*

BUTE SHINTY CLUB

The Shinty Year Book of 1977-78 mentions the formation of a club in Bute in 1898 and that of 1972-73 states that the season 1906-07 witnessed the formation of the Bute Club as the first properly organised club on the island. The club was re-formed in 1946, the meeting for that purpose being called by the father of the present Marquis of Bute and Sir Colin MacRae. There is record of a club called North Bute in 1912 and of North Bute (Rothesay) in 1924.

Home games are played at the Meadows. In 1991-92 there were two teams, in Divisions II and IV.

The club colours are red jerseys and white shorts.

The club has won several trophies over the years. The Sutherland Cup was not won until 1972 although the final of the competition had been reached in 1923. Other successes were the winning of the Southern League Championship (Fraser Cup) Skeabost Horn, Buteman Cup, McQuiston Cup, Campbell Cup, MacLellan Trophy, Balliemore Cup and Lady Margaret MacRae Trophy.

It has always been difficult to keep the game going mainly because of young men having to leave the community in search of employment. The club takes an interest in various matters concerning the Highlands and is a member of several associations. It has organised the Bute Highland Games for the last seventy years.

Among prominent personalities in the club were W.C. Duncan, a Vice Chieftain and player in the 1906 team, Donald Jenkins, Hector MacGillivray and John Dickie all past presidents and Jock Murray. Several members of the MacMillan family

(above): Civic Reception hosted by Argyll and Bute District Council on winning the Balliemore Cup. Raising his glass (centre) on the right of the Marquis of Bute is Jock Hunter who played for Bute in the first Sutherland Cup Final in 1923
(right) Balliemore Cup Winners, 1985

have appeared in Bute teams and acted as office bearers.

CABERFEIDH SHINTY CLUB

This club was formed in 1886 at a meeting held in the Spa Pavilion in Strathpeffer initiated by W.F. Gunn, factor of Cromartie Estates. Caberfeidh (Stag's antlers) is the crest of the Mackenzie clan, the chief being the Earl of Cromartie.

There are twenty-eight senior and thirty juvenile players. There are two senior teams and two juvenile ones, the Under-17 and the Under-14 team.

Home matches are played at Castle Leod, Strathpeffer, on the Cromartie estate, the castle being the home of the Earl of Cromartie. The club has always played there.

The club has been in existence since 1886 and for a period of two years in the 1920's it played as a junior club because of a dearth of experienced players following the first World War.

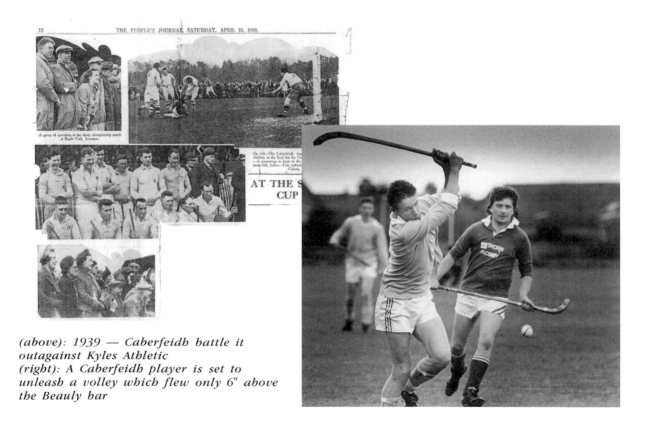

(above): 1939 — Caberfeidh battle it out against Kyles Athletic
(right): A Caberfeidh player is set to unleash a volley which flew only 6" above the Beauly bar

The colours are light-blue jerseys and white shorts. The badge is the Mackenzie crest.

The club has won a number of trophies, as can be seen in the results part of this book. Two memorable events were the winning of the Camanachd Cup in 1934 and 1939. The team of 1934 was the first team to win the Camanachd Cup, MacTavish Cup and MacGillivray League Cup in the same season.

A famous personality connected with the club was the late Earl of Cromartie, M.C., Chieftain. Mr. Kenneth A. MacMaster is Honorary President and was President of the Camanachd Association from 1970 to 1973. He has had a long connection as player and committee member. Three generations of players have been coached by him and he is still involved in coaching at Fodderty School. Mr. R.J. Macleod served as secretary of the club for 22 years and has been secretary of the Ross-shire Camanachd Association from 1951 to the present time.

The club has always been a family club with members of the same family playing for several generations. The renowned teams of the 1920's and 1930's had four Mackenzie brothers, four Cumming brothers, three MacMaster brothers and two Keir brothers.

COL-GLEN

Col-Glen Shinty Club was first formed in 1920 and by 1927 a strong team had emerged winning various trophies which were open to them with the exception of the Sutherland Cup.

In recent years the team has been weakened due to players going to other clubs and to population movement from the district, a sparsely populated one. At present it is difficult to raise a team, while in 1938 three teams and nine reserves could be raised.

Since 1979 the team has played in the Community Playing Field at Glendaruel where modern changing accommodation is available. The team colours are orange shirts and black shorts. In season 1991-92 the team was third in Division II of the Marine Harvest League South.

Before the Community Playing Field was available, games were played on various fields in the district offered by local farmers. Three teams from within the club competed for the Campbell Cup on a field at Lephinkill in 1938.

The club has never merged with another but it folded from 1966 to 1968 because of lack of players.

In 1956 the Buteman Cup was won and in 1983, under the captaincy of James Edgar, the Bullough Cup was won.

For some years there was a strong team in the local primary school which reached the final of the Mackay Cup. Had these boys been able to remain in the district, a fine pool of players would now be available.

In 1977 Col-Glen was awarded the Shinty Yearbook Trophy, showing that it had achieved much under difficult circumstances. This brought some distinction to the club and to the whole community.

Col. A. Fletcher of Dunans Castle, Glendaruel, whose family has had a long association with the glen and with shinty, was

Col-Glen's 1927 Cup winners

appointed Honorary President in 1968 and still holds that office. In 1973 he donated a cup which is played for by boys of two age groups at a six-a-side tournament. It is still held annually with over twenty teams competing.

A severe loss was sustained by the club in 1956. While returning by boat from Bute after the club had won the Buteman Cup, the then secretary and treasurer of the club, Mr Duncan Baxter, was accidentally drowned.

EDINBURGH UNIVERSITY

Shinty had been present at Edinburgh University from as early as the 1850's, but it was not until November 1891 that the official University Club was instituted. The beginnings of the club focused on a match between the Arts and Medical Faculties held at Inverleith Park. *The Student* newspaper noted that, "All the players went into the game with great enthusiasm and the fine playing of a great number augurs well for a successful team". The foundation of the club is attributed to Hugh Gunn.

In the early days fixtures were scarce and without doubt matches against Edinburgh Camanachd and Aberdeen University ensured the Club's survival. The club was set on firmer ground in 1899 with admission into the Camanachd Association when regular entry into the Association's Challenge Cup commenced. With these foundations in place some prominent teams were to emerge over the years. The period 1927 to 1933 is the most notable in the Club's history. Under the strong influence of M.C.

MacQueen, in partnership with Willie "El-lis" Stuart from Laggan and Charlie MacIn-tosh from Newtonmore the University retained the Littlejohn Vase (the Varsity cup) six years in succession. Much of the credit must go to M.C. MacQueen who went on to be a leading anaesthetist in Edinburgh but whether he put his opponents to sleep in his undergraduate days is not recorded! In those days the team was also competing in the Southern League and the Scottish Cup. Opponents of the time included Glas-gow Mid-Argyll, Glasgow Skye, Kyles Ath-letic and the Universities of Aberdeen and Glasgow.

After World War II the Club's revival is attributed to Archie Lamont and it was at this point in the Club's history that the Committee decided that "the Club should no longer be limited to hard-living, hard-drinking, Gaelic-speaking Highlanders". This period also saw the Club move to new pitches at East Fettes Avenue which were much superior to the old pitches at Craiglockhart and King's Buildings. The club must have enjoyed popularity in those post-war years as it was one of the few periods when a second team was fielded.

There was a much publicised match with Queen's University (Belfast) Hurling Club at the new ground. Edinburgh lost by the odd goal in five, Mackinnon getting both goals for the home team. The Irish team, how-ever, got a good taste of Highland and liq-uid hospitality. The Irish connection has continued to this day and many a game ver-sus Trinity College Dublin or Queen's Uni-versity on both sides of the water have been played (see Shinty Yearbook, 1992-93 "Crossing the seas and the centuries" by Brendan Harvey, Belfast).

Through the sixties and seventies the club remained strong. The seventies saw a long period of continuity for the club and as the Edinburgh Camanachd club was now de-funct, a new team, Tayforth, was spawned. There was a significant number of ex-E.U.

Reunion in 1991

players at Tayforth and the two teams have complemented each other ever since. In the eighties the club competed in Division Three (South) save for one regrettable year of isolation when fixtures were provided by the Littlejohn Vase. It is interesting to note how a University team's fortunes can fluctu-ate as the season 1986-87 saw the team narrowly miss promotion, 1987-88 saw demotion to Division Four.

In 1991 the club enjoyed its centenary year in which a grand reunion was organised. As news of the celebration spread, old contacts were re-established until every team since the 1920's could be represented at the Centenary Dinner. Guests of honour included Sorley MacLean who played for the club in the late twenties. The reunion proved a great morale booster for the club members (past and present) and that year the club decided not to pay their usual visit to Ireland but instead tour the North of Scotland from where a constant stream of players had sustained the club over the years. The tour brought in Inverness, Skye and Fort William over four days of Shinty washed down with the best of Highland hospitality.

FORT WILLIAM

There is newly-found evidence that Fort William were formed in 1893, but there is mention of a Fort William team playing Brae Lochaber at Blarour in January 1882 and of Fort William juveniles playing Blarmach-foldach in January, 1883. It would appear that this, in fact, was an annual New Year Game.

In March 1893 the newly formed Fort William club played and won its first match against Spean Bridge at Glen Nevis. James MacDonald, MacDonald Arms, was the chieftain at its formation and the first captain was R. Cameron, British Linen Bank.

This early victory was followed by another over Ballachulish, which was also won by four goals to nil.

One of the first trophies the club won was the Campbell Cup for six-a-sides shortly after the turn of the century and it was 1912 before the club entered for shinty's Blue Riband, the Camanachd Cup. And their finest hour came in 1992 when Fort William defeated Kingussie in the Final at Old Anniesland, Glasgow.

The Club's first senior honour was won during the previous season when Asti Cameron, whose brother the legendary Hugh "Horse" Cameron also served the club colours with distinction, became the first Fort captain to hold aloft a senior trophy.

Before 1992, the nearest the Fort had come to success in the Camanachd Cup was in 1937 when they were narrowly defeated by Oban Celtic in the semi-final and in the previous season to their historic victory when they were defeated by Kingussie at Inverness. The other main successes before 1992 were in the Torlundy Cup which was won in the mid-1950's and the Sir William Sutherland Cup, the junior championship, which was won in 1978 and 1984.

The club originally fielded only one team, drawing mainly on players from other areas who were drawn to Fort William for work. The club now supports teams from Under-14 through juvenile grades to a reserve team in Division Three and the senior team in Division One, North.

Originally the club played in Glen Nevis and then at King George V Park (formerly called Victoria Park) and then at Claggan before moving to An Aird in Inverlochy, near the town at the start of season 1982-83.

The club seems to have folded after the turn of the century, being re-formed in 1908. In 1923 it dropped out of senior shinty for a period but had a second team until about 1929, and was revived in 1932. The President then was Mr D. Livingstone and the Secretary Mr George Longbottom.

(above): Asti Cameron receives the Keyline MacAulay Cup from sponsors' representative Willie Griffen, Oban, 1991 (right): History was made at Old Anniesland with a single goal victory in the Camanachd Cup Final over Kingussie, June, 1992.

The club has played in the final of the MacTavish cup twice, in 1985 and 1989 and they won the Glenmhor Cup in 1976. Four league championships have been won — Division Two in 1984 and 1986 and Division Four in 1978 and 1987.

Throughout its history the club has had its fair share of personalities, most notably in recent years Peter Black and George Mac-Millan and on the field Iain "Copper" Mac-Donald, a North Player of the Year, and the late Joseph Toal who died on the field of play when representing Lochaber against Fort William. Perhaps the best known, however, is James "Ginger" Wilson who began playing for Nether Lochaber in 1923 and was renowned for his daring war-time escapades when escaped from captivity in Germany in 1940. Ginger's command of Gaelic is understood to have been the key to his eventual escape!

GLASGOW HIGHLAND SHINTY CLUB

In 1986 Glasgow Highland was formed by a nucleus of players some of whom formerly played for Glasgow University and other teams.

The club does not at present field a senior team but has thriving Under-14 and Under-17 teams.

Home games are played on a Glasgow District Council pitch at Bellahouston Park and the club has always played there. There are changing facilities close by.

The club which has continued since its formation has a badge and its colours are sky-blue tops.

In its first season, 1986-87, the team entered the Camanachd Cup competition and won promotion to the Weatherseal League South, Division II. The Fingal Shield was

Glasgow Highland Primary squad members with coach Angus Thorburn of Jordanhill College School (far left); School Rector William Bedborough (centre) and Gordon Smith, Primary head Teacher (far right). The School were the first non-Oban winners of the Lochgilphead Indoor Six-a-side championships.

won at the St Andrews six-a-side tournament and a team played in a tournament in London in 1987.

The Lorne Hotel and Queen's Cross Motors in Maryhill are sponsors.

The club has been instrumental in introducing the game to Jordanhill College School where Angus Thorburn, who is chairman and a founder of the club, is on the teaching staff. Another notable name in the club is Calum Maclean, the first president.

An entertaining article by Alexander Macdonald, ''Cliff-edge shinty — the ultimate in tall tales'', appears in the Shinty Yearbook of 1988.

GLASGOW MID ARGYLL

Glasgow Mid Argyll were formed in 1928 when Blawarthill Argyll changed their name on moving from Scotstoun in Glasgow to Whiteinch.

Blawarthill themselves had only been formed in 1923 by shinty enthusiasts principally from Lochfyneside. They had taken their name from the area of Scotstoun in which they were formed, where a local farmer provided a field. The site is now a housing estate.

Blawarthill quickly established themselves as rivals to the long-established Glasgow Cowal and won the Southern League (Fraser Cup) in 1924.

From its earliest days, the Mid Argyll club attracted players from all over Argyll. In addition to the former players from Inveraray and Furnace, players from Cowal, Kyles, Glendaruel and Strachur were joined by others from Ballachulish and Oban.

Donald Carmichael of Furnace and Dochie MacPhedran, Inveraray were the driving forces behind the formation of the club and the Carmichael Trophy was donated in Donald's memory. In 1930 Mid Argyll won their first major trophy, the Celtic Cup, and they went on to establish themselves as a force to be reckoned with, winning the same trophy in 1936 and the Southern League in successive years before the end of the decade (1938 and 1939).

During the post-war period Mid Argyll continued to hold a dominant position in the south, winning the league seven times in eight attempts between 1948 and 1955. With a new generation of players, led by the late Jock Black, Alec Maclean and Iain MacInnes, (all patrons of the Camanachd Association), the club ended the 1950's in some style, winning the Celtic Cup in 1957 and the Cup again, along with the Southern League, in 1959.

The club began the 1960's in confident mood, seeking to widen its horizons and meet new challenges. They were convinced they could compete with the best and win national competitions, but would require to play more games in a season and regularly meet the top teams. They were also at this time restricted by the small pitch at Victoria Park, having to play all their cup-ties on other available pitches in the city.

In 1960, Angus H. Cameron, formerly of North Ballachulish and the Club's Past President at the time, was elected as president of the Camanachd Association. During the journey to Fort William for his first

272

Glasgow Mid Argyll Shinty Club

Council meeting, Angus was involved in a road accident and died a few days later.

The Club moved to Luss on Loch Lomond-side in 1964, twenty-five miles out of the city and then joined the Dunn League, usually confined to teams from Argyll.

By now playing in the Dunn and Southern Leagues, with all home and cup-ties on a larger pitch, the club found that the changes paid immediate dividends when they won the Celtic Society Cup in 1964, in a final which was televised live on television. As winners of the Celtic Cup, they played Newtonmore (who had won the Mac-Tavish Cup) in the only Grampian Cup Final played between two club teams. The club also won the Southern League in the three consecutive seasons 1963-65.

Success could not be guaranteed by playing more games on a larger pitch, so regular training sessions began at Alan Glen's Rugby Club at Bishopbriggs in 1968. Fred Robertson, a former long distance runner, was appointed trainer and Donnie Mac-Niven as team coach.

By the club's previous standards, performances improved and greater success followed. The Celtic Cup was won again in 1969, 1971 and 1972. The ultimate honour, the Camanachd Cup, was then won in 1973 when Mid Argyll defeated Kingussie at Claggan Park, Fort William, in one of the wettest finals ever played.

In the 1970's, the club began to take on a more 'cosmopolitan' look with players being attracted from all the shinty-playing areas. Clubs with a greater experience of winning national competitions were also now enquiring of the formula required to sustain a successful team based in Glasgow.

The District Council then recognised the success of the club and provided a pitch at Maryhill in 1974. In 1975 a second team was formed which won the south's Division Three, the Ferguson Cup was won in 1978 Division Four, the MacLaren Cup followed in 1989 and then the club's second string reached the final of the Scottish Junior championship, the Sutherland Cup, in 1992, going down narrowly to the all-conquering Kingussie junior side.

The club also began to make a significant contribution to the work of the South of Scotland Shinty Association and the Camanachd Association in the 1970's. Club committee members were to be found in responsible positions in the administration of both associations and the management of the international team. Donald Skinner, the Association's Chief since 1986 was President of the Association from 1976-82. Iain Cameron, Donnie MacNiven and Fred Robertson managed and coached the national team during the 1970s.

The club also provided some key players to the international team over the years. Alastair Forbes, Iain Fraser, Iain MacMillan, Kenny MacNiven, Burton Morrison and Archie Robertson all played regularly for Scotland.

The club continues to make its contribution to the international dimension of the game. President Burton Morrison has been assistant national team manager with the promising young prospect Alan MacInnes having represented his country. Vice President Duncan Cameron is convenor of the Camanachd Association's development committee and Alan MacMillan, a regular first team player, was the game's first Team Sport Scotland Shinty co-ordinator.

The club began a re-building programme in the late 1980's and early 1990's, leaving it with prospects of a bright future as the century draws to a close. Great benefits are being achieved from a programme of local recruitment and coaching. Twenty youngsters from the Gaelic Medium Unit in a local primary school in Bishopbriggs regularly attend weekly coaching sessions.

GLASGOW UNIVERSITY

Via, Veritas, Vita

Glasgow University Shinty Club was formed in 1901, Aberdeen and Edinburgh Universities already being in existence for some years. The three founders were Angus MacVicar, Murdo Mackenzie and Murdo MacRae, and of these Angus MacVicar became the first captain.

In the 1950's the club fielded two teams but in recent years it has become more difficult to recruit shinty-playing students. The club is in Division II of the Southern League and its playing pitch is at Garscadden in the west of the city. The club colours are gold jerseys and black shorts and socks.

In the late 1950's and early 1960's the club had a most successful period, winning the Southern League in 1959-60 and the Littlejohn Vase in 1959-60, 1960-61 and in 1961-62. Some of these players came together again on the formation of Glasgow Kelvin. The final of the Sutherland Cup was reached for the first time in 1981 and the Skeabost Horn was won on several occasions.

Being a university club, it is run by the players themselves with financial support from the Glasgow University Athletic Club which also provides transport for away matches. Enthusiasm both on and off the field is of course required and this is occasionally recognized by the award of a University Blue which is highly regarded.

RAPE OF THE CAMAN

Our job it seems this season,
Is to support Division Two,
Not as mere spectators,
But the team who always lose!

Right from the throw up,
The ball was in our half,
Many's a home supporter
Did at Glasgow Uni. laugh.

From Tighnabruaich to Oban,
From Strachur to Col Glen,
The minibus wheels kept turning,
As the goals kept being knocked in.

Defeat seemed never ending,
Success was never there,
But us students played on regardless,
Camans everywhere!
'We'll show them', said our captain,

At the start of every game,
Unfortunately, yet we haven't,
But we're going to — that's our aim.

Our results have been improving,
I've even heard it said,
'The poor team that loses to Glasgow Uni.,
Will have faces pretty red.'

Within the team we don't mind,
The torment and defeat
'Cos a better bunch of losers
You're no likely e'er to meet.

Steven MacKenzie (1986 Yearbook)

Among notable characters in more recent times is Jack Asher who was awarded a Blue and is well known as a referee. He was one of the successful side of the 1950's and is now Honorary President. His son Gordon has become one of the stalwarts of the team.

   Much of the credit for keeping the club alive in the 1980's and running it goes to Derry Barton who consistently showed great

Glasgow University
1991

drive and enthusiasm. Fraser Gordon helped to promote university shinty during the same period and his immense contribution was recognized by the award of a Blue.

The efforts of David Bell and Daniel Dunn, from Glenurquhart and Kingussie respectively, did much to enable the team to move up to Division II and to win the Littlejohn Vase on three occasions. Both were awarded Blues.

Glasgow University has made, over the years, an important contribution to the game. New players have been trained and already established players have developed in skill. As they move on from University they help to develop it on the administrative side. Foremost among these are two leading authorities on all that pertains to the game, John W. Campbell, President of the Camanachd Association from 1982 to 1985 and Hugh D. MacLennan, journalist and broadcaster. Both were awarded Blues by the University in their playing days.

GLENGARRY

Old numbers of Inverness newspapers show that a team called Glengarry played Fort Augustus in 1882 and the club was active in the 1930's. After a long break, Alister Mac-Rae and James Patterson in 1976 formed the club again.

There are about thirty players with teams in Divisions II and IV. There are also twenty-four players with an Under-14 team and an Under-17 team.

Home games are played at Craigard, a new park donated by Mr Ellice of Glengarry. There is a pavilion with changing facilities. Games were previously played on a field of the Home Farm. The 1882 game was played at Aberchalder.

A club badge is being designed.

The club played up to the outbreak of war in 1939 and in 1948 amalgamated with Fort Augustus which also had difficulty in raising a team, to form Inveroich, a club which lasted for a few years. It was re-founded as Glengarry in 1976.

In season 1980-81 the Strathdearn Cup final was reached and in 1984-85 the Balliemore Cup final.

In 1987-88 and 1988-89 the Balliemore Cup was won.

In 1988-89 the final of the Qualifying Cup was reached and in the two following seasons the Valerie Fraser Cup final was reached. In 1990-91 Glengarry beat Newtonmore in the Under-14 League Final.

An unusual incident was seen about four years ago at the Canal Park at Kilmallie. After two minutes of play, a Glengarry forward, Jamie Paterson, collided with the goal posts, which collapsed and the game was abandoned.

Of notable persons connected with the club there is James Patterson who was behind the revival in 1976 and did much to foster the game among the local school children. Donald MacPhee was well known as President in the 1930's and Donald and Angus MacAskill were prominent players at that period. The present Chief, Mr Sandy

MacRae, Bank House, and the late W. Macdonald, Hill Cottage, rendered good service in having the present field brought into use. James Clark has been in the North Under-21 team in the past three seasons and has been twice in the Under-21 team in the Shinty/Hurling International, being captain of the 1992 side.

GLENORCHY CAMANACHD

Old letters and poetry show that organised shinty was played in Dalmally in and about 1880. These games were played by teams from each side of the River Orchy for a cup presented by a Mr Macdonald, who had returned from Australia. The contests took place on New Year's Day and continued up to 1932. While the game continued to be played in the district, it was not until 1947 that Glenorchy Camanachd was formed.

There are thirty-two players and two teams are run, one in Division I and another in Division III.

Home games are played at the Mart Park, Dalmally, and there are changing facilities at the Auction Market there. Apart from a pitch at Craig Farm when the Mart pitch was flooded, all home games since 1947 have been played at the Mart Park. The colours are black and white striped jerseys and white shorts.

After a period of some success in the 1950's, a severe shortage of players forced the club to fold in 1960 but it was re-formed in 1966 and has played continuously since then.

As a junior team the Munro Shield was won in 1952 and 1959, the Campbell Cup in 1958, the Bullough Cup in 1973 and the Sutherland Cup in 1990.

As a senior team the South League Championship was won in 1990.

Events which gave satisfaction were the winning of the Munro Shield in 1952, the club's first trophy, the winning of the Bullough Cup in 1973, the first triumph after a period of fifteen years, the winning of the Sutherland Cup and the championship of Division I in 1990.

Glenorchy has always been a small but enthusiastic village team which has had a struggle to remain sound financially. Of notable personalities connected with shinty in Glenorchy, there are Donnie MacDougall who got the club going again in 1966 and Mr and Mrs Kenny Campbell who did so much to encourage and coach boys at school. The team of boys, known as Cruachanside, has had considerable success.

The Door Nail at Stronmilichan
(Musing on the defeat of the Barnaclag
Shinty Club on January 1st, 1884)

Take away that ball and shinty; go and
*   hide them from my sight!*
Rob Ruadh's strong arm alone shall drag
*   me from my dismal room this night.*
Yet the peatreek round enfold me, as I
*   take my brochan here;*
Broken limbs reward the reckless; Ah!
*   that fight has cost me dear.*

Leave me here alone to ponder on that
hour of sore disgrace,
Then our pride was humbled lowly and
our friends we could not face;
Evil day wherein the glory of
Stronmilichan died away,
As the mist's wreaths on Ben Cruachan
vanish with the morning ray.

Alas! I see thro' gloom and darkness,
forms of giants dressed in blue,
And my comrades, fiercely striving
breathless all the ball pursue;
There the Redcaps all are scattered, hair
on end, and flashing eyes;
Fearful of their waning honour, and
MacDonald's worthy prize.

There they rush in wild disorder, eager to
o'er-come their foes,
And with energetic fury, deal at random
aimless blows;
Hark! The sound of Swan's shrill
bagpipes, echoing far thro' hill and
glen,
Screaming music emblematic of the
stormy minds of men;
Wails a chant, fierce yet solemn, not a
merry dancing tune,
Urging them to deeds of valour ere the
day be lost and won.

Rubbish, nonsense! Why these ravings?
Were we less expert than before,
When in days now nigh forgotten, stood
we victors on Dal Mhor?
My shinty bring, my Redcap fetch, my
warriors call to stern revenge,
Let MacVean, their Captain lead them,
like a band of wild Mahenge
McIntyre and fiery Currie, Baldy Ruadh
and Eoghain bean Eoghain,
Let us range them well together to avoid
being overthrown.

Samuel, never look so gloomy, bid your
dark despair adieu;
Quench your thirst in yonder pitcher, and
resume the strife anew.
Knew we how to dribble better, we had
soon reversed the score,
Had we but a little science we could foil
yon Para Mor;
Ah! Hear you not that cheer of triumph,
coming o'er the fields again,
If it comes from Barr-nan-Eiriornach,
then my followers fight in vain.

Had I thy counsel, sage Iain Rob, or thy
specs across my nose,
I might pierce the mystic future and
divine the combat's close;
Charge again, I say, at venture, 'tis not
bruised limbs we fear,
Tho' the odds are strong against us and
the prospects dark and drear;
Hold! My leg begins to stiffen, while the
sweat drops off my brow,
Yet, I must not cease revolving; woe is
me, where am I now?

Will that ghastly vision never leave me,
either day or night?
Must I still be haunted ever by the
shadow of that fight?
Yes, Stronmilichan knows no potion that
will quaff disgrace away,

*Barnaclag has no nepenths for the
    memories of that day.
Flowers may bloom, while zephyrs blow,
    but they soon will fade away,
As the snow-flakes quickly vanish in the
    waters of the Strae.*

*But when once conceit is humbled, what
    shall us revive again?*

*What shall soothe our wounded feelings,
    what shall cool our heated brain,
What is there in wide Glenorchy, that to
    us shall solace bring?
Fruitless yearnings, useless cravings,
    unavailing tho' they be,
Ah! The chances, Oh! The chances, that
    were lost to mine and me.*

GLENURQUHART SHINTY CLUB

At a meeting held at Blairbeg, Drumnadrochit, with Mr A. Douglas Campbell of Kilmartin as chairman, the club was formed as Glen Urquhart-Kilmartin Shinty Club. A match was arranged for New Year, 1885, the Kilmartin Challenge Cup (the oldest Challenge Cup) having been donated by Mr Campbell.

The playing strength of the club is a team in Division I, one in Division III, an Under-21 team, an under 17 team and an Under-14 team.

Home games are played at Blairbeg and there are changing rooms and showers at Blairbeg Public Hall.

The present field was levelled and lengthened after World War II. Before that games were played on available farm fields up and down Glen Urquhart.

The team colours are red and black jerseys and white shorts. The club has a badge worn on the jerseys.

There were sporadic appearances of the team between the famous matches with Strathglass in 1887 and 1888 and the 1920's when the club folded. It was revived in 1948 but folded again in the season 1951-52. There was a further revival in 1956 and the club has continued since then.

The contests with Strathglass in 1887 and 1888 attracted great interest at the time and helped considerably in encouraging the re-awakening of interest in the game.

A successful centenary programme, including a match with Kyles Athletic, was arranged and took place on Saturday, 17th August 1985.

The club's first appearance in a Camanachd Cup Final in 1988 was another memorable day.

One of the best known personalities connected with the club is Danny Fraser, Shewglie Farm, who was behind the revival of the

*(above): Action from Glenurquhart's most famous
day — the Camanachd Cup Final 1988.
(below left): Ali MacKintosh, Man of the Match, 1988
Camanachd Cup Final
(below right): Jamie Bell, North Player of the Year,
1991-92.*

club in 1948. A former player and president, he is now Chieftain. His wife, Dolly, has supported all aspects of club activities. Geordie Stewart, as player and coach, has given thirty-five years' service and is still active. Mr Alan Bell has been chairman for twenty-one years. Dr Peter English, a former player, has done immense work for the game and has written much in various num-bers of the Shinty Year Book. He is the author of a splendid history of the club.

To Glenurquhart (1984 season)

*Shinty is the game
Glen Urquhart is the name!
In a hundred years of the Shinty game,
Glen Urquhart's men have come to fame,*

*We've fought and hacked in rain and
mud,
And have been known to spill some blood.
Our team's won honour in the Glen.
By that stalwart side of Highland men.
And aye to help us, to the top,*

*Three chiefs come swinging from the 'Fort'.
Calvin, Graham and Stuart.*

Calvin Oliver

INVERARAY

The club was formed at a public meeting on January 12th, 1877 in the Argyll Arms Hotel with the first match taking place less than a month later. This was lost 4-1 to Vale of Leven at Govan and then in July 1878 it is recorded that Inveraray defeated Glasgow-Inveraray by five goals to nil.

The club currently fields two teams in Divisions One and Three of the Marine Harvest league in the south, numbering around forty players. There are also players at juvenile level and a mixed under-13 side.

The club's home ground is the Winterton Park, which is used by kind permission of His Grace the Duke of Argyll. Permission to play here was given in 1878.

The club played from its formation in 1877 until 1935-36 when it was banned from competition for eight years.

After World War II, the club joined with Furnace to become Loch Fyne-side. In 1957, Inveraray then re-formed and continued until 1972. The club was then wound up in 1979, but re-formed again three years later.

Up to 1879, the club took the field in blue knickerbockers and white jerseys, but the club colours are yellow and black. This is one of the club's nick-names, also being known as the Royal Burgh side and Aray Boys.

Inveraray — 1905

The Yellow and Black

Upon the banks of sweet Loch Fyne, a
little town doth stand—
Old Inveraray, famed afar for scenery so
grand;
Her daughters blithe and bonnie; while,
renowned for shinty play,
Her sons, who oft both met the foe and
bore the palm away.

Chorus:
Then hip, hurrah! for the Yellow and
Black,
For these are the colours gay,
Worn by the Inveraray boys
When they at shinty play;
And play they can, as they have proved
In many a well-fought fray;
Then give the boys three hearty cheers—
Hurrah! Hurrah! Hurrah!

In times of old the hardy "Slochs" well
knew the shinty game,
And in our days their gallant sons
uphold the ancient fame;
For never on the Winterton have they met
with defeat
Though matched against opponents who
were skilful, bold and fleet.

Ardkinglass sent a chosen team of stout
and stalwart men,
Who round the old grey stone soon found
they little chance had then
And tho' in later days the Rangers strove
with might and main
To vanquish Inveraray, yet their efforts
were in vain.

As firm as their own native rocks the
Furnace lads oft came,
Though manfully they played their part,
'twas aye a losing game;

And scarcely need I now repeat that
well-remembered tale,
Low on the Winterton were lowered the
colours of the Vale.

Lochgoilhead saw the struggle of the
Glasgow Camanachd Club,
And how the Inveraray boys so soundly
did them drub;
While Oban too, has witnessed her
defenders brave borne back,
And their fortress stormed by the bold
assault of the lads in Yellow and
Black.

The capital of Lorn beheld the heroes of
Glencoe—
A hardy band, victorious oft — upon her
fields laid low:
Undaunted to the last they fought like
lions grim at bay,
But Black and Yellow, as of yore,
resistless proved that day.

The Black and Yellow costumed lads have
met by Etive's tide
Dunollie's choicest hearts allied with
Cena's choicest pride;
All bootless was the well-laid scheme
their forces to combine,
For routed were they by the lads who
hailed from sweet Loch Fyne.

To the North the Yellow and Black stripes
have sped their way
And met the pride of Badenoch beside the
rolling Spey
Before the heroes of Argyll the Northern
Champions fell
For victory crowned the Western flag
upon Kingussie's Dell.

Despite its broken history, the club has experienced considerable success on the field of play.

The club have also featured in some of the most famous administrative wrangles involving the Camanachd Association, notably in 1903 when the Camanachd Cup was awarded to Kingussie as Inveraray had refused to travel to contest the replay of the final at Inverness, the first meeting at Perth having resulted in a draw.

The Sutherland Cup victory of 1969 was one of the most important modern victories in the club's fine history and the London Shield victory has shown that the youth policy being adopted is bearing fruit.

One of the most famous characters in the club's history is Donald Ban MacIntyre who featured in the 1930 team which won the Camanachd Cup and is the only shinty player to have won the famous Powderhall Sprint. Another is Hamish ''Skinner'' Stewart, a past chairman and member of both the Camanachd Association's Executive and Disciplinary Committee from 1966 to 1975.

Alex Blyth, one of the club's great modern players was captain of the Scottish international side which played against Ireland in the 1970's.

The current club was formed by Duncan MacKay and Alex ''Soda'' Campbell and the present chairman is Donald Clark of the George Hotel which is also one of the club's main sponsors, the others being Semple of Inveraray and Loch Fyne Oysters.

INVERNESS SHINTY CLUB

This club was founded in 1887, its title being Inverness Town and County Shinty Club to distinguish it from others formed in Inverness in that year. (These, the Highland Railway Locomotive Workshops Club and the Wanderers did not continue beyond 1890. A club called Clachnacuddin appeared briefly in 1901, competing in the Camanachd Cup.)

Inverness fielded two teams in 1991-92 in Divisions II and IV of the North League. Its colours are red jerseys and white shorts. From 1934 home games have been played in the Bught Park, the scene of many cup finals, where there are splendid facilities and a fine grandstand. Up to 1914 play took place at Millburn, Culcabock, Diriebught, Haugh (now Bellfield) Park and the Victoria Park. After 1919 a field at Lower Kessock Street was used and from 1923 to 1934 play was held in a field at the Bught, provided by Mr William MacBean, near the present fine pitch.

Camanachd Cup winners — the 1951 team

The club seems to have been dormant for about two years but was revived in 1893 and has continued without merging with any other.

Throughout its life many of the players were men from various Highland districts who had come to work in Inverness and the record of success in competitions has been modest. In 1921, to encourage the game in the district, the club organised a schools' shinty league in the town and vicinity and provided badges for the winning teams. The headmaster of Culcabock School and a former team player, J.D.M. Black, was prominent in this activity. Three members, Charles Mackintosh, Ewen MacQueen and W. Ellis Stuart, were behind the formation of the Schools Camanachd Association in 1937.

The season 1937-38 saw the team reach the final of the Camanachd Cup and 1951-52 was the most memorable as the Camanachd Cup was won.

Some of the leading personalities in shinty have been associated with the Inverness Club. In its early years John MacAskill was an energetic worker and was secretary of the Strathdearn Association from its inception in 1911. John Macpherson of the Sporting Stores had long been a player and office bearer and from 1896 annually presented a silver-mounted caman to the captain of the team winning the Camanachd Cup. Thomas J. Macpherson as player and office bearer for over fifty years was also involved in shinty administration generally. His brother Willie similarly served for many years. John W. MacKillop, who was a past president of the Camanachd Association, helped to revive the club after World War II and succeeded in getting the revenue authorities to recognize shinty as a national game exempt from entertainment tax. William MacKenzie was the only player to play in both Camanachd Cup Finals and Dennis Swanson has had a life-long connection with the club and with the Bught. Sandy Cumming, Tom MacKenzie and John W. Campbell rendered fine service and in recent years Mrs Liz MacInnes, Louis Stewart, Bill Kennedy, George Campbell, Malcolm Fraser and Murdo Maclean displayed much enthusiasm in various ways.

(left): fund-raising

KILMALLIE SHINTY CLUB

Kilmallie Shinty Club was formed in 1929 with the following as office bearers — Chairman, James Weir; Secretary, James A. Macintyre; Committee Members, Alistair Mackintosh and Hugh MacNaughton.

At present first and second teams are fielded along with Under-17 and Under-14 teams. There are school teams at Banavie and Caol.

Home games are played at Canal Park where there are changing rooms. From 1929 to 1970 games were played at Annat Park and then at Blackparks. The club colours are royal blue shirts with white shorts. The club has never folded or merged and there is no badge.

The securing of the Camanachd Cup in 1964 by beating Inveraray at Fort William was the most noteworthy event in the club's history. Another successful year was 1948 when both Sutherland and Strathdearn Cups were won.

The club owes a great deal to Mr James Weir of Annat Farm who did so much for it in the early days by providing a field and encouraging young players. The arrival of

(above): Kilmallie : Camanachd Cup Winners 1964 (rear): J.MacIsaac, Ian Sweeney, Charlie Fraser, Dougie McLachlan, Alastair MacIntyre, Hugh MacIntyre, Derek Fraser (front): Ronald Ferguson, Ian McIntosh, James Burnet (capt), Willie Brown, John Murphy

(above, right): The legendary Kilmallie 'Stonewall Defence' — (left) J. McIsaac and brothers Charlie and Derek Fraser

(right): Kilmallie : MacGillivray Senior League Champions, 1959

Mr. Walter Cameron as headmaster at Corpach also helped to maintain interest among boys in the district and the success of the juvenile team in the 1950's showed that his encouragement and training was of value in providing a succession of young players to fill vacancies in the senior team. Dick Cameron was another who helped greatly over the years. An article by 'Hail Judge' in the *Northern Chronicle* in 1948 touches on the fine sporting spirit of the club.

KILMORY CAMANACHD (SENIOR) FURNACE (JUNIOR)

The present Kilmory Club was formed in 1977, the players being school-leavers and some more-experienced players who had come to live in the Lochgilphead district.

After some years the playing strength was sufficient to form a second team which, in view of the number of players, officials and supporters from Furnace, was called Furnace, thereby reviving a famous name in shinty.

At present there is a senior team in Division I and a junior in Division IV. There are also Under-14 and Under-17 teams. There are fifty players, twenty-five adults and twenty-five schoolboys.

The club has the use of a field at Poltalloch but without facilities. Kilmory originally played at Lochgilphead before moving to Kilmartin and then to Poltalloch.

The Kilmory colours are maroon jerseys and black shorts. There is no club badge. The first team, Kilmory, flourished in the 1930's, inspired by Mr A. Greenshields from Tighnabruaich. It was re-formed after World War II as Kilmory United and from 1947 to 1955 played in the Southern League.

Kilmory played in Division III in 1977-78 and in Division II in 1978-79 when they topped it. After the season 1979-80 they were relegated and since then have been up and down between Divisions I and II.

The record of the original Furnace team is — 1900 Camanachd Cup finalists 1906; Celtic Cup won 1908; Camanachd Cup final-

Marine Harvest League Division Two (South) Champions, 1991-92

ists; Celtic Cup won 1909 and 1910; Camanachd Cup finalists 1912 and 1914; Celtic Cup won 1923; Camanachd and Dunn Cups won 1926; Sutherland Cup won 1958; Celtic Cup won 1959; MacAulay Cup won.

After World War II Furnace and Inveraray combined as Lochfyneside and won the Celtic Cup in 1949 and 1953 and reached the final of the Camanachd Cup in 1947 and 1950.

The 1923 winning of the Camanachd Cup was remarkable as Furnace did not concede a goal to any team, this feat earned them a place in the Guinness Book of Records. Of that team only Duncan MacColl survives. He lives in Furnace and retains a lively interest in shinty.

KINCRAIG

Newspaper reports show that a shinty club was formed at Kincraig in the parish of Alvie early in 1920. A club known as Alvie had been formed in 1891 and in the same year one at Insh came into being. These clubs had combined as Alvie and Insh by 1900 and by 1906 there was another club, or perhaps the same one, in the district known as Invereshie.

Alvie

In 1891 Mr F. MacBain was chairman of Alvie and Mr C.J.B. Macpherson of Balavil was president.

Balnespick and Invereshie are mentioned as places where the Insh Club held play in January 1893. Players mentioned were Malcolm Smith, Drumguish and Sam Macdonald, Village of Insh. A game described as ''a fine exhibition of play'' took place in the same year, the opposing team being Kingussie which by that time had a reputation for skilful play. The Alvie captain was Kenneth Grant, Dunachton and Duncan MacBain, Inspector of Poor; Alvie acted as referee. At a dinner of the Alvie Club about this time Duncan MacBain was described as Honorary Captain and Donald Macpherson, Speybank, as captain.

In the following year Alvie and Insh met at Invereshie, J. Tolmie being captain of Insh. In 1896 Alvie is found as one of the teams competing in the first year of Camanachd Cup Competition and the district was represented in that competition by Invereshie for some years after 1907.

The club at present has thirty playing members and two teams are fielded, in the Divisions II and IV. Since 1972 the pitch used has been at Invereshie; previously play was held on the old golf course and at Drumguish. Another field which had been used was where the council houses (Suidhe Crescent) now stand.

Little seems to be known of the club's record and it went into abeyance about 1955. It was re-formed in 1972 and has had occasional success. In 1976-77 the team was involved in the play-off, against Skye, for the championship of Division III. The Division IV championship was won in March, 1985 and the final of the Strathdearn Cup was reached in June of the same year.

During the Second World War the club sent camans to a Prisoner of War camp in Germany and among those who made use of them was Lachlan Macpherson (Lachie Ruadh).

KINGUSSIE

Kingussie are one of the game's premier clubs and have been the most influential and successful of recent years. Unfortunately there are no records of their early period, but they rank amongst the most illustrious names in the game.

The Kingussie Club played a crucial role in the development of the Camanachd Association which was formed in the village in 1893. They also have a unique link with the Camanachd Cup as the figure at the top of the trophy was modelled on J.C. Dallas, vice-captain of the first team to win the trophy in the first Final which was played at The Longman, Inverness in 1896.

Ally Dallas, a great grandson of John C. Dallas, is himself a Camanachd Cup-winning captain of the club, maintaining a unique link with the past. He features in Ewen Weatherspoon's evocative montage of pictures (see first colour plate).

Another important link between the club and the Association was the role played by John Campbell, the first Secretary of the Association, of whom much has been written in the early years following its formation. A special medal was presented to Mr Camp-

bell by the club for his contribution accompanied by a beautiful scroll to mark the occasion (see colour plate).

One of the most colourful characters to have featured in the early history of shinty as an organised sport was the Count de Serra Largo of Tarlogie, a great benefactor to the club. Interestingly, his appellation of Tarlogie, is co-incidental with the name of the spring from which the Glenmorangie Distillery Company take their water in their whisky-making process.

Kingussie, Grand Slam winners, 1987

The club in its modern guise has emulated the early success of the first winners of the Camanachd Cup in 1896 and has proceeded to create an astonishing list of records. There are four teams currently fielded at Under-14, juvenile, junior and senior levels.

All the major trophies have been won with regularity, but it is in the last twenty years that Kingussie have emerged as the dominant force, challenging the incomparable record laid down by their near neighbours and great rivals Newtonmore.

The clubs interestingly first met in the Camanachd Cup Final in 1984, although there have been many great clashes before then and, indeed later. The club's achievements are too great in the modern era alone to detail here, but a number are worthy of passing reference. An astonishing run of sixty-three matches undefeated was achieved by the senior squad which finally succumbed to Kyles in the Final of the MacAulay Cup in 1989.

A further run of one hundred unbeaten matches was achieved by the junior squad, being completed in the 1992-93 season. The club has as a result made a number of trophies virtually its own in recent years. Kingussie have dominated the national league competition since its inception in 1982, with eight wins; the Sutherland Cup has been won in each year since 1989.

Kingussie have used The Dell as their home field for many years and it has been re-furbished in this centenary year. Dunbarry was used while this work was being undertaken and a field at Kerrow has also been used in the past. An interesting name to appear in the club's past was the "Snowdrops" team which took part, along with others such as Kingussie Hearts, in local competitions.

The list of famous names which could be produced in connection with the club is virtually endless and they can count some of the greatest-ever players as members: John Dallas, K. Falconer, A. Borthwick, Andy Anderson and his son David, Ian Ross, Jimmy Murchie, Kevin Thain, Rab Muir, Donnie Grant; there are far too many to detail here and none should take offence at not having been included.

The Kingussie club's contribution to the history of the game is unique and they have upheld the best traditions of the game throughout their period of unprecedented success in modern years when they have swept the boards.

A full history of the club's great achievements is yet to be written.

KINLOCHSHIEL SHINTY CLUB

The club was formed by Duncan MacDonald, Bobby Gordon and Archie Cameron in 1958 in Duncan's house at Auchtertyre, Kyle, Wester Ross. The club is an amalgamation of the Kintail, Lochalsh and Glenshiel clubs.

There are thirty players and two teams are fielded in Divisions II and IV.

Home games are played on Kirkton shinty pitch leased from the National Trust for Scotland and the old byre, courtesy of K. Macleod, Nostie, is used as changing accommodation. The club has played every season since its formation and has never merged with another. The colours are blue jerseys and white shorts and there is a club badge.

The securing of the Sutherland Cup at Fort William in 1962 was a great event in the early years.

Grant Michael, who has played in several shinty/hurling internationals, is highly regarded as a player and as a very popular figure in the team.

John MacRae, (Johnnie 'Ach'), who has played in the team for 20 years, was the North Player of the Year in 1990-91, and Keith Loades also won the award.

(above): Glenshiel, Conchra Cup Winners, 1927
(right): Glenshiel Shinty team

(above): Grant Michael (left) and Michael MacLean with the Harrow Cup 1964

(above right): Strathdearn Cup Winners, 1975

Kinlochshiel
Shinty Club

KINTYRE CAMANACHD

Kintyre is one of the newest clubs in the Camanachd Association, having been formed in 1985. But there was shinty in Kintyre long before then and the re-emergence of the club after an absence of more than a hundred years was a matter of some pride to the local committee.

Donald Woodrow, one of the prime movers behind the re-establishing of the game, is the current club President. The current playing strength is almost twenty with an Under-14 team and primary school players aiming to join the older players in the club colours.

The club currently play on a pitch owned by Argyll and Bute District Council but are planning a move to their own pitch where they hope to have changing facilities. When the club first began, they relied on the help of local farmers who provided a field, but it has always retained its independence, with

The 1992 Division Four Champions with Club President Donald Woodrow (far left) and Douglas MacKintosh, Past President of the Camanachd Association, (far right)

several promising players emerging from the younger ranks.

It has not taken the club long to establish itself and in 1992 they won the Division IV Championship of the Marine Harvest League in the south. The championship was won with the last match of the season against Edinburgh University.

Kintyre also won the Munro Shield in 1992, defeating Furnace 5-4 after extra time.

The acquisition of a mini-bus has eased the club's travelling difficulties and an improved coaching scheme with more coaches in local schools has ensured that Kintyre will have a steady stream of young accomplished players for the future.

The club's main sponsors, Springbank Distillery, have helped considerably with the development of the club since its formation.

KYLES ATHLETIC

Few shinty clubs have a record to match that of the Kyles Athletic Football and Shinty Club which was formed in 1896, the same year as the first competition for the Camanachd Cup.

The club was formed mainly by two of the most famous families in the district, the Nicolsons and Jamiesons. There are two teams representing the club at senior and junior level and matches are played at the playing fields Tighnabruaich and Kilbride.

Kyles have never merged or folded as a club and play in a Royal Blue strip with white shorts. The first set of jerseys was presented by the Glasgow Rangers Football Club in 1900.

(above): Kyles have played in many of the great Camanachd Finals, including this one in season 1921-22, as Argyllshire teams dominated the game

(right): Kyles Athletic, Scottish Champions, 1983

In the club's first few years of existence, they played football and shinty on alternate Saturdays. They have played a crucial role in the game's competitions over the years and have won the Camanachd Cup on no less that nineteen occasions.

The Celtic Society Cup has been won on twenty-six occasions; the Dunn League twenty-four times; the MacAulay Cup nine times and the Sutherland championship on eight occasions.

One of their most notable victories was when the club won their first trophy, the Buteman Cup in 1901 and this was followed in 1901 by their first victory in the Celtic Society Cup.

One prominent name (amongst many) connected with the club in its early history was Neil Nicolson, the first President; another Nicolson, T.R., was captain in 1901 and later became British record-holder for throwing the hammer. There were also great players such as Ernest Smith, D.

Guthrie, D. MacPhail, D. Munro, Tommy MacArthur, A. & M. Sinclair and John S. Ferguson.

Others who contributed much to the reputation of the club were 'Dudie' Weir, Donald MacRae, a Vice-Chief of the Association, Willie MacKenzie, Donald Kent, John Kennedy, Robbie Mackintosh, John MacVicar, Archie Carmichael, and Archie Currie. Celly Paterson, who played before and after World War II, was also a great player who went on to become Chief of the Association.

In 1900 Kyles took over The Moss as their home ground and The Buteman referred to it as having " a surface like a billiard table, in tremendous order for a rousing game."

Kerr 'Barney' Crawford is another great player of his day who went on to become President of the club which has built up a unique relationship with the Newtonmore club, following many epic encounters when they strove to gain supremacy in the game.

The Macraes of Balliemore and Eilean Donan have been chieftains of Kyles over a long period and John Mackellar of Tighnabruaich was a legend also, being famous for his unique shinty balls. He was an official supplier of balls to the Camanachd Association.

Then good health to Kyles Athletic with a toast to every man,
Let us often think of the half-time drink frae the meal and water can,
That's our heritage that's been handed down from those mighty men of yore,
A respected name in our grand old game are the boys frae the Kerry shore.

LOCHABER CAMANACHD

The club was re-formed as Lochaber Camanachd in the season 1958-59 following a previous amalgamation in 1946 and subsequent split from 1949 to 1958 of the Brae Lochaber and Spean Bridge clubs. The club runs a team in Division II and in Division IV. There is also an Under-21 team.

Games are played on a field at Spean Bridge leased from a local landowner. The club was the first in the north to have its own changing rooms. Before playing on the present field in 1955 games were played at Blarour and Roy Bridge. The club colours are red and white hoops with white shorts.

(above left): Spean Bridge, MacTavish Cup Winners, 1933

(above right): Lochaber, Sir William Sutherland Cup Winners, 1965

(left): Highland Queen Indoor Six-a-side Champions, 1986

There is no club badge. The club was formed from Brae Lochaber (founded about 1887) which played at Roy Bridge and Spean Bridge (founded about 1894).

There was always great rivalry between Brae Lochaber and Spean Bridge both of which were prominent clubs in the early days. They were often drawn against each other in competitions and there was one occasion when, in the Camanachd Cup, the tie was drawn three times and had to be settled by a game which was played to a finish. It was won by Spean Bridge.

Two of the most notable personalities in the history of the game were connected with Lochaber. John Macdonald of Keppoch was captain of Brae Lochaber and was one of the principal men behind the formation of the Camanachd Association of which he was president from 1898 to 1914. His younger brother, Major A.W. Macdonald, D.S.O., of Blarour, held the same office from 1933 to 1939. They were grandsons of the famous 'Long John' Macdonald the distiller.

Three Lochaber men have acted as referee at Camanachd Cup finals — Angus Mackintosh in 1926, Donald Kennedy in 1949 and W. MacLachlan in 1985.

The Opening

It was a cold and wintry day
The ground was mantled white,
We made our way to Spean Bridge
To support the red and white.
We listened unto David,
The Reverences far and wide,
John Willie he was there himself

The box was by his side.
Oh Mrs Cameron she was there
A lady fine and grand,
She took a pair of scissors
And she cut the vital strand.
It opened up the complex
And things they were just right,
It was an honour to the boys
Who wear the red and white.

We then went up unto Roy Bridge
In Johnny's we took our stand,
We listened unto speeches there
From old players in the land,
There was MacIntyre and Batchen
And Tom from Inverness,
But most of all we can't forget
Mackenzie done his best.

Oh Duffie he was there himself
He was the best of crack,
He once played for Kilmallie
His position was at back.
Big Donald he was on the box
And made the people squeal,
He played a foxtrot and a waltz
And they danced a Highland reel.

There was hooching, there was dancing
The like was never seen,
And each and all the bodies there
Had a dram o' Highland Queen.
Now here my folks — the rally's o'er
And we are going home,
And each and all will thank compere
Our bearded Highland John.

by Archie MacPhee, on the opening of the Club's new changing room facilities at Spean Bridge.

(above left): Sir Stewart MacPherson presenting the Sir William Sutherland Cup to John MacLennan (butcher), the Lochcarron captain at Newtonmore, April 1939. Looking on (left) Dr Charles D Ferguson

(above right): Lochcarron, Dewar Shield winners 1970, complete with mascot

(right): Dr Charles G. MacKay — first president of Lochcarron

LOCHCARRON

In 1883 the club was founded and the in the same year another in the district, The Union, appeared but lasted only to 1884. The first game played by Lochcarron outside its own district was against Beauly in 1884. Before the founding of the club, and for many years after, an annual New Year Day game was played at the Battery Park between Janetown and Slumbay.

The club has one team which plays in Division II of the Northern League in season 1992-93.

The club colours are blue jerseys and white shorts. Home games are played at the Battery Park where there are first class changing rooms, etc.

In its early days the club played at Tullich and at New Kelso. While improvements were being carried out at the Battery Park in and after season 1980-81 games were played at Attadale.

The club has never folded although there were few games in the early years and there were some years in the 1920's when a team could not be raised. It was never amalgamated with another.

A notable event was the win over Caberfeidh in a Jubilee Day game at Tullich in

May, 1935. Caberfeidh at that time had a great reputation having won many honours. The years 1937 and 1939 were very successful in which several trophies were won and in its Centenary Year, 1983, which was fittingly celebrated with a dinner and a game with Beauly, the Strathdearn Cup once again returned to Lochcarron. A history of the club was also published.

Of outstanding personalities one of the earliest was William Lockhart Bogle, the founder, whose mother was the daughter of Rev. John MacRae, minister of Glenshiel and Glenelg. The first President was Dr Charles G. Mackay of the district and the first secretary was Mr Donald Beaton. Captain Archibald MacRae Chisholm, the founder of the Strathglass Club in 1880, was also associated with Lochcarron shinty. At a time when the club's fortunes were at a low ebb, in 1932, Dr Charles D. Ferguson came to the district and was the driving force behind its recovery and eventual success. Among those who rendered good service were Mr D. Maclennan who retired in 1922 after serving as secretary, Donnie MacKenzie ('Donnie Keeper') and Alex MacKenzie ('Jeck') who at the Centenary Celebrations in 1983 was the oldest living former player.

LONDON CAMANACHD

The club was formed in 1894, being an amalgamation of London Northern Counties and London Scots. After a long period in abeyance it was re-formed in 1982 by Hugh O'Kane and Sean Reid.

One team is fielded. The membership is very transient, being drawn from all over England and unattached players from Scotland. It is difficult to get twelve players together at one place and at one time. A 'feeder' school at Chipping Campden, Gloucestershire, where some pupils play shinty, provides some recruits. Of late the club has been restricted to play for the Camanachd Cup and Skeabost Horn and some six-a-side competitions in Scotland.

Official Association matches must be played in Scotland. Matches are played at the Bannister Sports Centre, Harrow or at Wormwood Scrubs, both hurling pitches. Between 1982 and 1989 play was held at Northolt. In earlier times play was held at Wimbledon Common, Parliament Hill, Kodak Grounds (Harrow) and probably elsewhere. Between 1873 and 1915 regular play was held on Good Friday and Boxing Day at Wimbledon. Of all the London clubs only London Camanachd continued until the 1920's and 1930's.

The only trophy won was the Skeabost Horn in 1985. Semi finals of both the Balliemore and Bullough Cups were reached in 1984-85. Nine matches were played that year, more than in any other, and the Shinty

Year Book Trophy was awarded for endeavour.

The club entered for the Camanachd Cup in 1896 and scratched to Glasgow Cowal as they could not afford the trip to London. As in its early years the club had the same difficulties in raising a team and finding money to travel to Scotland, local competitions were organized for such as Mr Macleod's Cup 1882, Inverness Association Cup (a silver-mounted ram's head) 1901, The Dewar Shield 1908, Young Cup 1913, London Challenge Cup donated by the chief, Mr R.T.S. Macpherson, in 1986. The club won this trophy for four years until 1990 when Fr. Murphy's G.A.A. won it. In 1991, Brian Boru, having entered every year, won it. The club's furthest advance in the Camanachd Cup was in 1984 when it lost to Skye in the quarter final. In 1989 the club donated the London Shield for the national juvenile play-off. Kilmory, Glasgow Highland and Scottish university teams have made the long trip to win the London Cup.

LOVAT SHINTY CLUB

Lovat shinty club, which celebrated its centenary in 1988, was formed as Kiltarlity. There are now senior and junior teams, as well as players at Under-17 and Under-14 levels.

Home games are played at Balgate where the club have built committee rooms and changing facilities. In the early years, matches were played at Culmiln, Bruiach and the Glebe, as well as at Beaufort Castle.

The club has never folded, but there was an amalgamation in 1912-13 with Beauly and a team entered and won the Camanachd Cup as Beauly.

The 'Beauly' amalgamation side with the Camanachd Cup.

Lovat/Beauly amalgamated team which won the Camanachd Cup under the name of "Beauly" in 1913

Lord Lovat presenting the Lovat Cup to Jimmy Gallagher after one of the New Year matches against Beauly in the 1980's.

The club plays in white stripes with black shorts. They also have a rallying song:

Amongst all those teams that Camanachd play,
It is Lovat from Beaufort who lead the way.
In the colours of white and black which they wear
There is no-one who with them that can compare.
chorus:
Then here's a health to the lads of the Aird,
Long to the field may their youth be spared.
To uphold forever the Camanachd game
And honour the homes which nurtured them.

All their rival teams from the past well know,
That they give of their best from the first up-throw,
But whether they win, or whether they lose,
It's the sporting game they always choose.

It's the joy of their youth to the old they bring,
As they speed on the ball, from wing to wing.
And the young boys dream of the coming day
When in Lovat's white and black they will play.

So it's ever to Lovat I'll be true
And I'll not look for colours of a different hue,
But shall proudly remember the players now gone,
And hold fast to traditions which they handed on.

Tune: Suaicheantas na h-Alba. The Thistle of Scotland.

The Lovat club reached the Final of the Camanachd Cup in 1925, but will always be remembered for their achievements in 1953 when they won all the available trophies at senior level including the Celtic Society Cup of that season.

Amongst the founders of the club were Malcolm Fraser, Revachkin, John Macrae, Fascaple, and Angus Maclean, Glaicbea, descendants of whom played and still play. Finlay MacRae, Eilean Aigas, whose sons were all players and later administrators, was a stalwart of his time and many stories are told about him.

A great player lost in World War 1 was Donnie MacDonald, Balgate and in the 1920's and 1930's there were the Rennie brothers, the Ramsay brothers, the Campbells, the Macrae brothers and the Kennedy brothers.

Tommy Fraser, The Glebe, was a magnificent goalkeeper in the 1940's and 1950's and he played alongside many great players including the Mackenzie brothers and Willie Cowie.

Among the office-bearers who have served the club with distinction are Bert Cameron, secretary in the 1950's, Jock Fraser (Jock 'Meechal'), treasurer, who was succeeded in that office by Mary Ann Henton and Colin Macrae who succeeded his brother Ashie as President in 1953. Colin's son Ally has been one of the most loyal servants of the club in recent years and one of the best players of his day in a number of positions, particularly as goalkeeper. Jackie Henton has also served the club in this position with distinction.

MULL

There is evidence that there was a Tobermory Shinty Club in 1877 and that there was a revival of the game in the district in 1921. The Mull team took part in the Dunn Cup competition in 1922-23.

The current club was formed in 1990 by Len MacRae, Jim MacLeod and Stuart Jackson when a memorial match for the former Kilmallie player Angus MacIntyre was played in Lochaline against a Kilmallie select which

Mull Camanachd

resulted in 5-0 win for Kilmallie with the island supplying the bulk of the team.

The club fields one team which played for the first time in Division IV of the south league in 1991-92.

Home games are played at Garmony Sports Field which is situated about three miles from both ferry terminals at Craignure and Fishnish. Changing facilities are due to be ready before the end of season 1992-1993. When work was being carried out at

Garmony, three home games were played at Glen Forsa fields near the air strip.

The club plays in white jerseys with black shorts.

Being a relatively new club, there have been no successes in terms of silverware, but the players have been delighted with their progress, winning four of their matches in Division IV during season 1992-93, drawing two others.

NEWTONMORE

Newtonmore, the record holders of the Camanachd Association Challenge Trophy with twenty-eight wins, are arguably the most famous name in shinty.

There are records of shinty having been played at Eilean Bheannchair since 1877,

but local legend has it that St Bridget's Mission Church teachers played on the Eilan. There are records, however, of the re-constitution of the club in 1895.

The club currently operates with a pool of around sixteen regular seniors; twenty

(above left): Highland Queen Trophy winners, Aviemore, 1988

(right): Peter Cullen of Glenmorangie presents club captain Jeffrey Kirk with the 1991 trophy

children at primary school level; another sixteen at Under-14 level and eighteen Under-17 players.

Newtonmore have always played at the Eilan, which they now own (they are thought to be the only club to own their own pitch) and modern changing facilities have been completed to mark the club's centenary which is being celebrated in 1993.

The club did not enter the Camanachd Cup competition for a few years at the turn of the century and then won it for the first time in 1907. They have never folded, although for a short period (described as "unfortunate" at best by some in the Newtonmore area), there was an amalgamation with Kingussie towards the end of the second decade. The team played as Kingussie initially, but then changed to Newtonmore and went on to win the Camanachd Cup in 1928-29 at Spean Bridge.

The club's badge was registered with the Lord Lyon, King of Arms just after the second World War and fourteen were presented to players by Captain J.C. Cattanach for sewing on to jerseys.

Newtonmore have a record second to none in terms of winning competitions. As well as their achievements in the Camanachd Cup, they have won the MacTavish Cup an unprecedented thirty times (including, remarkably, every year from 1970-80).

The club has always been at the centre of shinty, involved in some of its greatest contests and most controversial moments, notably the 1911 Camanachd Cup Final when Newtonmore's victory on the field of play was controversially set aside.

The club has enjoyed a great rivalry with the great Kyles Athletic and has built up a very special relationship with that club. The most intense rivalry is, however, still between Newtonmore and their nearest neighbours Kingussie.

The Newtonmore Roll of Honour would be long enough to fill this centenary volume and includes many of the most illustrious names in the game. They are too many to mention individually here, but a few are worthy of special acclaim: Jock Paul MacIntosh, Doddie Sellar, Dr John Cattanach (killed in action in World War I), Angie MacDonald, Dave 'Tarzan' Ritchie and Hugh Chisholm (who hold the record of twelve Camanachd Cup winners' medals), Johnnie Campbell, 'Honi' Ruadh Kennedy, John Fraser, his brother George and their father Gabriel, and John Mackenzie, the current club Chieftain.

A fuller reference to the many illustrious servants of this most famous club is being made in the club's own history, being produced to mark its centenary in 1993.

The Boys of the Eilan

(A song about Newtonmore's 1929 victory in the Camanachd Cup at Spean Bridge when they defeated Kyles Athletic 5-3)

Chorus:
Sing a song about camans and
 camanachd play,
And come let us all shout
 Hip-Hip-Hip-Hooray,
April the sixth was a glorious day,
For the brave Shinty boys of the Eilan.

On April the sixth, 1929,
A beautiful day, the weather was fine,
Three thousand spectators, stood round
 the line,

(above): Scottish Champions, season 1984-85

(above right): Newtonmore, 1985

(right): Newtonmore's next generation of stars, the MacTavish Juvenile Cup winning team of 1991

At Spean to witness the Final.

The goalman and backs and centres
    fought well,
And swift dashing forwards in play did
    excel,
Great was the cheer that rang through
    the Dell,
When they won back the Cup from the
    Kyles men.

In the annals of Shinty their name shall
    remain,
Right bravely they fought on the Lochaber
    plain,
And brought back the Cup to their own
    native vale,
Neath the shade of Craigdhu to the Eilan.

The gallant MacDonalds played bonnie
    and pure,

Budge and MacPhersons were steady and
    sure,
The Rosses and Cattanachs fought hard
    to secure,
The honour again for the Eilan.

Jim Guthrie in goal we will never forget,
For cool and successful he guarded the
    net,
Each dangerous onslaught with courage
    he met,
Defending the name of the Eilan.

Come now and give three cheers for the
    grand Committee,
And Hip-Hip-Hooray for the Dame
    Coig-na-Shee,
Also the trainer, I'm sure you'll agree,
They all did their best for the Eilan.

One other name we esteem and regard,

Our great Highland sportsman, the
*   Balavil Laird,*
Since the days of his youth we have
*   known him to be,*
A true friend of the boys of the Eilan.

I will mention another, you know his
*   address,*
John MacPherson, the Sports, Inverness,
Beautiful camans he gave to express,
His love for the game and the Eilan.

Another MacPherson who is worthy of
*   praise,*
Loyal to Shinty he has been all his days,
With his Pibroch, songs, reels and
*   Strathspeys,*
You can hear his sweet lilt on the Eilan.

Captain J.D. MacPherson of Keppoch near
*   Roy,*
True to the village a Newtonmore boy,
There is naught in the World that gives
*   him more joy,*
Than helping the lads of the Eilan.

From a field so historic and famous of
*   old,*

Your grandsires, remember, were warriors
*   bold,*
Play up descendants, bred from that fold,
Ye sons of Banchor Eilan.

It's an old Highland pastime, may the
*   game never die,*
From the far London Scot, to the Island
*   of Skye,*
From the Braes of Lochaber, to where
*   Islanders cry,*
Eskma, feasgama agus Eilan.

The cradle of Shinty is Badenoch we
*   know,*
Where the game has been played since
*   the Spey first did flow,*
When winter appears in its mantle of
*   snow,*
It's "Hello are you going to the Eilan?"

Now strike up the music, sing, dance and
*   rejoice,*
Let the young and the old use their lungs
*   and their voice,*
And give ringing cheers for our own
*   gallant boys,*
The Camanachd lads of the Eilan.

OBAN CAMANACHD

There is evidence that Oban Shinty Club
was in existence as early as 1881, although
the centenary was not celebrated until
1989. The club was re-formed in 1922.

Two teams are fielded now, the senior
team in Division One of the south league
and a junior team, founded in 1923 under
the name of Lochside Rovers, in Division III.
There is also an Under-17 team which won
the MacQuiston Cup in 1992.

(above): Oban Camanachd, Centenary Year
(above right): Lorne Robertson, captain of
Oban Camanachd's Under-17 team receives
the 1992 MacQuiston Cup from Neil
Campbell B.E.M, the Vice-Chief of the
Association
(right): Attendances at the AGM of Oban
Camanachd were better in the fifties and
sixties than in modern times

The Club plays in red and black striped jerseys and white shorts. It is amongst the most successful in the game, having won the Celtic Society Cup on six successive occasions from 1987. The Camanachd Cup has been won in 1933 and 1938 and the MacAulay Cup has been won on numerous occasions.

When the club was re-formed in 1922 the Chieftain was Alex MacKay of Glencruitten, the Honorary President was Sir William Sutherland, K.C.B., M.P. and the President was Provost Donald MacDonald Skinner.

Provost Skinner held office from 1922 to 1954 and was an office-bearer of the Camanachd Association. His son Hugh was well known as a referee and his grandson Donald is the current Chief of the Association.

Robert Galbraith, captain of the Camanachd Cup runners-up team of 1958, played for many years and was selected for Scotland in the Shinty/Hurling international. Another stalwart player, John MacInnes, acted as secretary and president and served on the Camanachd Association Executive Committee.

Duncan Cameron, who was President of the club, and a Vice-President of the Camanachd Association, contributed an article "Shinty in Oban" in the 1975-76 Shinty Yearbook.

The Canine Intrusion That Caused Such Confusion

Tune: Dancing in Kyle

*This tale's no invention, well it's no ma
   intention,*
Tae project such a queer shinty game.
*Oban Camanachd were riled, claimed the
   match had been spiled,*
And an innocent dog was to blame.

*Fur it caused a sensation, a great big
   Alsatian,*
Thought poultry had strayed off the park.
*The handsome big "cur" wis supporting
   Strachur,*
Sunk his fangs into poor "Chookie" Clark.

*Chookie let oot a howl as he yelled fur a
   foul,*
As he hopped roond aboot like a frog.
*While big shepherd Ernie shouts "surely
   that learns ye,*
*Tae watch oot fur 'One man and his
   Dog'."*

*Now the Camanachd story is covered in
   glory,*
*But thae recent events caused such a
   blow.*
*G.Y. shinty views have been making the
   news,*

Doon at Crufts famous old doggy show.

*Then the referee 'Teak' says, "it fair
   makes me "seeck",*
*And tae book a poor dug makes nae
   sense,*
*Ah'll control any temper but nae way
   distemper,*
Fur the Rule Book omits this offence."
*Much thought has gone into the Future of
   Shinty,*
Jack Richmond's been working like hell,
*Noo this canine intrusion will cause mair
   confusion,*
*Will he consult Barbara Woodhouse as
   well?*

*Be it dogs, be it bitches, poor Chookie's
   in stitches,*
A protest has been made, so they say.
*We will just wait and see if it makes real
   history,*
With a judgement on 'Dirty dogs play'.

*Thae adverts on TV will a' change noo
   ye'll see,*
Tho' each firm say their's cannot be beat.
*Keep yer Pal, Bonus, Chum, Oor dog
   prefers "Bum",*
*That's a new brand called "Chookie's dog
   meat."*

by I.M.A. Collie, The Kennels, Barking

OBAN CELTIC

In 1927, when the town of Oban fielded a senior and junior side, it was felt that there were enough good players who could not get a game for these teams, to form another side.

It was decided to field a junior side, and its name was decided by the toss of a coin. The choice was either Celtic or Rangers.

The club did not have to wait long for its first success, winning the Bullough Cup in

OBAN
SHINTY AND
Scottish Camanachd Cup

CELTIC
ATHLETIC CLUB
Winners, 1927, 1949, 1954, 1960, 1963

*Oban Celtic, Camanachd Cup
winners 1959-60*

1928. Teams are currently fielded at senior, junior, Under-17 and Under-14 level. The Under-14 team were beaten in the final of the Ken MacMaster national trophy in 1992, the first time the cup was played for.

Oban Celtic play in green and white hoops and use the facilities at Ganavan and Mossfield Park. For some time the club's ground was at Moleigh Farm, four miles outside Oban.

The club is rightly considered amongst one of the most respected in terms of its history. The Camanachd Cup has been won five times, with the club also having played in the Final on four other occasions.

The club decided to go senior in 1935. Two years later, in the Semi-Final of the Camanachd Cup, three Celtic players were ordered off. Three replacements were introduced from the junior side for the Final and

Celtic went on to defeat Newtonmore for a famous victory, their first ever in the Final.

The MacAulay Cup has also been won on five occasions and the Dunn Cup, the Division One Championship in the south, on eleven occasions. The club have also won the Sutherland Cup (once) and Celtic Society Cup (twice) and the Torlundy Cup (three times) amongst many other trophies.

Harry Dunn (Jnr), son of the Harry Dunn who presented the Division One Championship Trophy, went on to become President of the Camanachd Association (1957-60). Others connected with the club who have rendered splendid service in the game's administration include Jock Douglas and the highly respected John Craig (Club President) who has been associated with the club for over fifty years.

SAINT ANDREWS UNIVERSITY

Shinty was started in St Andrews in the summer term of 1967 by a group of medical students who sold the idea to colleagues as the "in" thing to do. They allegedly scraped a win against the Aberdeen University second team at home, but that was their only success.

The following season, 1967-68, saw the club on a more solid foundation and former players with other clubs, now studying at the University came to the club's aid. One of these, Allan MacInnes, went on to represent and captain the Scottish University select side at the end of the decade.

In season 1969-70, the club scored notable successes, defeating Glasgow University at home, and drawing with the Aberdeen first team away from home.

The club has always drawn heavily on the experience of hockey players, mainly from England, but players of many nationalities have represented the club, always in the most sporting and sociable fashion.

Amongst those who went on to represent the Scottish Universities select later was Garry Gray in the seventies.

St Andrews also hosted a very successful six-a-side competition and their efforts as a club were recognised in 1975, when they became the first winners of the Shinty Yearbook Trophy, donated by Tom MacKenzie of Inverness. The trophy is awarded annually to club chosen for ''its earnest and successful endeavour in furthering the game of camanachd''.

SKYE CAMANACHD

There was a Portree Shinty Club in 1888 and one in Bernisdale at the same time. The club was originally Portree Athletic Club, 'Athletic' being dropped later and from 1895 the title became Skye Camanachd.

Before the formation of the club play used to be held, usually at Old New Year, at Bugha Mor, Kilmuir common, Armadale and elsewhere in the island.

In the early years games were played at Portree Home Farm and for some time the pitch has been in the King George V Park at Portree. A field at Skeabost was also used. The club colours are white jerseys and blue shorts. There are two teams, in Divisions I and III, also a juvenile team and there is a very active schools league.

At no time has the club gone into abeyance or merged with another.

The club, an original member of the Camanachd Association, entered for the Camanachd Cup in 1895-96 and also in subsequent years despite attempts to have it

The unique first MacTavish Cup medal, by courtesy of the MacKinnon family, Uig

(above): Camanachd Cup winners, 1990
(above middle): Skye's captain, Caley MacLean, with spoils of war
(above right): Martin MacDonald of Skye is author of an excellent history of the club published in 1992
(right): Willie Cowie of Skye was the first winner of the Marine Harvest National Player of the Year Award in 1990
(far right): an observant Sorley MacLean (centre)

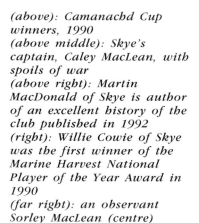

excluded from the competition unless it was agreed that all ties would be played on the mainland.

In the early days the well known J.G. Mackay was prominent in the club's affairs along with Myles MacInnes, Kenneth MacRae and Norman MacLean, father of 'Kaid' MacLean. Dr D.D. MacDonald and Lawrence Skene also rendered valuable service. William Ross was one of several of the club who fell in the war of 1914-18. Nearer the present time, much of the recent success was due to the efforts of such as D.R. Macdonald, Donnie MacKinnon, John Angus Morrison, Kenneth Macpherson and Hugh Clark. The well known Gaelic bard, Sorley Maclean, is an Honorary Vice President.

STRACHUR AND DISTRICT SHINTY CLUB

There is evidence that a club was formed at Strachur in 1880 and that in the annual games on New Year's Day, sixty players from Succoth Glen took part

At present, the club has around thirty players and home games are played at Strachur Park, where the club has always played. It has never folded or merged with another club. The colours are blue and white.

One of the club's greatest days was the Camanachd Cup Final of 1983 which was played at Fort William. Strachur were beaten by Kyles by the odd goal in five, but had Ewen Paterson selected as man of the match. Another young player who has made his mark in modern times is Alister Paterson, who has represented Scotland with distinction.

The club has reached the Final of the Sutherland Cup on five occasions — 1934, 1955, 1985, 1986 and 1988. The Celtic Cup has been won on two occasions, in 1982 and 1985, with the south league championship being won in 1977 and 1978. Two other Finals which were contested were the MacAulay Cup in 1983 and the Celtic Society Cup in 1910.

Two of the earliest matches in which Strachur took part were played against Glasgow Cowal. The first took place at Dennistoun Park, Glasgow, in April, 1880 and it resulted in a draw, four hails each.

In May, 1881, the teams met again on Glasgow Green and play was stubbornly contested. The result was again a draw, three hails each.

Sir Fitzroy MacLean, formerly M.P. for Bute and North Ayr is a Chieftain of the Club.

(above): Strachur, 1908

(right): Strachur at the Meadows, Rothesay, 1935-36

STRATHCLYDE POLICE SHINTY CLUB

This club was founded in 1963 as the Glasgow Police Shinty Team. The current title was adopted in 1975 when regionalization began.

The club can only field one team and the average age of players is higher than that of other clubs. Home games take place on Strathclyde Police Recreation Association Playing Fields at Lochinch, Glasgow. The clubhouse there has splendid changing facilities, etc. Previously play was held at Victoria Park and at Pollock Park, Glasgow.

Policemen in Glasgow from shinty-playing districts founded the club as a means of continuing to play the game.

The colours are blue jerseys with thin white vertical stripes and blue shorts. There is a badge with a motto, *Ludus et Otium, Play and Leisure.* The club has continued since its inception.

The club played in the old South of Scotland League Division I but was relegated in the season 1979-80 and has remained in Division II.

Division II was won in 1979-80 and the Skeabost Horn has been won several times too.

An unusual incident in the life of the club was a day spent at Luss when an episode in the West Highland 'soap' opera *Take the High Road* was being filmed. The Police club was asked to provide the opposition in a game held in connection with the filming.

The late Dr John Murchison, at the time of the disbanding of Glasgow Skye in 1959, conceived the idea of having a club consisting of serving police officers. In addition to Norman Crowe and Ian Bain, others who took part in the formation of the club were Hugh MacGillivray, Kenny Ross and Duncan MacDougall. The last named was most energetic in getting the club off to a good start in its early years. In the social side of the club's activities, Mrs Sheena MacInnes has taken a leading part.

STRATHGLASS SHINTY CLUB

Strathglass which was always one of the strongholds of the game in olden times has had a club since 1880 and a constitution and rules were drawn up by the club in that year.

At present the club has teams in Divisions II and IV and in addition there are Under-21, Under-17, Under-14, and primary teams.

Games are played at Cannich Playing Field and changing facilities etc., are being planned. From 1920 to 1957 games were played at Struy and at Invercannich and Kerrow from 1960 to 1968 when the field at Cannich came to be used.

The colours of the club are maroon and light blue jerseys and light blue shorts. The club has a badge with the motto *Vi aut Virtute, By strength or rather by skill.*

Some games were played towards the end of last century but there was not much competitive shinty from 1900 to 1914. The club was active in the 1920's but folded about 1938. It was active for a time after 1946 but there was no team from 1957 to 1960. There were some competitive games between 1960 and 1964 and after the latter year the club competed regularly and from 1979 fielded a second team.

The contests with Glenurquhart in 1887 and 1888, which helped with the revival of the game in the north, were the most noteworthy events in the club's history. The most notable personality connected with the club was Captain Archibald Macra Chisholm of Glassburn who was its founder and was first Chief of the Camanachd Association from 1893 to the time of his death in 1897. Mr Duncan Chisholm, Raonabhraid, was the first secretary and in the years after 1946 Mr James Grant held that office. From 1963 the secretary was Mr Murdo Mackenzie in whose years of office there was something of a revival. Mr Colin MacRae who was an Honorary Vice-President was also a well known and highly respected figure in shinty. The Macdonald Cup for which

(above): The Mackenzie family — Strathglass stalwarts

(below): Club Badge

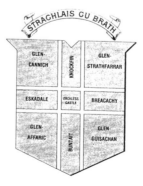

Strathglass — 1991-92
North Division Two
champions

Strathglass and Glenurquhart compete each year was presented in 1948 by Mr James

Macdonald, Tomich, the last survivor of the famous game of 1887.

TAYFORTH CAMANACHD

The club was formed at a meeting in the City Mills Hotel, Perth in 1973 bringing together the shinty and hurling backgrounds of Barry Nesbitt and Father Eugene O'Sullivan. There has been a strong Irish presence in the form of John Joe Moran, Rory O'More and Morris Lyons.

One team is fielded from about twenty players scattered throughout Perth, Edinburgh, Livingston and south-east Scotland.

The club has always played on the South Inch at Perth where there are changing facilities provided by Perth and Kinross District Council.

The club which has never merged with another began with one team in 1973. In 1975 Roy Whitehead and Ron Macdonald started shinty in Perth High School and in

1976 girls from the High School played against Cumbernauld and Whitburn. By 1980 a second team was formed as some former university players and boys who had played at the High School had become available. By 1987 the second team ceased due to retirals and shortage of players in southern Scotland. By 1990 several players joined Tayforth on the folding of Livingston.

In 1980-81 the club gained the Division II championship (Fraser Cup) and having gained promotion, remained in Division I for ten consecutive seasons. In 1986 there was a victory over Kyles Athletic in the last game of the season enabling the club to remain in Division I. The Mod Cup was won in 1980 and in 1986. There have been several visits to Kilkenny to win 'Ye Fair Cities'

Cup. In 1988 the semi-final of the Camanachd Cup was reached and in 1990 the Aviemore National Six-a-side competition was won.

The club suffered a great loss in the death of Willie Dowds who held a special place in the history of shinty. He was involved in the founding of clubs in Perth, Dundee and Glenrothes and in 1977 led a group of Tayforth Camanachd to London to receive an Irish Post Community award from the Irish Ambassador.

The club publishes its own magazine and runs an annual 12-a-side one day Tournament — The Frews Cup.

The founding fathers: (right) Ron MacDonald; (above right) Father Eugene O'Sullivan (shinty's "sporting priest") and John Jo Moran (far right)

(above, middle): Club badge

TAYNUILT

Shinty has been played intermittently in Taynuilt for as long as people can remember and between both world wars a team competed in most of the local junior cups such as the Sutherland Cup in 1935.

In the late 1970's a team once again began to compete in Division III South and later in Division II. It was playing in Division II in 1984 and 1985.

The club colours are tangerine jerseys with black shorts.

An unexpected success was the winning of the Colintraive Cup at Glendaruel when Strachur were beaten 2 — 0 in 1982.

A primary school team reached the final of the Aviemore Six-a-side competition in 1988.

The club declined and went into abeyance in 1990 and although the game is at present at a low ebb in the district it is hoped that the tide will turn.

Taynuilt

THE OLD GAME

The shinty game is failing
Throughout the Northern Land
Whilst we stand here bewailing
And raise no helping hand.

Let Gaels all stand together,
As steadfast as the Bens,
To see that stick on leather
Keeps echoing in our glens.

At the drying peats I'm sitting
And back from days of yore
Some sounds of crisp, clean hitting,
The cheers, the clever score.

The jousting and the swinging,
The subtle, silken slip
From men, whose way of winning
Despised the hack and trip.

An' the great names I am minding
Flood back from yester year;
The list's too long, I'm finding,
To put them all down here.

From Oban up to Spean,
From Newtonmore to Kyles,
Come stalwarts all worth seein'
Fell skilled in shinty wiles.

Strong men from far Lochaber,
All upright, broad and tall;
With strength to toss a caber,
Or hit a pitch-length ball.

Fleet-footed men from Furnace,
And Inveraray Town,
Went north to Ballachulish
To throw the gauntlet down.

A challenge that was taken,
In battles fierce to see,
When valiant hearts were shaken
In the famous "Jubilee".

Kingussie, cute an' cunning,
Clever, sharp an' slick
Were always in the running,
Old maestros of the stick.

And cheering on the players,

The Bodachs let it rip,
Wi' no words found in prayers—
An' "snifters" at their hip.

It wass not there for boozin',
For that was neffer done;
TO COMFORT YOU WHEN LOOSIN'
AND CHEER YOU WHEN YOU WON.

Tho' you seldom had the notion,
You sometimes made so bold,
As to swig an extra potion,
IN CASE YOU GOT THE COLD.

No man of rightful thinking
Could overdo "THE STUFF"
For he might get keen on drinking,
AN' WAN BOTTLE WASS ENOUGH.

No yelling an' no shouting,
No beer-cans on the sward;
Nor "Polis" busy clouting,
For that we thank the Lord.

Just skill an' manly striving
In shinty's ancient arts,
That kept the old game thriving,
And gladdened Highland hearts.

All storms the Game will weather,
Both strong an' proud will stand,
If brave we fight together
Throughout this Bonnie Land.

To keep our shinty living,
With hand an' heart engage;
START WORKING AND START GIVING
TO SAVE OUR HERITAGE!

Angus MacIntyre
Shinty Yearbook, 1971

MAKING THE CAMAN

a progressive sequence of studies of Mabel & John Sloggie taken by Donald Mackay in 1980

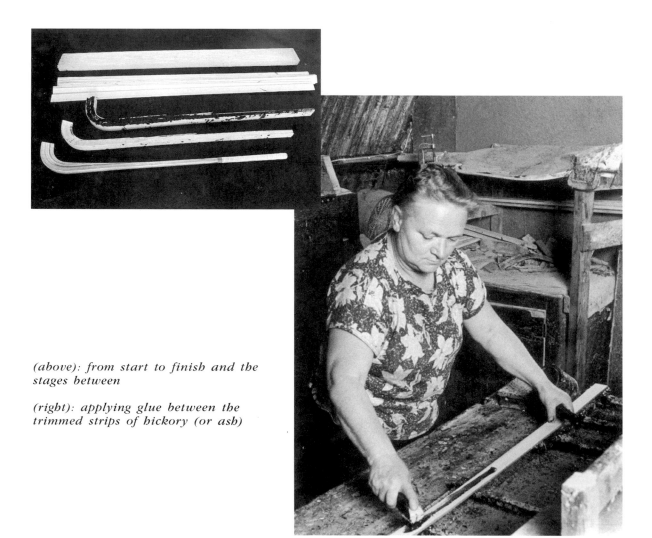

(above): from start to finish and the stages between

(right): applying glue between the trimmed strips of hickory (or ash)

(left & below): the stick is squeezed into correct shape between two templates

320

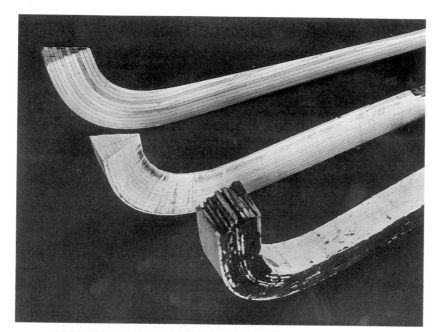

(left, below & opposite): achieving the final shape requires steady hand and eye — Robert Baxter at work

John Sloggie uses plane, rasp and much experience to achieve the required finish

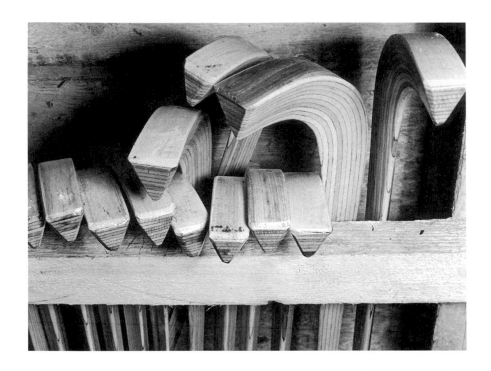

(above): ready for export and sale

(right): Mabel & John Sloggie outside their home in 1980

Celebrations!

(above from left to right): Camanachd Association Chief, Donald Skinner; President, Ken Thomson; Glenmorangie's Commercial Director, Peter Cullen; Team Sport Scotland's first Shinty Co-ordinator, Alan MacMillan

(left) Peter Black of Fort William trying to wear the Camanachd Cup as a hat — he didn't know it was full of Glenmorangie!

Supporters...

(above): Pipe-band leads Kingussie and Fort William
on to the field for the Camanachd Cup Final
at Old Anniesland, Glasgow

Paperwork at Dunbarry, Kingussie

H.R.H. Prince Edward joined Team Sport Scotland for a day. Perth 1992

A royal stick for the Princess of Wales at Bute Highland Games

Donnie Grant trying to sign Ian Botham!

John Willie Campbell (*centre*) was the BBC's *Voice of Shinty* for over 20 years until 1991.
BBC staff and former colleagues marked his contribution with a special presentation

Oban Shinty Select with the Volante Cup, 1960's, at Mossfield Park, Oban

Oban Camanachd's first Mod Cup win, October 1992

1992 Marine Harvest National League winners, Kingussie (Mossfield Park, Oban)

Caberfeidh Centenary 1986,
with (*centre left*) the Earl of Cromartie, beside the legendary Ken MacMaster

The Scotland Under-21 squad, 1988, Inverness

SHINTY.

A COMPENDIUM OF FACT AND FIGURE

ASSOCIATION CHIEFS

1893-1898	Captain Chisholm of Glassburn
1898-1933	Lord Lovat
1933-1940	Colonel A.W. MacDonald, D.S.O., of Blarour
1946-1961	Lord Lovat, M.C., D.S.O.
1961-1966	Captain Duncan MacRae, Balliemore
1966-1971	Ian MacLeod, Esq., Inverness
1971-1974	Ex-Provost Donald Thomson, Oban
1974-1979	Walter P. Cameron, Esq., Banavaie
1979-1980	Duncan MacRae Eaq., Tighnabruaich
1980-1985	Tom MacKenzie, Esq., O.B.E., M.M., J.P., Inverness
1985-1986	Celly Paterson, Esq., Tighnabruaich
1986-	Donald Skinner, Esq., Glasgow.

ASSOCIATION PRESIDENTS

1893-1898	Lord Lovat
1898-1914	John MacDonald, Esq., Keppoch
1919-1925	Colonel A.W. MacDonald, D.S.O., Blarour
1925-1931	Provost Donald M. Skinner, Oban
1931-1934	William MacBean, Esq., Inverness
1934-1937	John C. Dallas, Esq., Kingussie
1937-1948	William Paterson, Esq., Beauly
1948-1951	J.W. MacKillop, Esq., C.B.E., Inverness
1951-1954	Archibald MacPherson, Esq., Skye
1954-1957	Ewen Ormiston, Esq., Newtonmore
1957-1960	Harry Dunn, Esq., Oban
1960-1961	A.H. Cameron, Esq., Glasgow
1961-1966	Walter P. Cameron, Esq., Banavie
1966-1969	Hume D. Robertson, Esq., Kiltarlity
1969-1970	Dr John D. Murchison, Esq., Glasgow
1970-1973	Kenneth A. MacMaster, Esq., Strathpeffer
1973-1976	Tom MacKenzie, Esq., O.B.E., M.M., J.P., Inverness
1976-1982	Donald Skinner, Esq., Glasgow
1982-1985	John Willie Campbell, Esq., Gorthleck
1985-1990	Douglas S. Mackintosh, Esq., Newtonmore
1990-	Ken Thomson, Esq., Inverness

FORMATION

The following list has been compiled from the earliest references to the formation of clubs, The names of clubs, some of which folded after a very short time, are followed by the earliest date found, and the source of that date.

It has not been possible to definitely source the formation of some clubs due to scarcity of records. For the same reason, some clubs may be celebrating their centenaries at slightly different points to the date of the the original formation.

Some short quotations which are of interest are also included from the various sources which have been located. The list does not claim to be a complete one of all the clubs formed.

Abbreviations: **BR** *Badenoch Record*; **Cam** *Camanachd* Roger Hutchinson, 1989; **CM** *Celtic Monthly*; **H** *Highlander*; **HN** *Highland News*; **IC** *Inverness Courier*; **ID** *Inverness-shire Directory*, 1885; **NC** *Northern Chronicle*; **OT** *Oban Times*; **RJ** *Ross-shire Journal*; **SH** *Scottish Highlander*; **SYB** *Shinty Yearbook*.
Clubs still in existence are in **bold**

Aberdeen Camanachd 1968 (IC 3/9/1968) 'withdrew from competitive shinty five years ago' and revived 1982-83 (SYB 1983)
Aberdeen North of Spey by 1849 (IC 11/1/1849)
Aberdeen University 1861 (Cam) (See IC 24/12/1889, 'first match the University Club ever played', also 20/12/1910, 2/12/1949)

Achnacarry   by 1907 (IC 22/1/1907)
Achnasheen   by 1930 (NC 26/11/1930)
Achnashellach 1961 (IC 12/9/61)
Airdrie   1895 (CM Vol 111)
Alvie   1891 (IC 17/2/1891) 'newly reconstructed club'
Appin   by 1948 (IC 28/9/1948)
Ardgay   1894 (IC 23/11/1894)
Ardgour   1882 (IC 5/1/1882)
Ardkinglass (Rangers) by 1895 (SYB 1980)
Ardvaasar   by 1934 (IC 27/11/1934)
Argyll Pack Battery (Oban) 1924 (IC 17/10/1924) Oban Pack Battery (IC 25/12/1923)
Avoch   1896 (NC 1/4/1896)
Balfour Beatty's Club Fort William 1925 (IC 18/12/1925)
Ballachulish by 1893 (Cam)
Ballifeary   1928 (IC6/3/1928)
Beauly   1884 (NC 2/1/1884); (NC 15/4/1896; IC 13/4/1897; IC 8/2/1898 - 'Greens')
Benderloch by 1948 (IC 5/11/1948)
Ben Nevis 1882 (IC 5/1/1882) (1885, Inverness-shire Directory)
Ben Slioch Rovers 1892 (Cam)
Bernisdale   1888 (OT 29/12/1888)
Boat of Garten c1909 (NC 29/2/1939)
Boleskine 1927 (IC 29/11/1927) Amalgamation of Foyers and Stratherrick
Bolton Caledonian 1877 (H 5/1/1878)
Bonawe   by 1881 (H 27/4/1881) 'between the Oban club and the Granite' at Bonawe
Brae Lochaberby 1887 (IC 26/1/1882, 15/2/1887); IC 13/4/1897 'Lochaber white, Beauly green'
Braes   1907 (IC 5/3/1907; IC 29/11/1932)
Brahan   1947 (IC 23/12/1947)
Breakish   by 1894 (IC 9/2/1894)
Broadford   by 1922 (NC 12/4/1922; IC 8/11/1927)

Bute 1898 (SYB 1977-78); formerly known as North Bute

Caberfeidh 1886 (SYB 1987) (IC 6/2/1891) 'Reds' Mountaineers (Garve) 'Blues'

Cameron Highlanders Depot 1887 (IC 18/3/1887); Cameron Depot (NC 27/2/1907) 'Camerons took up shinty that year'

Cameron Highlanders, 1st Battalion, Fort George 1903 (IC 23/10/1903)

Cairndow 1960 (IC 2/9/1960)

Caol 1967 (IC 20/10/1967)

Carr Bridge 1912 (IC30/1/1912)

Clanranald 1953 (IC 15/9/1953)

Colglen by 1949 (IC 27/9/1949)

Colintraive by 1922 (IC 19/12/1922)

Colintraive and Glendaruel by 1932 (IC 6/12/1932)

Conon 1887 Played at Dingwall (IC 25/1/1887); Formed as a junior club (NC 28/11/1923)

Contin by 1899 (NC13/12/1899)

Cumbernauld by 1973 (IC 16/1/1973)

Cumbrae by 1912 (IC13/2/1912)

Dalmally 1892 (CM Vol I)

Dingwall 1887 Club formed (IC 18/1/1887) Mention of Nelson (Dingwall) IC 24/12/1889

Dochgarroch 1930 (IC 7/3/1930)

Drumguish 1948 (IC 28/9/1948)

Dulnain Bridge c1909 (NC 29/2//1939)

Dunollie by 1886 (SYB 1975-76)

Dunoon 1984? (SYB 1985)

Dunstaffnage by 1949 (IC 27/9/1949)

Duror by 1921 (IC 6/12/1921)

Edinbane 1907 (IC 5/3/1907)

Edinburgh Camanachd 1870 (H 26/2/1876) 'this the premier club' (NC 9/1/1884); 6th Anniversary (H 26/2/1876); revived 1933 (IC 19/9/1933)

Edinburgh Northern Counties by 1896 (IC 1/12/1896)

Edinburgh Sutherland by 1894 (CM Vol III)

Edinburgh University 1891 (SYB 1991-92)

Elgin 1899 (IC 17/10/1899)

Evanton by 1906 (SYB 1988)

Fairburn 1920 (IC 23/11/1920)

Falkirk 1898 (IC 7/3/1899) 'being raised'

Feochan United, Oban 1933 (IC 24/10/1933 and 8/12/1933)

Fodderty by 1899 (IC 18/4/1899)

Forres by 1905 (IC 5/12/1905)

Fort Augustus 1885 (IC 14/3/1885); (NC 23/1/1884); (IC 19/2/1889 'no uniform, only caps with yellow and black stripes'; IC 9/1/1891 Lovat 'Blues', Fort Augustus 'Whites' Revived 1955 (IC 20/9/1955)

Fort William 1893 (IC 21/2/1893); Revived 1932 (NC 9/11/1932)

Fort William Celtic 1933 (IC 10/12/1933)

Foyers 1898 (IC 11/3/1898)

Furnace by 1878 Described as 'Excelsior Furnace'; (H 5/1/1878) Revived 1986 (SYB 1987)

Garve 1890 'Mountaineers' (IC 4/2/1890)

Glasgow Caledonian 1899 (IC 20/10/1899)

Glasgow Camanachd 1875 (H 27/11/1875) Also Ossian, a branch of Glasgow Camanachd

Glasgow Cowal 1877 (H 10/3/1877) Withdrew (IC 13/11/1934)

Glasgow Fingal 1877 (H 28/4/1877) Became Glasgow Glenforsa (H 30/4/1880)

Glasgow Highland by 1986 Won Division III that year See list of cup winners, also SYB 1992-93

Glasgow Inveraray 1877 (H 10/3/1877)

Glasgow Inverness-shire (IC 12/2/1924)

Glasgow Islay 1922 NC 14/11/1922) To 1923 (IC 30/11/1923)

Glasgow Kelvin 1966 (IC 1/11/1966)

Glasgow Kyles 1920 (IC 14/12/1920)

Glasgow Mid Argyll 1923 as Blarwarthill Argyll (SYB 1986)

Glasgow Oban & Lorne by 1913 (NC19/11/1913)

Glasgow Ossian 1876 (H 23/12/1876)

Glasgow Police 1963 (SYB 1986)

Glasgow Skye 1879 Ossian became Glasgow Skye (H 21/3/1879)

Glasgow University 1901 (SYB 1971)

Gleann Mór (Fort Augustus) 1907 ''Newly formed team'' (NC 30/10/1907)

Glencoe 1879 (12/9/1879) Re-formed 1893 (Cam)

Glendaruel 1879 (H 11/1879)

Glenelg 1961 (IC 12/9/1961)

Glengarry 1882? (NC 23/1/1884)

Glenmoriston by 1930 (IC 4/3/1930)

Glenorchy 1896 1932 (SYB 1980)

Glenshiel   by 1922 (NC 28/11/1923)

Glenurquhart 1884 (IC17/1/1885 (See IC 15/2/1887, Also in ID 1885); (23/2/1886 — 'red caps and red bands on their arms and light knickerbockers'; 16/3/1886 — 'wearing red and white'

Govan   1901 (IC 3/12/1901)

Grantown   by 1894 (IC 9/10/1894)

Greenock   877 (H 20/1/1877) (CM Vol III 1894) (IC 17/10/1905)

Insh   1891 (IC 27/1/1893) 'recently formed' (SH 8/1/1891, 27/1/1891); IC 27/1/1893 'Red coats' Alvie and Insh Shinty Club by 1900 (IC 9/11/1900) 'Newly formed' (IC 17/10/1905)

Inveraray   1877 (H 24/2/1877) Ceased 1979 (SYB 1983) Revived (SYB 1983)

Invereshie   by 1907 (NC 6/3/1907)

Invergarry   1977 (SYB 1977-78)

Invergordon   1893 (CM Vol 11)

Inverlochy   by 1938 (IC 21/10/1938); 1946 (IC 27/8/1946)

Invermoriston   1886 (IC 16/2/1886); (IC 14/3/1885); 'blue and white caps'; (IC 19/2/1889 — 'wore red jerseys, stockings, caps and white knickerbockers')

Inverness Celtic 1938 (IC 9/12/1938) 1938-39 only

Inverness Clachnacuddin 1901 (IC 19/4/1901) Only 1901

Inverness   (Town and County) March 25, 1887 (See IC 29/3/1887 Highland Railway Workshop Club 1887 (IC 12/4/1887); (IC 24/1/1888) 'town and County wore red tunics'

Inverness Wanderers 1887 (NC 23/3/1987) Only 1887

Inveroich   1948 (IC 21/9/1948) Amalgamation of Glengarry and Fort Augustus

Kames   by 1924 (IC 10/12/1924)

Kelburn (Oban) by 1909 Won Bullough Cup that year See list of cup winners

Kilfinan   by 1921? (SYB 1985)

Kilmallie   by 1932 (IC 6/12/1932, 1/10/1946)

Kilmorack   1933 (IC 12/12/1933)

Kilmory   by 1914 (SYB 1985) 'Kilmory United' (IC 28/9/1948) Revived 1977 (SYB 1977-78)

Kincardine   1896 (NC 19/2/1896)

Kincraig   1920 (IC 17/2/1920) Re-formed 1973 (SYB 1977-78)

Kingarth   by 1912 (IC13/2/1912)

Kingussie   c1887 (BR 12/2/1948; NC1/2/1888, played Newtonmore; 'Kingussie club formed over two years ago' 1890; IC 5/4/1892); NC 15/4/1896 'Kingussie red and black, Beauly Green'

Kinlochewe Rovers 1890 (IC 4/2/1890 and 28/3/1893)

Kinlochshiel 1960 Amalgamation of Kintail, Glenshiel and Lochalsh (IC 21/10/1960)

Kintail   by 1923 (NC 28/11/1923)

Kintail/Glenshiel by 1950 (IC 13/10/1950)

Kintyre   1985 (SYB 1986)

Kirkhill   1887 (IC 25/2/1887) Revived 1920 (IC 14/12/1920

Kirn   1880 (H 26/3/1880)

Kyles Athletic 1896 (SYB 1977-78)

Laggan   by 1892 (IC 18/3/1892)

Lairg   1898? (IC 15/3/1898)

Lanarkshire Highlanders 1923 (IC 30/11/1923) mainly Irish hurling players

Livingston   1977 (SYB 1977-78, 1987)

Lochaber Camanachd 1946 Amalgamation of Spean Bridge and Brae Lochaber (IC 17/9/1946)

Lochalsh   1922 (NC 26/4/1922)

Lochbroom Camanachd 1992 (IC 30/10/1992)

Lochcarron   1883 'some months ago the club formed'; (IC 17/12/1883); in November 1883 (IC 17/12/1883)

Lochcarron, Union 1883 (NC 2/1/1884) Only to 1884

Lochfyneside 1946 (SYB 1985)

Lochgilphead by 1925 (IC 18/12/1925)

Lochgoilhead 1878 (H 20/4/1878)

Lochloy   1896 (IC 6/10/1896)

Lochside Rovers (Oban Camanachd) 1923 (SYB 1975-76)

Lochyside   by 1953 (IC 29/9/1953)

London Caledonian 1894 (IC 9/10/1894)

London Camanachd 1894 to 1939 and revived 1981 (Cam)

London Clans Shinty Club 1900 (Cam)

London Highland Camanachd Club 1878 (H 5/1/1878; 19/1/1878)

London Highland Athletic Club Shinty Team 1897 (Cam)

London Inverness-shire Association Camanachd Club 1883 (Cam) then became London

Northern Counties Camanachd Club
(IC 1/1/1886; IC 11/2/1884)

London Ross-shire Association Camanachd Club 1884 (Cam)

London Scots Shinty Club by 1892 (NC 6/1/1892)

Lovat 1887? as Kiltarlity (IC 18/1/1887; 30121887) 'Blues' Lovat (IC 9/1/1891)

Manchester 1877 (H 7/4/1877) 'Another being formed in Manchester'

Manchester Camanachd by 1876 (H 22/4/1876)

Manchester and Salford 1876 (H 23/12/1876; 7/4/1877)

Mid Ross 1925 (IC24/11/1925) 'arrangement between Caberfeidh and Strathconon'

Millhouse by 1921 (SYB 1985)

Minard 1923 (IC 13/11/1923)

Motherwell 1924 See Lanarkshire Highlanders (IC 21/10/1924)

Moy 1903 (IC 9/10/1903)

Muir of Ord 1898 (IC 18/3/1898)

Mull 1921 (IC 25/10/1921); (SYB 1975-76; 1991 re-formed (SYB 1992-93)

Nairn 1893/1895? (H 26/1/1878; IC 20/11/1894; NC 8/1/1896)

Ness Athletic 1949 (IC 13/9/1949)

Nether Lochaber by 1932 (IC 6/12/1932)

Nethy Bridge 1905 (IC 18/4/1905)

Newtonmore c1887 'played Kingussie' (BR 21/2/1948; NC 1/2/1888); 'formed anew' 2nd January, 1895 (IC 5/4/1892); IC 6/2/1891 'team appeared in uniform'

North Ballachulish 1927 (IC 4/11/1927)

North Bute by 1912 (IC 13/2/1912) North Bute (Rothesay) (IC 9/12/1924)

North Lorne (Kinlochleven) 1951 (IC 18/9/1951)

Oban Camanachd by 1881 (H 27/4/1881) Re-constituted 1922 (SYB 1975-76)

Oban Celtic 1928 (SYB 1975-76)

Oban Lorne 1948 (SYB 1975-76)

Paisley 1908 (HN 22/5/1909; 1st AGM)

Perth 1898? (IC 23/9/1898)

Portree or Skye 1892 (IC 8/3/1895); described as 'Skye' (NC 5/2/1896; 15/2/1888)

Redcastle by 1887 (IC 15/2/1887)

Renton 1880? (H 27/10/1880)

Rogart 1894 (IC 9/4/1895)

Ross County 1920 (RJ 26/11/1920) 1921 in Camanachd Cup

Rothesay by 1912 (IC 13/2/1912; 4/12/1923)

Scottish Pulp and Paper Mill, Corpach 1973 (IC 6/3/1973) See Caol above

Seaforth Highlanders 1911 (IC 10/1/1911)

Skye Camanachd See Portree

Sleat by 1932 (IC 29/11/1932)

Spean Bridge by 1894 (IC 13/4/1894)

Spean Bridge Celtic 1935 (NC 17/4/1935)

Springburn 1876 ('club is newly formed' H 29/4/1876)

St Andrews University 1967 (SYB 1971)

Stornoway 1893 (HN 6/12/1893)

Strachur by 1880 (H 16/4/1880; 4/5/1881)

Strath, Skye 1921 (IC 6/12/1921)

Strathcarron by 1920 (RJ 5/3/1920)

Strathclyde Police 1975 (SYB 1986)

Strathconon by 1920 (RJ 5/3/1920)

Strathdearn 1898 (IC 4/1/1898)

Stratherrick by 1890 (IC 3/2/1890; 11/2/1890)

Strathglass 1880 (H 13/1/1880)

Strathnairn 1923 (IC 14/12/1923)

Straths Athletic 1947 (Amalgamation of Stratherrick and Strathnairn) (IC 9/9/1947)

Sutherland (Lairg and Rogart) 1900 (IC 13/11/1900)

Tain 1896 (NC 19/2/1896); Proposal to form a club in Tain (IC 19/11/1895) Revived 1924 (IC 30/12/1924)

Tayforth by 1974 (SYB 1975-76)

Taynuilt by 1935 (IC 13/12/1935)

Tighnabruaich 1879 (H 11/1/1879)

Tobermory (1877 H 10/2/1877) (IC 4/1/1921)

Uig by 1888 (NC 15/2/1888)

Vale of Laroch 1879 (H 12/9/1879)

Vale of Leven 1854 (H 19/2/1876) 'been in existence for 22 years'

Vale of Oich by 1881 (IC 5/11/1946)

Wester Ross 1908 (RJ 6/3/1908; 1912 — (IC 23/4/1912; 1920 — IC 19/10/1920) 1949 (IC 13/9/1949)

Wimbledon and District Scots Association Shinty team 1910 (Cam)

RULES

1 The field of play

a) Dimensions.

The Field of Play shall be rectangular, its length being not more than 170 yards (155 metres) nor less than 140 yards (128 metres) and its breadth not more than 80 yards (73 metres) nor less than 70 yards (64 metres).

b) Marking.

The Field of Play shall be marked with distinctive lines, the longer boundary lines being called the side-lines and the shorter bye-lines The lines across the goals, joining the goal-posts, shall be called the goal-lines.

A flag on a post not less than 3 feet 6 inches (1 metre) high and having a non-pointed top shall be placed at each corner.

The centre of the field shall be indicated by a suitable mark and a circle of 5 Yards (5 metres) radius shall be marked round it.

c) Ten Yard Area (Nine Metre Area)

In front of each goal a line shall be drawn, 12 feet (3.66 metres) long, parallel to and 10 yards (9 metres) from the goal-line. The line shall be continued each way to meet the bye-line by quarter circles, having the inside of the goal-posts as centres. The space enclosed by this line and the bye-line, shall be known as the Ten yard Area (Nine Metre Area).

d) Corner Area

From each corner flag-post a quarter circle, having a radius of 2 yards (2 metres) shall be drawn inside the Field of Play.

e) Penalty Spot

At each end of the Field of Play, a suitable mark shall be made in front of the goal, 20 yards (18 metres) from the mid-point of the goal-line. These shall be the penalty-hit marks. A semi-circle of 5 yards (5 metre) radius shall be drawn behind each penalty-hit mark.

f) The Goals

The goals shall be placed at the centre of each bye-line and shall consist of two upright posts, equidistant from the corner flags and 12 feet (3.66 metres) apart (inside measurement), joined by a horizontal cross-bar, the lower edge of which shall be 10 feet (3.05 metres) from the ground. The width and depth of the uprights and the cross-bar shall not be more than 4 inches (10cms) and not less than 3 inches (7.5 cms).

The goal shall be provided with nets attached to the uprights and cross-bars, and fixed square with the goals at a distance of not less than 3 feet (1 metre) behind the goal-line and cross-bar.

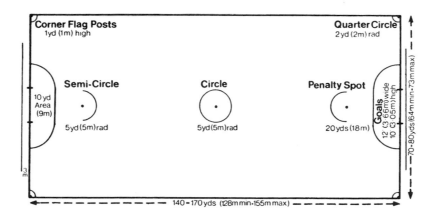

Decisions of Interpretation

For semi-final and final ties the field of play shall be not less than 160 yards (146 metres) long and 80 yards (73 metres) wide.

All lines, with the exception of the goal-line, should be a minimum of 1$\frac{1}{2}$ inches wide (4 cms) and a maximum of 3 inches (7.5 cms) wide.

The goal-line shall be the same width as the upright.

The Field of Play shall be fenced off at a distance of not less than 6 feet (2 metres) outside the bye-lines and the side-lines.

Where it is not possible to protect the whole field of play with a fence, both goals must be protected in the rear by a fence of wood, wire or rope over a minimum distance of 15 feet (5 metres) from either side of the goalposts and not less than 6 feet (2 metres) behind the goal-nets.

Where it is not possible to protect the rear of the goals with a fence, a line must be drawn 10 feet from the parallel to the bye-line. Only the goal-judges shall be permitted between this line and the bye-line during play.

The cross-bars and the uprights must be made of wood or metal and shall be painted white. They may be square, rectangular in shape, and no bar, strut or board, except at the top, shall connect the uprights and the posts supporting the goal-nets.

2 Number of Players

A match shall be played by two teams, each consisting of not more than twelve players, one of whom shall be the goal-keeper.

Substitutes, up to a maximum of two per team, shall be permitted during a match, except in representative matches where the maximum number permitted shall be four per team. The referee shall be informed of the names of substitutes (if any) before the change is made.

Punishment

If, without being notified, a player, or a named substitute, changes place with the goal-keeper during the game, or at any interval during the game in which extra time is played, and then handles the ball within the Ten Yard Area, (Nine Metre Area), a penalty hit shall be awarded.

Decisions of Interpretation

A competitive match shall not be considered valid if there are fewer than eight players in either team. Names of substitutes must be included in team lines, any two of whom shall be eligible to play.

A player who has been replaced shall not take any further part in the game. The referee must be informed if a player is to be substituted. A substitute may only be permitted to enter the field of play at the mid-point of either side-line, during a stoppage in the game and after he has received a signal from the referee authorising him to do so. A substitute shall be deemed to be a player and shall be subject to the jurisdiction of the referee whether called upon to play or not.

3 The Ball

The ball shall be spherical — the interior shall be cork and worsted, the outer cover shall be of leather or some other approved material. The circumference of the ball shall be not more than eight inches (20 cms) and not less than 7$\frac{1}{2}$ inches (19 cms). The weight of the ball at the start of the game shall not be more than 3 ounces (85 gms) nor less than 2$\frac{1}{2}$ ounces (70 gms). The ball shall not be changed during the game unless authorised by the referee.

4 Players' Equipment

Teams shall play in distinguishing colours and goal-keepers shall wear colours which distinguish them from outfield players and the referee.

A player shall not wear anything which is dangerous to another player nor shall a player use a caman which is in a condition which is dangerous to another player.

Boots must conform to the following standard:

a) bars shall be made of leather, rubber or plastic which extend the total width of the boot. The bars must be flat and rounded at the corners.

b) Studs shall be made of leather, rubber, plastic or similar material and shall be solid. Other than the metal seating for screw type of studs, no metal shall be allowed.

The caman must conform to the following standard:

a) The head of the caman must not be of a size larger than can pass through a ring of diameter of 2$\frac{1}{2}$ inches (6.3 cms).

b) No plates, screws, or metal in any form shall be attached to or form part of the caman.

No equipment should be used in any competition run under the auspices of the Camanachd Association unless first approved by the Executive Council.

Decisions of Interpretation

A player whose caman is broken during a game may play the ball before obtaining a replacement caman, providing the broken caman is not in a condition which is dangerous to himself or another player. A player changing his caman must do so at the side-lines or bye-lines.

5 Referees

A referee shall be appointed to officiate in each game. His authority and the exercise of the powers granted to him by the Rules of Play commence as soon as he enters the field of play. His power of penalising shall extend to offences committed when play has been temporarily suspended, or when the ball is out of play.

His decisions on points of fact connected with the play shall be final, so far as the result of the game is concerned.

He shall—

a) Enforce the Rules of Play

b) Refrain from penalising in cases where he is satisfied that, by doing so, he would be giving an advantage to the offending team.

c) Keep a record of the game; act as a time-keeper and allow the full or agreed time, adding thereto all time lost through accident or other cause.

d) Have discretionary power to stop the game for any infringement of the Rules and to suspend or terminate the game whenever, by reason of the elements, interference by spectators, or other cause, he deems such a stoppage necessary. In such a case he shall submit a detailed report, which should be posted within three working days, to the competent authority under whose jurisdiction the match was played.

e) From the time he enters the field of play, caution any player guilty of misconduct or ungentlemanly behaviour and, if he persists, suspend him from further participation in the game; send off the field of play any player who, without any previous caution, is guilty of violent conduct, serious foul play, or the use of foul or abusive language. In such cases the Referee shall send the name of the offender to the competent authority, posted within three working days, and in accordance with the provisions of the Disciplinary Machinery.

f) Allow no person other than the players, Goal Judges and Linesmen to enter the field of play without his permission.

g) Stop the game if, in his opinion, a player has been seriously injured, have the player removed as soon as possible from the field of play, and immediately resume the game. If a player is lightly injured, the game shall not be stopped until the ball has ceased to be in play.

h) Signal for re-commencement of the game after all stoppages.

Decisions of Interpretation

The referee shall report to the appropriate authority misconduct or any misdemeanour on the part of the spectators, officials, players, named substitutes, or other persons, which take place either on the field of play or in its vicinity at any time prior to, during, or after the match in question so that appropriate action can be taken by the authority concerned.

In no case shall the referee consider the intervention of a Goal Judge if he himself has seen the incident and, from his position on the field, is better able to judge.

The referee can only reverse his decision so long as the game has not restarted.

If the referee has decided to apply the advantage clause and to let the game proceed, he cannot revoke his decision if the presumed advantage is not realised, even though he has not, by any gesture, indicated his decision. This does not exempt the offending player from being dealt with by the referee.

The referee shall not allow any person to enter the field until play has stopped, and only then if he has given them a signal to do so. This applies to club trainers, etc.

In the case of serious injury, the referee should exercise extreme care before removing the injured player from the field and, if possible, seek the opinion of any qualified medical person in attendance.

6 Goal Judges

Two Goal Judges shall be appointed, whose duty (subject to the decision of the Referee) shall be to indicate—

a) When a goal is scored.

b) When the ball is out of play over the bye-line and whether a bye-hit or a corner should be awarded.

c) When an attacking player is off-side.

They shall assist the Referee to control the game in accordance with the Rules.

In the event of undue interference or improper conduct by a Goal Judge, the Referee shall dispense with his services and arrange for a substitute to be appointed. (The matter shall be reported by the Referee to the appropriate authority.)

Decisions of Interpretation

Goal Judges, where neutral, shall draw the Referee's attention to any breach of the Rules of Play of which they become aware if they consider that the Referee may not have seen it; but the Referee shall always be the judge of the decision to be taken.

Goal Judges shall not change ends at half-time.

7 *Linesmen*

Four linesmen shall be appointed where available whose duty (subject to the decision of the Referee) shall be to indicate when the ball is out of play over the side-lines, and which side is entitled to the hit-in. Each linesman shall be responsible for one half of a side-line.

Decisions of Interpretation

Linesmen shall not change over at half-time.

8. *Duration of the Game*

The duration of the game shall be two equal periods of 45 minutes, subject to the following:

a) Allowance shall be made in each period for time lost due to injury.

b) Time shall be extended to permit a penalty-hit being taken at, or after, expiration of the normal period in each half.

The half-time period shall be of not more than ten minutes' duration.

The ball must be in play when each half is terminated.

Decisions of Interpretation

The duration of the game may be less than 90 minutes if a shorter period is mutually agreed upon and it is permissible under the Rules of the Competition. The agreed time shall be divided into two equal periods.

9 *Start of Play — The Throw-up*

a) At the beginning of the game, choice of ends shall be decided by the toss of a coin.

The Referee, having blown his whistle, shall start the game by throwing up the ball to a minimum height of 12 feet (4 metres) between the two opposing players standing at the centre spot, at least 3 feet (1 metre) apart, with their camans crossed above head level. The players shall not shift their stance until the ball is struck in the air, or touches the ground. No other player shall be within 5 yards (5 metres) of the centre spot until the ball has been played. A goal scored direct from a throw-up shall count.

b) After a goal has been scored the game shall be restarted in like manner.

c) After half-time (when re-starting after half-time) ends shall be changed and the game restarted in like manner.

d) After any temporary suspension (when restarting after a temporary suspension for any cause not mentioned in these Rules of Play, provided immediately prior to the suspension the ball has not passed out of the field of play), the Referee shall throw the ball up at the place where it was when play was suspended.

Decisions of Interpretation

If the ball, when thrown up by the Referee, strikes one or both camans, it shall again be thrown up to the required height by the Referee.

If the two centre players are one left-handed and the other right-handed, each shall have choice of his side in the throwing up for one half of the match.

If one player should use his caman to hold his opponent's caman and prevent his opponent playing the ball, or shift his stance, he shall be penalised by the award of a free-hit to his opponent.

If the ball is within the Ten Yard Area (Nine Metre Area) when play is temporarily suspended, the Referee shall restart the game with a throw-up outside the area at the spot nearest to where it was when play was suspended.

10. *Method of Scoring*

A goal is scored when the whole of the ball has passed over the goal-line and under the cross-bar, except when resulting directly from a free-hit or when it has been kicked, carried or propelled by hand or arm by a player of the attacking side.

The team scoring the greatest number of goals during a game shall be the winner; if no goals, or an equal number of goals are scored, the game shall be termed a 'draw'.

Decisions of Interpretation

Rule 10 defines the only method according to which a match is won or drawn; no variations whatsoever can be authorised. A goal cannot be allowed if the ball has been prevented by some outside agency from passing over the goal-line. If this happens in the normal course of play, other than at the taking of a penalty-hit, the game must be stopped and restarted by the Referee throwing up the ball outside the Ten Yard Area (Nine Metre Area) at a point nearest to where the interference took place.

11. Ball In and Out Play

The ball is in play at all times from the start of the match to the finish including—

a) If it rebounds from a goal post, cross-bar or corner flag-post into the field of play.

b) If it rebounds off the referee.

c) In the event of a supposed infringement of the Rules of play, until a decision is given.

The ball is out of play—

a) when it has wholly crossed the goal-line, bye-line or side-line, whether on the ground or in the air.

b) when the game has been stopped by the Referee.

12. Fouls and Misconduct

A player who intentionally commits any of the following offences—

a) Kicks the ball;

b) Kicks or attempts to kick an opponent;

c) Jumps at an opponent;

d) Charges an opponent from behind;

e) Charges an opponent in a violent or dangerous manner;

f) Uses his caman in a violent or dangerous manner;

g) Pushes an opponent;

h) Trips an opponent, i.e. throwing or attempting to throw him by use of the legs or caman;

i) Strikes, or attempts to strike an opponent with his hand, arm or caman;

j) Strikes, deflects or impedes an opponent's caman, except to 'block' or 'hook' a caman which is within striking distance of the ball;

k) Throws his caman;

l) Attempts to participate in the game without his caman in his hand;

m) Holds an opponent or an opponent's caman;

n) Obstructs an opponent, i.e. running between the opponent and the ball or interposing the body so as to form an obstacle to an opponent;

o) Handles the ball, i.e. carries, strikes, or propels the ball with his hand or arm; NOTE:— The goal-keeper is permitted to stop and slap the ball with his open hand within the Ten Yard Area (Nine Metre Area).

p) Heads the ball;

He shall be penalised by the award of a free-hit to be taken by the opposing side at the place where the offence occurred.

Should a player from the offending side commit one of the above-mentioned offences within the Ten Yard Area (Nine Metre Area) he shall be penalised by the award of a penalty-hit.

A penalty-hit can be awarded irrespective of the position of the ball, if in play, at the time the offence is committed within the Ten Yard Area (Nine Metre Area).

A player shall be cautioned if—

1) He persistently infringes the Rules of Play

2) He shows by word or action, dissent from any decision given by the Referee;

3) He is guilty of ungentlemanly conduct;

4) He swing recklessly even when attempting to play the ball;

5) He enters or re-enters the field of play to join or re-join his team after the game has commenced, or leaves the field of play during the progress of the game (except through accident or as covered in the off-side rule) without, in either case, first having received a signal from the Referee showing him that he may do so.

6) He uses foul or abusive language;

A player shall be sent off the field of play if -

7) In the opinion of the Referee he is guilty of violent conduct or serious foul play;

8) He commits a cautionable offence after having received a caution.

9) He is guilty of a serious violation of any of the above offences.

Decisions of Interpretation

A player may stop the ball with one foot provided that it is at rest on the ground at the moment of contact. If both feet are off the ground at the moment of contact, the Referee shall be the sole judge of whether or not the player intentionally kicked the ball.

A player is allowed to play an opponent's caman with his own caman only to 'block' or 'hook' the swing of a caman which is within playing distance of the ball, except in the case of blocking an opponent about to strike the ball or in shielding the ball while in possession.

If, in the opinion of the Referee, a player deliberately hits the ball out of play to waste time, the Referee shall caution the player for ungentlemanly conduct and award a free-hit.

13 Off-side

An attacking player shall be off-side if he is within the Ten Yard Area (Nine Metre Area) when the ball enters that area either on the ground or in the air. Note:— The Ten yard Area (Nine Metre Area) includes the goal area between the goal-line and the nets and the lines bounding it.

Punishment

For an infringement of this rule a free-hit shall be taken by a player of the defending side from the place where the infringement occurred.

Decisions of Interpretation

A player is considered to be off-side if any part of his body or stick is within the Ten Yard Area (Nine Metre Area) before the ball enters that area. A player who steps over the bye-line to avoid being off-side shall not be allowed to enter the field of play while the ball is within the Ten Yard Area (Nine Metre Area).

14 Bye-hit

When the whole of the ball passes over the bye-line, either in the air or on the ground, having been last played by one of the attacking side, it shall be hit direct into play from a point within the Ten Yard Area (Nine Metre Area).

The striker shall not play the ball a second time until it has touched or been played by another player. No player shall be within 5 yards (5 metres) of the striker when the hit is being taken.

A goal from such a hit shall count.

Punishment

If a player taking a bye-hit plays the ball a second time before it has been played by another player, a free-hit shall be awarded to the opposing team, or, if the infringement occurred inside the Ten Yard Area (Nine Metre Area), a penalty hit shall be awarded to the opposing team.

15 Corner-hit

When the whole of the ball passes over the bye-line, either in the air or on the ground, having last been played by one of the defending team, a member of the attacking team shall take a corner-hit from the quarter circle at the nearest flag-post, which must not be removed. A goal may be scored direct from a corner hit.

No player shall be within 5 yards (5 metres) of the striker when the hit is being taken. The striker shall not play the ball a second time until it has been touched or been played by another player.

Punishment

If a player taking a corner-hit plays the ball a second time before it has been played by another player, a free-hit shall be awarded to the opposing side.

16. Hit-in

When the whole ball passes over the side-line, whether in the air or on the ground, it shall be hit into play, by an overhead hit, by a player of the team opposite to that of the player who last touched it.

In taking the hit, the player shall stand outside the side-line, facing the field of play, with both feet on the ground and in a position square to the side-line. The caman shall be withdrawn directly overhead and at the time of contact both the caman and the ball shall be directly overhead.

If the player taking the hit misses the ball entirely, the opposing team shall be awarded the hit-in. The striker shall not play the ball a second time until it has been touched by a second player. No player shall be within 5 yards (5 metres) of the striker when the hit is being taken. A goal may be scored direct from a hit-in.

Punishment

a) If the ball is hit-in improperly, the hit-in shall be taken by a player of the opposing side.

b) If a player taking a hit-in plays the ball a second time before it has been played by another player, a free-hit shall be awarded to the opposing team.

17. Free-hit

A free-hit is awarded for any infringement of the Rules, except by a defending player within the Ten Yard Area (Nine Metre Area) and shall be taken by the opposing side, from the place where the offence occurred.

The ball must be struck by the club, or scooped and it shall not be deemed in play until it has travelled the distance of its own circumference.

No player shall be within 5 yards (5 metres) of the striker when the hit is being taken. The striker shall not play the ball a second time until it has touched or been played by another player. A goal from such a hit shall NOT count.

Punishment

If a player taking a free-hit plays the ball a second time before it has been played by another player, a free-hit shall be awarded to the opposing team.

Decisions of Interpretation

The Referee has the discretionary power to refrain from awarding a free-hit, if, in his opinion, it will benefit the offender. If any player stands within 5 yards (5 metres) of the striker when the hit is being taken, the Referee has the discretionary power to order the hit to be re-taken.

18. Penalty-hit

A penalty-hit is awarded for any infringement of the Rules by a defending player within the Ten Yard Area (Nine Metre Area) and shall be taken by the opposing side from the penalty spot. When the hit is being taken, all players, with the exception of the player taking the hit and the defending goal-keeper, shall be within the field of play but outside the 5 yard (5 metre) semi-circle behind the penalty spot.

The defending goal-keeper must stand, without moving his feet, on his own goal-line until the hit is taken.

If the ball on being struck does not reach the goal-line or bye-line, the hit shall be held to be a bye.

The player taking the hit shall not play the ball a second time until it has touched or been played by another player. If necessary, time of play shall be extended at half-time or at full-time to allow a penalty-hit to be taken. A gaol from such a hit shall count.

Punishment

For any infringement of this Rule—

a) by the defending team, the hit shall be retaken if a goal has not resulted;

b) by the attacking team other than the player taking the hit, if a goal is scored it shall be disallowed and the hit re-taken;

c) by the player taking the hit, committed after the ball is in play, a player of the defending side shall take a free-hit at the place where the infringement occurred.

Decisions of Interpretation

If a re-take has been awarded, a change of penalty taker is permissible.

NOTE: Provided the principles of these rules be maintained, they may be modified in their application to players of school age as follows — (a) size of playing pitch; (b) Size, weight and material of ball; (c) width between the goalposts and height of the cross-bar from the ground; (d) the duration of the periods of play.

BIBLIOGRAPHY

Cumaidh sinn suas an cluidh-iomain
Cluidh is grinn' a tha fo'n ghréin.

This bibliography represents a comprehensive list of the primary sources used in researching this book. It is by no means a complete record of all the material ever written about shinty.

Information has also been included on sources which are useful in pursuance of material on other related matters such as Highland culture in general and the Gaelic language in particular.

Sources have been detailed by author where applicable (surname first) and first word of title where no individual author available.

Abraham, J.W. and Wilton, M.J., (eds), *Report on the Evaluation of the Continuing Supply of Camans and Balls for Shinty.* Highlands and Islands Development Board. Inverness, 1981

An Teachdaire Gaelach, Edinburgh, 1830, 1831

Bannerman, John, *Studies in the Early History of Dalriada.* Edinburgh, 1974

Barron, Hugh. *The First Hundred Years. A short history of Inverness shinty club,* 1887-1987. Inverness, 1987

Barron, Hugh (ed), *The Third Statistical Account of Scotland.* Vol XVI. The County of Inverness. Edinburgh, 1985

Barron, Hugh and Campbell, J.W., *A History of Comunn Camanachd Strathghlais,* Strathglass Shinty Club. Inverness, 1980

Barron, Hugh, Campbell J.W., and MacLennan, H.D., *Lochcarron Camanachd* 1883-1983. Inverness, 1983

Barron, James, *The Northern Highlands in the 19th century.* Three volumes. 1800-1856. Inverness, 1913

Beauly Camanachd - Centenary, 1892 - 1992, Inverness, 1992

Caberfeidh Shinty Club, Centenary. 1886-1986. Dingwall, 1986

Cameron, Iain, *The "terrible parochialism" that is stifling shinty — and what needs to be done.* In North 7, published by the Highlands and Islands Development Board, Inverness, November/December, 1979

Campbell, J.F., *Popular Tales of The West Highlands.* 1861

Campbell, Muirne A.N., *Scottish Camanachd, a study of the traditional, historical and cultural background with an outline of the modern organisation.* Unpublished MA Thesis, Aberdeen University, 1971. (See also Shinty Yearbook, 1971)

Canny, Liam, *The Irish game of Hurling', in Folklife: A Journal of Ethnological Studies*, Society of Folk Life Studies, Vol 19, 1981

Cox, Allan, A History of Sports in Canada 1860-1900 (nd)

Dagg, T.S.C., *Hockey in Ireland, The Kerryman,* 1944

Dillon, Myles and Chadwick, Nora, *The Celtic Realms.* 1967

De Burca, Marcus, *The GAA. A History of the Gaelic Athletic Association.*, Wolfhound, 1980

English, Peter R., *Glen Urquhart. Its places, people, neighbours and its shinty in the last 100 years and more.* Aberdeen, 1985

Finlay, Ian, *Columba.* London, 1979

Fullam, Brendan, *Giants of the Ash.* Wolfhound, 1991

Grant, Isabel, F., *Highland Folk Ways.* 1961

Hunter, James, *Scottish Highlanders. A People and their Places.* 1992

Hunter, James and MacLean, Cailean, *Skye : The Island.* 1986

Hutchinson, Roger, Camanachd: *The Story of Shinty.* Mainstream, 1989

Hurling: *Some Notes on The History of The Game.* The Columban Record, 1914

Huyshe, Wentworth, *The Life of Saint Columba by Saint Adamnan.* 1914

Kelvin, Dr Jones and Vellathottam, George T., *"The Myth of Canada's National Sport"*, in Camper Journal, September-October, 1974

Lovat Shinty Club. Centenary 1888-1988. Inverness, 1988

Lindsay, P.L., *A History of Sport in Canada 1807-1867* (nd)

Littlejohn Album, 1905. (Held in Aberdeen University Library)

Lucas, A.T., *"Hair Hurling Balls"*, in Journal of the Cork Historical and Archaeological Society, Vol **57**, 1952

Lucas, A.T., *"Two Recent Finds : Hair Hurling Balls from Co. Limerick"*, in Journal of the Cork Historical and Archaeological Society, Vol 59, 1954

Lucas, A.T., *"Hair Hurling Balls from Limerick and Tipperaray"*, in Journal of the Cork Historical and Archaeological Society, Vol 76, 1971

Lucas, A.T., *"Hair Hurling Ball from Knockmore, Co. Clare"*, in Journal of the Cork Historical and Archaeological Society, Vol 77, 1972

MacArthur, E. Mairi, *Iona : The Living Memory of a Crofting Community.* 1990

MacDonald, Alexander, *Shinty, Historical and Traditional*, in Transactions of the Gaelic Society of Inverness, Vol XXX. Inverness, 1924

MacDonald, Colin M., (ed) *The Third Statistical Account of Scotland.* Vol. IX. The County of Argyll. Edinburgh, 1961

MacDonald, Rev. J. Ninian, OSB, *Shinty. A Short History of The Ancient Highland Game.* Inverness, 1932

MacDonald, Martin, *Skye Camanachd. A Century Remembered.* Portree, Skye. 1992

MacIntyre-North, C.N., *Leabhar Comunn nam Fior Ghael*, Vol II, 1881

MacKay, John G., *Life in The Highlands a Hundred Years Ago.* (Address to The Gaelic Society of Glasgow) 1890

MacKenzie, Rev., George, *Student Life at Aberdeen Two Centuries Ago.* 1892

Mackinnon, Roddy, *Beauly Camanachd Centenary*, Inverness 1992

MacLean, Calum, *The Highlands*, Edinburgh, 1990

MacLennan, Hugh D., *An Gearasdan : Fort William Shinty Club's first hundred years.* Inverness, 1993

MacLennan Hugh D., Shinty: *Rules of Play and Coaching Manual.* Camanachd Association 1983

MacLennan Hugh D., and Richmond J., *A History of Newtonmore Camanachd.* Inverness 1993

MacPherson, Angus, *A Highlander looks back. Oban,* no date

MacPherson, Margaret, *The Shinty Boys.* 1963

MacVicar, Rev. A.J., *Hebridean Heritage,* 1966

Martin, Martin, *A Late Voyage to St Kilda.* 1698

Mather, Alexander S. (ed), *The Third Statistical Account of Scotland.* Vol XIII. The County of Ross and Cromarty. Edinburgh, 1987

Nicholls, Kenneth, *Gaelic and Gaelicised Ireland in the Middle Ages.* 1972

Nicolson, Alex, *History of Skye,* **1930**

O'Caithnia, Liam P., *Sceal na hIomana.* Dundalgan Press, 1980

O'Maolfabhail, Art, *Caman : 2,000 Years of Hurling in Ireland.* Dundalk, 1973

Prebble, John, *The Lion in the North.* 1971

Redmond, G., *The Scots and Sports in the Nineteenth Century* Canada (nd)

Richmond, Jack, (ed), *Shinty Forum Report*, The Camanachd Association, 1974

Richmond, Jack, (ed), *Future of Shinty Report,* The Camanachd Association, 1981

Ross, R. J., and Hendry, J., (eds) *Sorley MacLean : Critical Essays.* 1986

Sage, Rev Donald, *Memorabilia Domestica.* 1899.

Shinty in Eigg, (Transcript of a conversation with Hugh MacKinnon) In Tocher 36-36, Published by The School of Scottish Studies, Edinburgh, 1982

Shinty Yearbook Published annually since 1971, various editors.

Smyth, Alfred P., *Warlords and Holy Men.* 1984

Thomson, Derick, *An Introduction to Gaelic Poetry.* Gollancz 1974

Thomson, Derick, (ed), *The Companion to Gaelic Scotland.* 1983

"We shall keep up the shinty play, the finest game under the sun".

RESULTS

THE CAMANACHD ASSOCIATION CHALLENGE CUP

1896	Kingussie 2	Glasgow Cowal 0 [Inverness]
1897	Beauly 5	Brae-Lochaber 0 [Inverness]
1898	Beauly 2	Inveraray 1 [Inverness]
1899	Ballachulish 2	Kingussie 1 [Perth]
1900	Kingussie 1	Furnace 0 [Perth]
	(after a drawn game at Inverness)	
1901	Ballachulish 2	Kingussie 1 [Inverness]
1902	Kingussie 3	Ballachulish 1 [Inverness]
1903	[Kingussie were awarded the Cup after a drawn game at Perth, with Inveraray, who refused to play at Inverness]	
1904	Kyles Athletic 4	Laggan 1 [Kingussie]
1905	Kyles Athletic 2	Newtonmore 0 [Inverness]
1906	Kyles Athletic 4	Newtonmore 2 [Inverness]
1907	Newtonmore 7	Kyles Athletic 2 [Kingussie]
1908	Newtonmore 5	Furnace 2 [Inverness]
1909	Newtonmore 11	Furnace 3 [Glasgow]
1910	Newtonmore 6	Furnace 1 [Kingussie]
1911	Ballachulish 3	Newtonmore 1 [Lochaber]
	(the first game at Inverness, Newtonmore won 3 2 but a protest was granted to Ballachulish.)	

1912	Ballachulish 4	Newtonmore 2 [Perth]
1913	Beauly 3	Kyles Athletic 1 [Kingussie]
1914	Kingussie 6	Kyles Athletic 1 [Glasgow]
1915-1919	[There was no competition because of World War 1]	
1920	Kyles Athletic 2	Kingussie 1 [Glasgow]
	(after a drawn game 0-0, at Inverness)	
1921	Kingussie 2	Kyles Athletic 1 [Inverness]
1922	Kyles Athletic 6	Beauly 3 [Oban]
1923	Furnace 2	Newtonmore 0 [Inverness]
1924	Kyles Athletic 2	Newtonmore 1 [Kingussie]
	(after a drawn game 3-3, at Glasgow)	
1925	Inveraray 2	Lovat 0 [Inverness]
1926	Inveraray 3	Spean Bridge 2 [Oban]
1927	Kyles Athletic 2	Newtonmore 1 [Inverness]
1928	Kyles Athletic 6	Boleskine 2 [Glasgow]
1929	Newtonmore 5	Kyles Athletic 3 [Spean Bridge]
1930	Inveraray 2	Caberfeidh 1 [Oban]
1931	Newtonmore 5	Inveraray 1 [Inverness]
1932	Newtonmore 1	Oban 0 [Glasgow]

The first ever Camanachd Cup medal of 1896 — (left) front (right) reverse

1933	Oban 3	Newtonmore 2 [Keppoch]
	(after a drawn game, 1-1, at Corpach, Fort William)	
1934	Caberfeidh 3	Kyles Athletic 0 [Inveraray]
1935	Kyles Athletic 6	Caberfeidh 4 [Inverness]
1936	Newtonmore 1	Kyles Athletic 0 [Spean Bridge]
	(after a drawn game, 2-2, at Oban)	
1937	Oban Celtic 2	Newtonmore 1 [Keppoch]
	(after a drawn game, 2-2, at Inverness)	
1938	Oban 4	Inverness 2 [Oban]
1939	Caberfeidh 2	Kyles Athletic 1
1946	[There was no competition because of World War 2]	
1947	Newtonmore 4	Lochfyneside 0 [Oban
1948	Newtonmore 4	Ballachulish 2 [Inverness]
1949	Oban Celtic 1	Newtonmore 0 [Glasgow]
1950	Newtonmore 4	Lochfyneside 2 [Oban]
1951	Newtonmore 8	Oban Camanachd 2 [Inverness]
1952	Inverness 3	Oban Celtic 2 [Glasgow]
1953	Lovat 4	Kyles Athletic 1 [Fort William]
	(after a drawn game, 2-2, at Oban)	
1954	Oban Celtic 4	Newtonmore 1 [Inverness]
1955	Newtonmore 5	Kyles Athletic 2 [Glasgow]
1956	Kyles Athletic 4	Kilmallie 1 [Oban]
1957	Newtonmore 3	Kyles Athletic 1 [Spean Bridge]
1958	Newtonmore 3	Oban Camanachd 1 [Inverness]
1959	Newtonmore 7	Kyles Athletic 3 [Glasgow]
1960	Oban Celtic 4	Newtonmore 1 [Oban]
1961	Kingussie 2	Oban Celtic 1 [Fort William]
1962	Kyles Athletic 3	Kilmallie 1 [Inverness]
1963	Oban Celtic 3	Kingussie 2 [Glasgow]
1964	Kilmallie 4	Inveraray 1 [Fort William]
1965	Kyles Athletic 4	Kilmallie 1 [Oban]
1966	Kyles Athletic 3	Newtonmore 2 [Inverness]
1967	Newtonmore 3	Inveraray 0 [Glasgow]
1968	Kyles Athletic 2	Kingussie 1 [Oban]
	(after a drawn game, 3-3, at Fort William)	
1969	Kyles Athletic 3	Kilmallie 1 [Oban]
1970	Newtonmore 7	Kyles Athletic 1 [Kingussie]
1971	Newtonmore 7	Kyles Athletic 1 [Inverness]
1972	Newtonmore 6	Oban Celtic 3 [Glasgow]
1973	Glasgow Mid-Argyll 4	Kingussie 2 [Fort William]
1974	Kyles Athletic 4	Kingussie 1 [Oban]
1975	Newtonmore 1	Kyles Athletic [Fort William]
	(after a drawn game, 3-3, at Kingussie)	
1976	Kyles Athletic 4	Newtonmore 2 [Inverness]
1977	Newtonmore 5	Kyles Athletic 3 [Glasgow]
1978	Newtonmore 3	Kyles Athletic 2 [Fort William]
1979	Newtonmore 4	Kyles Athletic 3 [Oban]
1980	Kyles Athletic 6	Newtonmore 5 [Kingussie]
1981	Newtonmore 4	Oban Camanachd 1 [Glasgow]
1982	Newtonmore 8	Oban Celtic 2 [Inverness]
1983	Kyles Athletic 3	Strachur 2 [Fort William]
1984	Kingussie 4	Newtonmore 1 [Oban]
1985	Newtonmore 4	Kingussie 2 [Kingussie]
1986	Newtonmore 5	Oban Camanachd 1 [Glasgow]
1987	Kingussie 4	Newtonmore 3 [Fort William]
1988	Kingussie 4	Glenurquhart 2 [Inverness]
1989	Kingussie 5	Newtonmore 1 [Oban]
1990	Skye 4	Newtonmore 1 [Fort William]
1991	Kingussie 3	Fort William 1 [Inverness]
1992	Fort William 1	Kingussie 0 [Glasgow]

Camanachd Cup medals:
(left): 1908
(right): 1992

1923	Newtonmore 3	North Bute 2 [Keppoch]
1924	Kyles Athletic 3	Newtonmore 2 [Oban]
1925	Lochside Rovers 2	Newtonmore 0 [Keppoch]
1926	Furnace 4	Caberfeidh 3 [Newtonmore]
1927	Newtonmore 4	Kyles Athletic 0 [Oban]
1928	Newtonmore 4	Col-glen 0 [Oban]
1929	Lochside Rovers 4	Strathglass 3 [Spean Bridge]
1930	Strathconon 2	Col-glen 1 [Kingussie]
1931	Kyles Athletic 3	Kingussie 1 [Keppoch]
1932	Kyles Athletic 4	Newtonmore 1 [Oban]
1933	Lochside Rovers 3	Strathconon 1 [Keppoch]
1934	Nether Lochaber 5	Strachur 2 [Oban]
1935	Kyles Athletic 5	Caberfeidh 2 [Keppoch]

1936	Lochside Rovers 5	Nether Lochaber 1 [Oban]
1937	Lochside Rovers 1	Newtonmore 0 [Keppoch]
1938	Newtonmore 6	Kyles Athletic 2 [Fort William]
1939	Lochcarron 5	Kilmallie 4 [Newtonmore]
1940-1946 [There was no competition due to World War 2.
1947	Oban Celtic 4	Newtonmore 3 [Fort William]
		(after a drawngame, 1-1, at Fort William)
1948	Kilmallie 7	Straths Athletic 1 [Fort Augustus]
1949	Ballachulish 3	Lochcarron 2 [Inverness]
1950	Portree 5	Newtonmore 4 [Beauly]
1951	Spean Bridge 4	Straths Athletic 3 [Corpach]
1952	Beauly 5	Col-glen 2 [Oban]
1953	Newtonmore 3	Dunstaffnage 1 [Fort William]
1954	Beauly 4	Appin 2 [Fort William]
1955	Lochcarron 1	Strachur 0 [Fort William]
1956	Beauly 1	Lochside Rovers 0 [Spean Bridge]
1957	Beauly 3	Kilmallie 2 [Spean Bridge]
1958	Kilmallie 4	Skye 2 [Beauly]
		(after a drawn game, 3-3, at Beauly)
1959	Newtonmore 7	Inveraray 5 [Oban]
1960	Lochside Rovers 2	Glenurquhart 1 [Spean Bridge]
1961	Kyles Athletic 6	Newtonmore 1 [Oban]
1962	Kinlochshiel 5	Kyles Athletic 4 [Fort William]
1963	Glenurquhart 3	Kyles Athletic 2 [Spean Bridge]
1964	Boleskine 4	Kyles Athletic 0 [Strachur]
1965	Lochaber 3	Ballachulish 1 [Fort William]
1966	Boleskine 4	Kyles Athletic 2 [Fort William]
1967	Lochcarron 4	Inveraray 2 [Fort William]
1968	Lochcarron 2	Ballachulish 1 [Inverness]
1969	Inveraray 5	Ballachulish 3 [Dalmally]
1970	Lochcarron 4	Ballachulish 2 [Spean Bridge]
1971	Ballachulish 2	Skye 0 [Inverness]
1972	Bute 2	Aberdeen University 1 [Spean Bridge]
1973	Aberdeen Univ 7	Bute 2 [Oban]
1974	Aberdeen Univ 6	Oban Celtic 4 [Kingussie]
1975	Kyles Athletic 6	Newtonmore 3 [Oban]
1976	Kingussie 3	Lochaber 1 [Newtonmore]
1977	Kinlochshiel 9	Glenorchy 1 [Fort William]
1978	Fort William 6	Oban Celtic 3 [Inveraray]
1979	Skye 3	Kyles Athletic 2 [Fort William]
1980	Kyles Athletic 4	Kingussie 3 [Oban]
1981	Skye 3	Glasgow University 1 [Oban]
1982	Glenorchy 2	Lochaber 1 [Fort William]
1983	Lochaber 6	Col-glen 1 [Taynuilt]
1984	Fort William 1	Bute 0 [Spean Bridge]
1985	Skye 2	Strachur 1 [Inveraray]

The Sutherland Cup

1986	Kingussie 5	Strachur 0 [Fort William]
1987	Kyles Athletic 7	Glenurquhart 5 [Taynuilt]
		(after extra time)
1988	Skye 7	Strachur 2 [Strathpeffer]
1989	Kingussie 6	Lochside Rovers 1 [Taynuilt]
1990	Kingussie 4	Lochside Rovers 0 [Inverness]
1991	Kingussie 13	Inveraray 1 [Inveraray]
1992	Kingussie 5	Glasgow Mid-Argyll 3 [Spean Bridge]

THE BALLIEMORE CUP

1985	Bute 3	Glengarry 2 [Spean Bridge]
1986	Strathglass 4	Col-glen 2 [Inveraray] (after extra time)
1987	Lochaber 4	Bute 0 [Inveraray]
	(after a drawn game, 1-1, at Newtonmore)	
1988	Glengarry 2	Bute 1 [Inveraray]
1989	Glengarry 5	Kilmory 3 [Fort William]
1990	Glenurquhart 8	Col-glen 0 [Taynuillt]
1991	Glenurquhart 5	Ballachulish 0 [Beauly]
1992	Kilmallie 4	Kilmory 2 [Taynuilt]

The Balliemore Cup

NATIONAL LEAGUE FINAL

1982	Kingussie 3	Kyles Athletic 0 [Oban]
1983	Newtonmore 1	Kyles Athletic 0 [Inverness]
1984	Kingussie 3	Kyles Athletic 2 [Oban]
1985	Newtonmore 4	Kyles Athletic 1 [Glasgow]
1986	Kyles Athletic 4	Kingussie 2 [Inverness]
1987	Kingussie 3	Kyles Athletic 0 [Oban]
1988	Kingussie 6	Kyles Athletic 2 [Oban]
1989	Kingussie 5	Oban Camanachd 1 [Inverness]
1990	Kingussie 8	Glenorchy 2 [Inverness]
1991	Kingussie 4	Oban Camanachd 2 [Fort William]
1992	Kingussie 6	Kyles Athletic 2 [Oban]

LONDON SHIELD winners & venues

1989	Inveraray 4	Kingussie 1 (Fort William)	1991	Glenurquhart 4	Oban Celtic 3 [Beauly]
1990	Kingussie 4	Oban Celtic 1 [Taynuilt]	1992	Oban Camanachd 2	Newtonmore 0 [Oban]

NORTH QUALIFYING CUP

1989	Lochaber 3	Glengarry 1 [Fort William]	1991	Glenurquhart 5	Kinlochshiel 2 [Kiltarlity]
1990	Kinlochshiel 2	Glenurquhart 0 [Inverness]	1992	Glenurquhart 6	Strathglass 1 [Inverness

SOUTH QUALIFYING CUP

1989	Kilmory 5	Tayforth 1 [Grangemouth]	1991	Inveraray 4	Ballachulish 2 [Oban]
1990	Inveraray 5	Tayforth 2 [Strachur]	1992	Ballachulish 3	Kilmory 2 [Taynuilt]

CAOL CUP

1991	North 2	South 1 [Inveraray]	1992	North 3	South 1 [Portree]

two MacAulay medals

1963 Argyll [Oban]	1969 North [Fort William]	1977 North [Perth]	1987 North [Kingussie]
1964 Newtonmore [Inverness]	1970 Badenoch & Lochaber [Spean Bridge]	1978 North [Inveraray]	1988 South [Beauly]
1965 Badenoch & Lochaber [Fort William]	1971 Badenoch & Lochaber [Fort William]	1979 North [Skye]	1989 North [Newtonmore]
1966 Badenoch & Lochaber [Fort William]	1972 North [Fort William]	1980 South [Spean Bridge]	1990 North [Kingussie]
1967 Badenoch & Lochaber [Fort William]	1973 Central [Oban]	1981 North [Spean Bridge]	1991 North [Kiltarlity]
1968 Badenoch & Lochaber [Fort William]	1974 Central [Fort William]	1982 North [Taynuilt]	1992 North [Oban]
	1975 North [Oban]	1983 South [Strathpeffer]	
	1976 North [Fort William]	1984 North [Ballachulish]	
		1985 North [Drumnadrochit]	
		1986 South [Rothesay]	

MACAULAY CUP winners

The MacAulay Cup

1947 Newtonmore	1970 Kingussie
1948 Lovat	1971 Kyles Athletic
1949 Newtonmore	1972 Kyles Athletic
1950 Oban Celtic	1973 Kingussie
1951 Kyles Athletic/Newtonmore final not played	1974 Kingussie
1952 Oban Camanachd	1975 Newtonmore
1953 Lovat	1976 Newtonmore
1954 Oban Camanachd	1977 Kyles Athletic
1955 Inverness	1978 Kyles Athletic
1956 Kyles Athletic	1979 Newtonmore
1957 Oban Camanachd	1980 Newtonmore
1958 Kyles Athletic	1981 Kingussie
1959 Furnace	1982 Kingussie
1960 Oban Celtic	1983 Kingussie
1961 Kyles Athletic	1984 Kingussie
1962 Kingussie	1985 Newtonmore
1963 Oban Celtic	1986 Newtonmore
1964 Kingussie	1987 Kingussie
1965 Oban Celtic	1988 Kingussie
1960 Kyles Athletic	1989 Kyles Athletic
1967 Newtonmore	1990 Kingussie
1968 Kingussie	1991 Fort William
1969 Oban Celtic	1992 Kingussie

The MacTavish Cup

THE MACTAVISH CUP winners

1898	Skye	1924	Newtonmore	1952	Ballachulish	1974	Newtonmore
1899	Beauly	1925	Spean Bridge	1953	Lovat	1975	Newtonmore
1900	Laggan	1926	Lovat	1954	Newtonmore	1976	Newtonmore
1901	Kingussie	1927	Newtonmore	1955	Newtonmore	1977	Newtonmore
1902	Newtonmore	1928	Lovat	1956	Newtonmore	1978	Newtonmore
1903	No competition	1929	Newtonmore	1957	Kingussie	1979	Newtonmore
1904	No competition	1930	Newtonmore	1958	Newtonmore	1980	Newtonmore
1905	Beauly	1931	Newtonmore	1959	Kilmallie	1981	Kingussie
1906	Lovat	1932	Caberfeidh	1960	Newtonmore	1982	Kingussie
1907	Inverness	1933	Spean Bridge	1961	Kilmallie	1983	Newtonmore
1908	Wester Ross	1934	Caberfeidh	1962	Kingussie	1984	Kingussie
1909	Fort Augustus	1935	Caberfeidh	1963	Newtonmore	1985	Newtonmore
1910	Fort Augustus	1936	Newtonmore	1964	Newtonmore	1986	Newtonmore
1911	Inverness	1937	Caberfeidh	1965	Kingussie	1987	Newtonmore
1912	Inverness	1938	Ballachulish	1966	Newtonmore	1988	Kingussie
1913	Beauly	1939	Newtonmore	1967	Kilmallie	1989	Kingussie
1914	Kingussie	1940-1946 World War 2		1968	Newtonmore	1990	Kingussie
1915-1919 World War 1		1947	Lovat	1969	Kilmallie	1991	Kingussie
1920	Newtonmore	1948	Ballachulish	1970	Newtonmore	1992	Kingussie
1921	Kingussie	1949	Lovat	1971	Newtonmore		
1922	Spean Bridge	1950	Newtonmore	1972	Newtonmore		
1923	Newtonmore	1951	Newtonmore	1973	Newtonmore		

1925	Stratherrick	1937	Kingussie	1955	Kingussie	1967	Newtonmore
1926	Caberfeidh	1938	Caberfeidh	1956	Newtonmore	1968	Kingussie
1927	Caberfeidh	1939	Newtonmore	1957	Newtonmore	1969	Newtonmore
1928	Caberfeidh	1940-1946	World War 2	1958	Newtonmore	1970	Newtonmore
1929	Caberfeidh	1947	Newtonmore	1959	Kilmallie	1971	Newtonmore
1930	Caberfeidh	1948	Lovat	1960	Kilmallie	1972	Newtonmore
1931	Caberfeidh	1949	Lovat	1961	Newtonmore	1973	Beauly
1932	Caberfeidh	1950	Lovat	1962	Kingussie	1974	Newtonmore
1933	Caberfeidh	1951	Newtonmore	1963	Caberfeidh		
1934	Caberfeidh	1952	Lovat	1964	Newtonmore		
1935	Caberfeidh	1953	Lovat	1965	Kilmallie		
1936	Newtonmore	1954	Newtonmore	1966	Lovat		

MACGILLIVRAY JUNIOR LEAGUE CUP winners

1949	Straths Athletic	1963	Glenurquhart
1950	Kilmallie	1964	Lochaber
1951	Straths Athletic	1965	Lochaber
1952	Beauly	1966	Boleskine
1953	Beauly	1967	Newtonmore
1954	Newtonmore	1968	Ballachulish
1955	Newtonmore	1969	Lochaber
1956	Kilmallie	1970	Ballachulish
1957	Kilmallie	1971	Ballachulish
1958	Kilmallie	1972	Newtonmore
1959	Newtonmore	1973	Beauly
1960	Glenurquhart	1974	Newtonmore
1961	Newtonmore		
1962	Lochcarron		

The MacGillivray Challenge Cup

Division One (Trophy-MacGillivray Senior Cup)

1974-1975	Newtonmore	1979-1980	Kingussie	1984-1985	Newtonmore	1989-1990	Kingussie
1975-1976	Newtonmore	1980-1981	Kingussie	1985-1986	Kingussie	1990-1991	Kingussie
1976-1977	Newtonmore	1981-1982	Kingussie	1986-1987	Kingussie	1991-1992	Kingussie
1977-1978	Newtonmore	1982-1983	Newtonmore	1987-1988	Kingussie		
1978-1979	Newtonmore	1983-1984	Kingussie	1988-1989	Kingussie		

two MacTavish medals
(left): 1910-11
(right): 1938

Division Two (Trophy — MacGillivray Junior Cup)

1974-1975	Kilmallie	1979-1980	Lochcarron	1984-1985	Kinlochshiel	1989-1990	Strathglass
1975-1976	Kinlochshiel	1980-1981	Caberfeidh	1985-1986	Fort William	1990-1991	Glenurquhart
1976-1977	Lochaber	1981-1982	Skye	1986-1987	Lochaber	1991-1992	Strathglass
1977-1978	Lovat	1982-1983	Lochaber	1987-1988	Caberfeidh		
1978-1979	Inverness	1983-1984	Fort William	1988-1989	Kinlochshiel		

Division Three (Trophy-John MacRae Cup)

1974-1975	Newtonmore	1979-1980	Kinlochshiel	1984-1985	Kingussie	1989-1990	Kingussie
1975-1976	Kingussie	1980-1981	Kingussie	1985-1986	Kingussie	1990-1991	Kingussie
1976-1977	Skye	1981-1982	Kingussie	1986-1987	Kilmallie	1991-1992	Kingussie
1977-1978	Newtonmore	1982-1983	Kingussie	1987-1988	Kingussie		
1978-1979	Newtonmore	1983-1984	Newtonmore	1988-1989	Kingussie		

Division Four (Trophy — John Fraser Cup)

1977-1978	Fort William	1981-1982	Beauly	1985-1986	Kilmallie	1989-1990	Caberfeidh
1978-1979	Kinlochshiel	1982-1983	Lochaber	1986-1987	Fort William	1990-1991	Boleskine
1979-1980	Kingussie	1983-1984	Kinlochshiel	1987-1988	Newtonmore	1991-1992	Lochaber
1980-1981	Caberfeidh	1984-1985	Kincraig	1988-1989	Lovat		

VALERIE FRASER CUP

1987	Caberfeidh	1989	Strathglass	1991	Glenurquhart
1988	Caberfeidh	1990	Glenurquhart	1992	Kinlochshiel

STRATHDEARN CUP winners

1911	Inverness	1925	Foyers	1935	Caberfeidh	1952	Beauly
1912	Foyers	1926	Foyers	1936	Lovat	1953	Newtonmore
1913	Foyers	1927	Caberfeidh	1937	Lochcarron	1954	Beauly
1914	Carrbridge	1928	Caberfeidh	1938	Lovat	1955	Beauly
1915-1919 World War		1929	Strathglass	1939	Lochcarron	1956	Beauly
1920	Stratherrick	1930	Strathdearn	1940-1947 World War 2		1957	Kilmallie
1921	Grantown on Spey	1931	Strathconon	1948	Kilmallie	1958	Lochcarron
1922	Stratherrick	1932	Strathconon	1949	Newtonmore	1959	Lochcarron
1923	Beauly	1933	Strathconon	1950	Straths Athletic	1960	Glenurquhart
1924	Lovat	1934	Foyers	1951	Kingussie	1961	Kinlochshiel

The Strathdearn Cup

1962	Glenurquhart	1970	Lochcarron	1978	Aberdeen University	1986	Skye
1963	Newtonmore	1971	Ballachulish	1979	Aberdeen University	1987	Kingussie
1964	Boleskine	1972	Glenurquhart	1980	Caberfeidh	1988	Kingussie
1965	Lochaber	1973	Aberdeen University	1981	Newtonmore	1989	Kingussie
1966	Kinlochshiel	1974	Newtonmore	1982	Strathglass	1990	Kingussie
1967	Strathglass	1975	Kinlochshiel	1983	Lochcarron	1991	Kingussie
1968	Lochcarron	1976	Kinlochshiel	1984	Newtonmore	1992	Kingussie
1969	Lochcarron	1977	Glenurquhart	1985	Kingussie		

MACTAVISH JUVENILE CUP winners

1921	Inverness Academy	1932	Beauly	1949	Kingussie	1960	Kilmallie
1922	Beauly	1933	Beauly	1950	Kingussie	1961	Kilmallie
1923	Foyers	1934	Ballachulish	1951	Kingussie	1962	Kilmallie
1924	Beauly	1935	Kingussie	1952	Lovat	1963	Beauly
1925	Abbey School	1936	Kingussie	1953	Lovat	1964	Beauly
1926	Newtonmore	1937	Kinlochleven	1954	No competition	1965	Newtonmore
1927	Newtonmore	1938	Ballachulish	1955	Kingussie	1966	Newtonmore
1928	Newtonmore	1939	Kingussie	1956	Kilmallie	1967	Newtonmore
1929	Ballachulish	1940-1946	World War 2	1957	Newtonmore	1968	Glenurquhart
1930	Ballachulish	1947	Kilmallie	1958	Newtonmore	1969	Newtonmore
1931	Kingussie	1948	Kilmallie	1959	Kilmallie	1970	Fort William

1971	Lovat	1983	Skye
1972	Kingussie	1984	Kingussie
1973	Kingussie	1985	Kingussie
1974	Newtonmore	1986	Kingussie
1975	Newtonmore	1987	Beauly
1976	Skye	1988	Beauly
1977	Skye	1989	Kingussie
1978	Newtonmore	1990	Kingussie
1979	Lochaber	1991	Glenurquhart
1980	Kingussie	1992	Newtonmore
1981	Strathglass		
1982	Skye		

A special Strathdearn medal — struck by the Tomatin Estate in 1930

W. J. CAMERON TROPHY winners

1969	Newtonmore	1976	Newtonmore	1983	Skye	1990	Kingussie
1970	Fort William	1977	Skye	1984	Kingussie	1991	Newtonmore
1971	Lovat	1978	Newtonmore	1985	Kingussie	1992	Newtonmore
1972	Fort William	1979	Lochaber	1986	Kingussie		
1973	Skye	1980	Skye	1987	Beauly		
1974	Skye	1981	Kingussie	1988	Newtonmore		
1975	Newtonmore	1982	Skye	1989	Kingussie		

STRATHDEARN JUVENILE SIX-A-SIDE CUP winners

1956	Fort William	1964	Glenurquhart	1972	Kilmallie	1980	Strathglass
1957	Beauly	1965	Newtonmore	1973	Fort William	1981	Beauly
1958	Fort William	1966	Dingwall Academy	1974	Kingussie	1982	Glenurquhart
1959	Newtonmore	1967	Glenurquhart	1975	Newtonmore	1983	Kingussie
1960	Banavie	1968	Fort William	1976	Skye	1984-1990	No competition
1961	Banavie	1969	Fort William	1977	Newtonmore	1991	Lovat
1962	Banavie	1970	Fort William	1978	Glenurquhart	1992	Kingussie
1963	Plockton	1971	Fort William	1979	Lochaber		

The W.J. Cameron Cup

SOUTH COMPETITIONS

GLASGOW CELTIC SOCIETY CUP *winners*

1879 Glasgow Cowal	1905 Glasgow Cowal	1925 Inveraray	1947 Oban Camanachd
1880 Vale of Leven	1906 Furnace	1926 Inveraray	1948 Oban Celtic
1881 Glencoe	1907 Glasgow Cowal	1927 Kyles Athletic	1949 Lochfyneside
1882 Glencoe	1908 Furnace	1928 Kyles Athletic	1950 Lovat
1883 No competition	1909 Glasgow Cowal	1929 Kyles Athletic	1951 Lovat
1884 No competition	1910 Kyles Athletic	1930 Glasgow Mid-Argyll	1952 Ballachulish
1885 Vale of Laroch	1911 Oban	1931 Glasgow Inverness-shire	1953 Lochfyneside
1886 Dunollie	1912 Furnace	1932 Glasgow Skye	1954 Kyles Athletic
1887 Inveraray	1913 Glasgow Skye	1933 Kyles Athletic	1955 Oban Lorn Athletic
1888-1898 No competition	1914 Furnace	1934 Inveraray	1956 Kyles Athletic
1899 Oban	1915-1919 World War	1935 Inveraray	1957 Glasgow Mid-Argyll
1900 Oban	1920 Kyles Athletic	1936 Glasgow Mid-Argyll	1958 Furnace
1901 Kyles Athletic	1921 Kyles Athletic	1937 Oban Camanachd	1959 Glasgow Mid-Argyll
1902 Glasgow Caledonian	1922 Kyles Athletic	1938 Oban Camanachd	1960 Kyles Athletic
1903 Kyles Athletic	1923 Kyles Athletic	1939 Kyles Athletic	1961 Glasgow Mid-Argyll
1904 Oban	1924 Inveraray	1940-1946 World War 2	1962 Oban Celtic

1963	Kyles Athletic	1971	Glasgow Mid-Argyll	1979	Kyles Athletic	1987	Oban Camanachd
1964	Glasgow Mid-Argyll	1972	Glasgow Mid-Argyll	1980	Glasgow Mid-Argyll	1988	Oban Camanachd
1965	Kyles Athletic	1973	Oban Camanachd	1981	Kyles Athletic	1989	Oban Camanachd
1966	Kyles Athletic	1974	Inveraray	1982	Strachur	1990	Oban Camanachd
1967	Kyles Athletic	1975	No competition	1983	Kyles Athletic	1991	Oban Camanachd
1968	Inveraray	1976	Kyles Athletic	1984	Kyles Athletic	1992	Oban Camanachd
1969	Glasgow Mid-Argyll	1977	Kyles Athletic	1985	Strachur		
1970	Kyles Athletic	1978	Glasgow Mid-Argyll	1986	Kyles Athletic		

DUNN SENIOR CUP winners

1932	Inveraray	1957	Oban Celtic
1933	Furnace	1958	Oban Celtic
1934	Oban Camanachd	1959	Kyles Athletic
1935	Oban Camanachd	1960	Oban Celtic
1936	Oban Camanachd	1961	Kyles Athletic
1937	No competition	1962	Kyles Athletic
1938	Kyles Athletic	1963	Oban Celtic
1939	Oban Camanachd	1964	Oban Celtic
1940-1946 World War 2		1965	Kyles Athletic
1947	Oban Camanachd	1966	Kyles Athletic
1948	Ballachulish	1967	Inveraray
1949	Ballachulish	1968	Kyles Athletic
1950	Kyles Athletic	1969	Inveraray
1951	Kyles Athletic	1970	Inveraray
1952	Oban Celtic	1971	Inveraray
1953	Oban Celtic	1972	Kyles Athletic
1954	Oban Celtic	1973	Kyles Athletic
1955	Oban Celtic	1974	Kyles Athletic
1956	Oban Celtic		

The Celtic Society Cup

FRASER CUP winners

1901	Glasgow Cowal	1907	Glasgow Cowal
1902	Glasgow Cowal	1908	Edinburgh University
1903	Glasgow Cowal	1909	Glasgow Skye
1904	Glasgow Cowal	1910	Glasgow Cowal
1905	Glasgow Cowal	1911	Glasgow Skye
1906	Glasgow Cowal	1912	Glasgow Skye

1913	Glasgow Skye	1931	Glasgow Inverness
1914	Glasgow Skye	1932	Glasgow Skye
1915-1920 World War		1933	Glasgow Mid-Argyll
1921	Glasgow Kyles	1934	North Bute
1922	Glasgow Skye	1935	North Bute
1923	Glasgow Skye	1936	Cup withheld
1924	Blawarthill Argyll	1937	Edinburgh Camanachd
1925	Glasgow Cowal	1938	Glasgow Mid-Argyll
1926	Glasgow Skye	1939	Glasgow Mid-Argyll
1927	Glasgow Skye	1940-1946 World War 2	
1928	Glasgow Inverness	1947	Glasgow Skye
1929	North Bute	1948	Glasgow Mid-Argyll
1930	Glasgow Inverness	1949	Glasgow Mid-Argyll

1950	Glasgow Mid-Argyll	1963-1965 No competition	
1951	Glasgow Mid-Argyll	1966	Edinburgh University
1952	Glasgow Mid-Argyll	1967	Edinburgh University
1953	Edinburgh Camanachd	1968-1970 No competition	
1954	Glasgow Mid-Argyll	1971	Glasgow Police
1955	Glasgow Mid-Argyll	1972	Glasgow Inverness
1956	Bute	1973	Bute
1957	Bute	1974	Glasgow Police
1958	Glasgow Skye	1975	Glasgow University
1959	Glasgow Mid-Argyll	1976	Glenorchy
1960	Glasgow University	1977	Glenorchy
1961	Strachur	1978	Bute
1962	Strachur		

Division One (Trophy — Dunn Cup)

		1983-1984	Kyles Athletic
1974-1975	Kyles Athletic/Oban Camanachd — shared	1984-1985	Kyles Athletic
1975-1976	Glasgow Mid-Argyll	1985-1986	Kyles Athletic
1976-1977	Kyles Athletic	1986-1987	Kyles Athletic
1977-1978	Kyles Athletic	1987-1988	Kyles Athletic
1978-1979	Kyles Athletic	1988-1989	Oban Camanachd
1979-1980	Kyles Athletic	1989-1990	Glenorchy
1980-1981	Kyles Athletic/Oban Celtic shared	1990-1991	Oban Camanachd
1981-1982	Kyles Athletic	1991-1992	Kyles Athletic
1982-1983	Kyles Athletic		

*Torlundy Cup medals
(left): 1952
(right): 1962*

SOUTH LEAGUES winners

Division Two (Trophy — Fraser Cup)

1978-1979	Kilmory	1986-1987	Bute
1979-1980	Strathclyde Police	1987-1988	Bute
1980-1981	Tayforth	1988-1989	Glenorchy
1981-1982	Glenorchy	1989-1990	Inveraray
1982-1983	Ballachulish	1990-1991	Ballachulish
1983-1984	Glenorchy	1991-1992	Kilmory
1984-1985	Bute		
1985-1986	Kilmory		

Two Celtic Society Cup medals
(above): from 1881
(below): from 1959-60

Division Three (Trophy — Ferguson Cup)

1976-1977	Oban Celtic
1977-1978	Glasgow Mid-Argyll
1978-1979	Oban Celtic
1979-1980	Livingston
1980-1981	Oban Celtic
1981-1982	Oban Celtic
1982-1983	Aberdeen Camanachd
1983-1984	Strachur
1984-1985	Glenorchy
1985-1986	Glasgow Highland
1986-1987	Inveraray
1987-1988	Inveraray
1988-1989	Livingston
1989-1990	Lochside Rovers
1990-1991	Inveraray
1991-1992	Lochside Rovers

Division Four (Trophy — McLaren Cup)

1983-1984 Kilmory	1986-1987 No competition	1989-1990 Inveraray
1984-1985 Ballachulish	1987-1988 Edinburgh University	1990-1991 Oban Celtic
1985-1986 Inveraray	1988-1989 Glasgow Mid-Argyll	1991-1992 Kintyre

BULLOUGH CUP winners

1906 Ballachulish	1923 Lochside Oban	1949 Oban Celtic	1962 Inveraray
1907 Ballachulish	1924 Ballachulish	1950 Appin	1963 Oban Celtic
1908 Ballachulish	1925 Lochside Oban	1951 Dunstaffnage	1964-1967 No competition
1909 Kelburn (Oban)	1926 Lochside Oban	1952 Appin	1968 Ballachulish
1910 Inveraray juniors	1927 Lochside Oban	1953 Appin	1969 Oban Celtic
1911 Inveraray juniors	1928 Oban Celtic	1954 Appin	1970 Oban Celtic
1912 Oban juniors	1929 Oban Celtic	1955 Strachur	1971 Lochside Rovers
1913 Oban juniors	1930 Oban Celtic	1956 Lochside Rovers	1972 Lochside Rovers
1914 Glencoe	1931 Oban Celtic	1957 Lochside Rovers	1973 Glenorchy
1915-1919 World War	1932 Lochside Rovers	1958 Inveraray	1974 Oban Celtic
1920 Ballachulish	1933 Lochside Rovers	1959 Inveraray	1975 Oban Celtic
1921 Oban juniors	1934 Lochside Rovers	1960 Lochside Rovers	1976 Glenorchy
1922 Duror juniors	1935-1948 No competition	1961 Inveraray	1977 Strachur

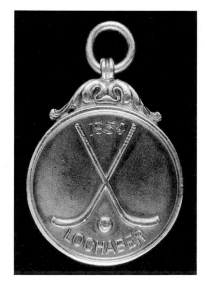

Lochaber Six medal
(left): front
(right): reverse

1978	Strachur	1982	No competition	1986	Glenorchy	1990	Inveraray
1979	Kilmory	1983	Col-glen	1987	Kyles Athletic	1991	Ballachulish
1980	Ballachulish	1984	Glenorchy	1988	Glenorchy	1992	Kilmory
1981	Ballachulish	1985	Glenorchy	1989	Lochside Rovers		

SKEABOST HORN winners

1926	Glasgow Skye	1937	Edinburgh Camanachd	1957	Bute	1984	Glasgow University
1927	Glasgow Skye	1938	Glasgow Mid-Argyll	1958	Glasgow Mid-Argyll	1985	London Camanachd
1928	Glasgow Skye	1939	Glasgow Mid-Argyll	1959-1970	No competition	1986	Strathclyde Police
1929	Glasgow Skye	1940-1947	World War 2	1971	Glasgow Inverness	1987	Glasgow Highland
1930	Glasgow Skye	1948	Glasgow Skye	1972-1974	No competition	1988	Strathclyde Police
1931	Glasgow Inverness	1949	Glasgow Mid-Argyll	1975	Cumbernauld Caberfeidh	1989	Strathclyde Police
1932	Glasgow Skye	1950	Glasgow Mid-Argyll	1976-1978	No competition	1990	Glasgow University
1933	Glasgow University	1951	Glasgow Mid-Argyll	1979	Edinburgh University	1991	Tayforth Camanachd
1934	Edinburgh Camanachd	1952	Glasgow Mid-Argyll	1980	Tayforth Camanachd		
1935	Glasgow University	1953-1955	No competition	1981-1982	No competition		
1936	Glasgow Inverness	1956	Bute	1983	Glasgow University		

MUNRO SHIELD winners

1923	Lochside Rovers	1937	Oban Celtic	1962	Unknown	1976	Strachur
1924	Lochside Rovers	1938	Ballachulish	1963	Oban Celtic	1977	Oban Celtic
1925	Lochside Rovers	1939-1949	World War 2	1964	Unknown	1978	Glenorchy
1926	Lochside Rovers	1950	Oban Celtic	1965	Ballachulish	1979	Unknown
1927	Lochside Rovers	1951	Appin	1966	Unknown	1980	Unknown
1928	Oban Celtic	1952	Glenorchy	1967	Oban Celtic	1981	Ballachulish
1929	Lochside Rovers	1953-1954	No competition	1968	Ballachulish	1982	Strachur
1930	Lochside Rovers	1955	Lochside Rovers	1969	Unknown	1983	Glenorchy
1931	Lochside Rovers	1956	Lochside Rovers	1970	Oban Celtic	1984	Glenorchy
1932	Lochside Rovers	1957	Lochside Rovers	1971	Strachur	1985	Glenorchy
1933	Oban Celtic	1958	Unknown	1972	Oban Celtic	1986	Glenorchy
1934	Lochside Rovers	1959	Inveraray	1973	Unknown	1987-1991	No competition
1935	Lochside Rovers	1960	Glenorchy	1974	Oban Celtic	1992	Kintyre
1936	Lochside Rovers	1961	Inveraray	1975	Strachur		

COLINTRAIVE CUP *winners*

1978	Bute	1982	Taynuilt	1986	Edinburgh University	1990	Lochside Rovers
1979	Glenorchy	1983	Glenorchy	1987	Livingston	1991	Inveraray
1980	No competition	1984	Kilmory	1988	Lochside Rovers	1992	Lochside Rovers
1981	Oban Celtic	1985	Glenorchy	1989	Lochside Rovers		

NATIONAL MOD CUP *winners*

1969	Newtonmore	1975	Glasgow Mid-Argyll	1981	Lochaber	1987	Livingston
1970	Oban Celtic	1976	Aberdeen Camanachd	1982	Skye	1988	Glenorchy
1971	Glasgow Mid-Argyll	1977	Glenurquhart	1983	Glasgow Mid-Argyll	1989	Skye
1972	Lovat	1978	Oban Celtic	1984	Inverness	1990	No competiton
1973	No competition	1979	Lochcarron	1985	Glengarry	1991	Caberfeidh
1974	Aberdeen Camanachd	1980	Tayforth	1986	Tayforth	1992	Oban Camanachd

Oban Camanachd won the Mod Cup for the first time in 1992 when the Royal National Mod returned to the town
(left): Ken Thomson, President of the Camanachd Association, Dave MacUish, captain of Oban Camanachd, and Donald MacRitchie, President of An Comunn Gàidhealach

Camanachd gu bràth!

To a very special friend

Jim Henson
President
21/5/53.